BLOW THE GAP

"Hit the deck!" Freeman yelled.

A heavy roar drowned out the battle's din for the prone men. The whole gap area spouted water, smoke, wood, sand, and steel high into the air. It was 0655, only 22 minutes after the team's boat touched bottom. The gap was blown clean, a 5-yard-wide lane open from sea to shore. In tribute to his men's letter-perfect performance, Chief Freeman gasped: "God, it was right out of the damned book."

NAKED WARRIORS

THE STORY OF THE U.S. NAVY'S FROGMEN

CDR. FRANCIS DOUGLAS FANE, USNR (RET.)
and DON MOORE

Foreword by Adm. Richmond Kelly Turner, USN (Ret.)
New introduction by Rear Adm. Irve C. Le Moyne, USN

St. Martin's Paperbacks

Originally published by Appleton-Century-Crofts, Inc.

Published by arrangement with Naval Institute Press

NAKED WARRIORS

ISBN: 0-312-95985-0

Printed in the United States of America

Naval Institute Press hardcover edition published in 1995
St. Martin's Paperbacks edition/October 1996

St. Martin's Paperbacks are published by St. Martin's Press, 175 Fifth Avenue, New York, NY 10010.

10 9 8 7 6 5 4 3 2 1

*To all men who have served with
Underwater Demolition Teams*

Contents

Introduction	*ix*
Foreword	*xi*
Preface	*xv*

1. The Naked Warriors	1
2. The First Demolitioneers	10
3. Baptism in an Atoll	25
4. Demolition Drill	41
5. The Bloody Sands of Normandy	49
6. Fire in the Hole!	67
7. Push-Button Warfare	74
8. Swimmer Search at Saipan	81
9. "Welcome, Marines!"	109
10. Surprise Attack	123
11. Peleliu—Portal to the Philippines	132
12. The Navy Returns MacArthur	149
13. Through Hell and High Water	157

14. Intrepidity at Iwo   170

15. A Thousand Swimmers   189

16. The Blasting of Balikpapan   210

17. Samurai Surrender to Naked Warrior!   227

18. Korean Mines and Guerrillas   236

19. Over the Horizon   270

20. UDT Submerges   277

    Index   *303*

Introduction

CDR. DOUG FANE'S BOOK, *THE NAKED WARRIORS*, STANDS UP
well to the test of time. It is a highly entertaining, accurate,
and unglamorized account of the origins of the Underwater
Demolition Teams (UDTs) and their development in World
War II and the Korean War.

The Marine assault on Tarawa in November 1943 cast in
the starkest possible terms the importance of amphibious force
commanders having accurate reconnaissance information on
the underwater geography of landing beaches. This book
gives a vivid portrayal of how the U.S. Navy and Marine
Corps reacted to this requirement and set about, in a dedicated fashion, to develop the organizations and techniques
needed to get this vital intelligence for future amphibious
landings.

The Naked Warriors was an important work when it was first
published in 1956. The Navy's UDTs were among the truly
pioneering organizations for underwater work. Scuba diving
was just coming into its own in the early and middle 1950s,
and UDTs were at the leading edge of this emerging
technology.

The book remains important because it outlines the evolu-
tionary process in the development of UDTs' capabilities. It
sets the stage for what has transpired since, with the creation
of the Navy's sea-air-land (SEAL) teams. The book is a must

read for Navy SEALs and everyone else with an interest in the performance of unusual and dangerous missions. Commander Fane's book gives clear insight into the development of the U.S. Navy's combat-swimmer capability.

First came Combat Demolition Units, composed of one officer and six enlisted men. Their heroism was truly magnificent on the bullet-swept beaches of Normandy. In the Pacific Fleet, Combat Demolition Unit personnel used rubber boats to take themselves and their explosives to the beach for reconnaissance and obstacle removal.

These Combat Demolition Units were later combined into larger Underwater Demolition Teams. By the end of World War II, there were more than thirty UDTs preparing for the amphibious invasion of the Japanese home islands. Their operational skills had been finely honed in the many amphibious assaults conducted by the Navy and Marines across the Pacific.

The need for the men of the UDTs to abandon rubber boats, swim onto enemy beaches for reconnaissance, and later transport explosives to these same beaches for obstacle demolition became apparent as combat experience grew. This was an operational discovery generated by the men planning and carrying out the missions. This approach remains the foundation for today's generation of these "naked warriors," our Navy SEALs—men dedicated to accomplishing their difficult, dangerous missions, no matter how high the odds.

Rear Adm. Irve C. Le Moyne, USN

Foreword

BETWEEN THE TWO WORLD WARS THE U.S. NAVY, SPARKED by its Marine Corps, exerted much effort in the development of amphibious doctrines and techniques, since it was evident that American participation in any war in the Pacific Ocean would involve extensive amphibious operations. Our progress in actual training was hampered by a shortage of personnel, and by a lack of money for the construction of better attack transports, landing craft, and other specialized equipment. After the start of World War II in Europe, funds gradually became available for some improvement in these respects. It was then that the U.S. Army joined in the Navy's preparation for amphibious warfare. We were thus enabled to lay a reasonably sound foundation for the future.

Amphibious warfare requires the landing of troops from their sea transports against *immediate* enemy opposition. When opposition does not exist, it is not very difficult to put troops and their mountains of supplies and equipment ashore, even where harbors and docks do not exist. Naturally, attacking military forces much prefer unopposed landings! But often in World War II there was no choice. Hostile positions had to be seized for future exploitation or for eliminating enemy forces that threatened further Allied progress.

It is the general American practice in amphibious warfare for the Navy to command operations on and in the water, and

for the Army or Marines to command operations ashore above
the high-water mark. The Navy operates all floating equipment, with a few exceptions—as, for example, Army
"DUKWs" and Marine amphibious tractors ("alligators").
These amphibians perform much of their duty on shore in
support of combat, and therefore are manned by troops. Air
elements, initially under command of the Navy, as events tran-
spire gradually are replaced by shore-based aircraft under the
high troop command.

Landing "beaches" (often rock or coral ledges) are selected
after careful consideration of thousands of aerial and submarine periscope photographs; of known or estimated winds,
waves, currents, tides, water depths, and offshore and inshore
obstacles; and of the value of the positions with respect to tactical deployment.

Landing operations start with massive sea and air bombardment. Transports, six to eight thousand yards off the beaches,
unload their troop-filled landing boats and alligators, which
then move to the Line of Departure. Here, four thousand
yards from shore, these small craft form into boat waves and
thence, on a strict time schedule, proceed over reefs or shoal-
ing water to their designated landing points. Once ashore, the
troops first establish a firmly held beachhead, wide and deep
enough to protect further landings of men and material.

Traversing this zone, from the Line of Departure to the
Beachhead Line, is the really tough part of an amphibious operation. How successful the little landing boats will be in
putting the soldiers ashore depends largely on how safely they
can pass through enemy gunfire, and avoid the material obstacles that Nature and Man have placed across their way.

In our early amphibious operations of World War II we had
found no sure method of detecting and then destroying dangerous underwater obstructions close inshore, where
minesweepers could not penetrate. Nor could we ever be sure
of the depths of water in the shallows. We proceeded by edu-
cated guesswork—and some of the guesses were not good. It
was after Tarawa in the Pacific, but before Normandy in Eu-

rope, that we recognized the imperative need for a better method—a method that would acquaint us with the true underwater geography between the Line of Departure and the beach, and that would ensure either the removal or the safe avoidance of static dangers.

The method adopted was the employment of swimming scouts—Underwater Demolition Teams. It became the duty of these teams to chart the beach approaches, and to find and destroy underwater obstructions that might prevent or even retard the troop landings. Since Navy cognizance runs from the deep sea to the high-water mark, these scouts properly were provided by the Navy.

I am glad this book, *The Naked Warriors,* has been written about the daring, skillful men who were members of the Underwater Demolition Teams. Unknown to the public (and usually to the enemy) during the war, they deserve that their exploits should now be disclosed. Their efforts always reduced losses to troops and boats' crews and greatly facilitated the landing of men and cargo. Their value to the Amphibious Forces was immense.

Does the reader hold the view that young American men are soft and timid? Well, here before you is a true tale of some that aren't that way. Volunteers all, they knew before they joined that even their own officers believed that heavy combat losses were inevitable. But still, many more volunteers came forward than were needed. And they never failed us.

To these Naked Warriors: Hail! You earned and have my sincere admiration and respect.

Adm. Richmond Kelly Turner, USN

Preface

THIS IS THE STORY OF THE DEVELOPMENT AND THE COMBAT experiences of the U.S. Navy Underwater Demolition Teams, who are engaged in a new technique of warfare at sea. It is written as much as possible in the words of the men themselves, resulting from scores of personal interviews. The text is based on the reports of UDT returning from the wars and far-flung reconnaissance operations with the Amphibious Forces.

I commenced this book in order to record the history of UDT. Another need to relate the story has arisen from the growing interest of the public in the underwater world. It is also my aim to answer the hundreds of letters I am receiving at Underwater Demolition Unit One from the youth of our land, requesting information on how to become "Frogmen." It is hoped that this unvarnished account will answer their queries and whet their interest in the U.S. Navy and the sea. I take this opportunity to welcome all skin-divers aboard to meet the men of UDT. It is my hope to show that in this age of mechanized, push-button warfare, the courage, strength, and skill of unarmed men can still play a major part.

The grateful acknowledgment of the authors is due to the many UDT personnel who have contributed to this book. In addition to those named in the text, the authors wish to thank:

Admiral Richmond Kelly Turner, USN (Ret.), for his detailed review and helpful suggestions.

Admiral Richard L. Conolly, USN (Ret.); Rear Admiral B. Hall Hanlon, USN; Rear Admiral R. H. Rodgers, USN (Ret.); Captain Draper L. Kauffman, USN; Captain Joseph H. Gibbons, USNR; Mr. John T. Koehler; Mr. E. R. Fenimore Johnson; Doctor Christian J. Lambertson; Frank D. Morris; Photographer's Mate First Class Gerald E. Darrah, USN; to Mrs. J. W. Riggar, Chief Yeoman Jack W. Riggar, USN, and Yeoman Second Class Kenneth D. Knudsen, USN, for their many hours of labor typing the manuscript and revisions.

Thanks are also given to the Office of the Chief of Naval Information and to the staff of the Director of Naval History. I received encouragement and help from Rear Admiral John B. Heffernan, USN (Ret.), the Director of Naval History.

Background information concerning U.S. Fleet actions and incidents relative to UDT operations has been drawn from official records and Rear Admiral Samuel Eliot Morison's series on U.S. Navy Operations in World War II; from "Battle Report" by Captain Walter Karig; and from "The U.S. Marines and Amphibious Warfare" by Jeter A. Isely and Philip A. Crowl.

To all of the above and also to Mr. Stewart Johnson of Appleton-Century-Crofts, Inc., my thanks.

Cdr. Francis Douglas Fane, USNR (Ret.)

NAKED WARRIORS

1. The Naked Warriors

Ships have changed greatly throughout the generations that our Navy has guarded United States interests in the world's oceans. . . . But it is the spirit and skill of the seagoing men themselves which will remain the key to success in battle.

ADMIRAL ARLEIGH A. BURKE, USN,
CHIEF OF NAVAL OPERATIONS

THE BROWN, NAKED TORSO OF A SWIMMER LAY AWASH IN THE surf breaking on a dazzling-white sand beach. The beach stretched away from the sea to a grove of swaying, tossing coconut palm trees. Beyond the trees, hills rose gradually up into a mountain. The green upland slopes, the face of the cliffs, and the dense jungle foliage were dotted with white puffs of smoke. Despite the brilliant tropical sun beating hotly down on the back of the naked man, he shivered. For the palm trees were not swaying in the gentle Trade Winds; they were rocked by the detonation of heavy explosions, their fronds stripped from decapitated trunks. The beach under the man shook and trembled. Spouts of water jetted up from the sea around him; the concussion of exploding mortar shells slapped his naked body. He ducked down under the surf as machine-gun bullets whined over his head and ripped into the sea behind him. He had reason to fear, for he knew that less than 100 yards ahead of him and deployed in the hills were thousands of crack Japanese troops. Heavy Japanese shore batteries fired out to sea, seeking to destroy the ships from whence he came. The only weapon of this naked American warrior was a sheath knife.

The swimmer was not alone; he was part of a team. Up and

1

down the surf line were other near-naked men, a total of 56 if everyone had made it alive. They were stretched flat in the surf, keeping as much of their bodies under water as possible. For the water was their best protection from the exploding mortar shells, and rifle and machine-gun bullets. From their position near the beach the swimmers could clearly see the enemy positions. They plotted the data on slates, then slid back into the surf and swam to the safety of deep water.

The swimmers felt the honest fear of men facing death. Yet although nearly unarmed, they were far from unprotected. A few hundred yards offshore a division of rocket ships poured 40mm shells into the shattered palms. Close behind the rocket ships a division of destroyers bombarded the slopes of the hills with 5-inch projectiles. The destroyers were backed by cruisers whose 6-inch and 8-inch batteries shattered Japanese gun emplacements in the cliffs. From point-blank range two battleships engaged the heavy Japanese shore batteries. Out to seaward of the battlewagons were aircraft carriers hull down over the horizon and far beyond the sight of the naked warriors. They had given evidence of their presence to our men during the swim into the beach, when a squadron of "smoker" airplanes had laid a smoke screen between them and their enemies. The warships and airplanes were components of a Task Element of the United States Navy, the Gunfire Support Group, throwing thousands of tons of shells and bombs onto the beach to keep the Japanese down while these swimmers executed their audacious mission.

The assignment of the naked warriors was a vital one. Before the Naval Amphibious Force could land troops to wipe out the enemy on the island, it was necessary for the Underwater Demolition Team (UDT) to survey the beach for the best landing site, to demolish enemy-made obstructions which would be a barrier to landing craft, and to search out and destroy mines.

On island after island, throughout the vast expanse of

the Pacific Ocean, similar scenes were repeated—in the Marshalls, the Marianas, the Palaus, the Philippines, Iwo Jima, Okinawa, and Borneo—as well as in the Normandy and Southern France landings in Europe. During World War II, the naked warriors became one of the spearheads of amphibious assault. And more recently the beaches of Korea, Indo-China, the Taichen Islands, the Arctic and the Antarctic have become familiar shores to UDT.

A primary function of the United States Navy is to seek out the enemy wherever he may be, and to destroy him. A powerful weapon system devoted to this task is the Amphibious Force. This great sea train of assault transport, laden with troops and armored equipment, screened by destroyers, supported by cruisers, battleships and aircraft carriers, has the ability and mobility to land an overwhelmingly powerful attack on enemy targets. The directive "to seek out and destroy the enemy" may require that the Amphibious Force be landed on unknown and fiercely defended beaches.

Tarawa was such a place. It was here that the need for underwater swimmers was first found to be critical. Rear Admiral Richmond Kelly Turner, USN, the Commander of the Fifth Amphibious Force, was ordered to destroy the Japanese defenders of this Central Pacific atoll. The assault was well planned, every existing means of intelligence being used before the transports arrived off the right-angled triangle of barrier reef dotted with islands which surrounded Tarawa Lagoon.

The target was Betio Island, a narrow, tapering triangle, some two miles long and no more than six hundred yards wide near its broad western end. From the beach an L-shaped pier ran some seven hundred yards over the reef to deep water in the lagoon. By counting the outhouses built on piers over the reef and knowing how many men the Japanese allotted to each hole, intelligence experts figured that there were just under 5,000 enemy troops on the island—privy information which proved surprisingly accurate.

Before the arrival of the fleet, a submarine circled the

island, taking soundings and periscope photographs. Airplanes photographed vertical panoramas, then flew low along the reefs, taking oblique stereo-pair pictures to give a three-dimensional view. But although these photographs showed the dug-in, sandbanked honeycomb of pillboxes, coconut-log sniper pits, and gun emplacements that ringed and filled the island as well as the obstacles and mines strewn over the reef and beaches, they did not show the depth of water over the reefs.

According to most of the island traders and residents who had fled the Japanese seizure almost two years earlier, these reefs should have been covered by four or five feet of water at high tide, enough to let the landing craft put troops dry-shod on the beach in front of the barricade.

Admiral Turner's Operation Plan warned against the danger of "dodging tides," a little-known and unpredictable local condition of wind and current which, during neap tides, would cause the water to ebb and flow several times in twenty-four hours. The neap tide range was only four feet. The date of the attack, November 20, 1943, was to be in the neap tide period—and, probably due to strong southwest winds, "dodging" tides would prevail on D-Day.

A half-moon was three hours high that night beyond Betio Island when the Marines, burdened with combat packs and guns, scrambled down the cargo nets on the sides of their transports into bobbing open-cockpit boats. Men of the first three waves transferred into low, open, partially armored amtracs, or amphibian tractors, being unloaded from ships or rolling out of the open bow doors of tank landing ships over sea-level ramps.

These amtracs were rectangular, open-cockpit metal boxes with caterpillar tracks along their sides, powered by gasoline motors. Watertight, they could swim at four and a half knots, crawl up shelving reefs, and run at 15 miles an hour inland. Developed from tractors used in the Florida Everglades, the first models were promptly nicknamed "alligators." Officially they were Landing Vehicle, Tracked (LVT).

Previously used to ferry supplies ashore after the North Africa and Solomons landings, they were used to carry troops as a landing spearhead for the first time at Tarawa.

A shore battery fired on the fleet offshore. Guns of battleships, cruisers and destroyers, of the largest invasion fleet America had yet assembled, fired back, covering the tiny island with heavy smoke from fires of exploding fuel and ammunition dumps. The ships' guns poured three thousand tons of shells onto the island, the heaviest naval bombardment in World War II up until then. It was not enough. Transports had to retire seaward. The Marines had a long, slow ride which delayed H-Hour. They were crowded in low amtracs which chugged at a slow four knots seven miles through the recently mineswept pass into the lagoon. The spray-soaked Marines were anxious for action as they stared at the flat coral island, its palm treetops shattered by shellfire.

First to land on Tarawa was a lone amtrac with men of Lieutenant William D. Hawkins' Scout-Sniper Platoon and Lieutenant Alan G. Leslie's Flamethrower Platoon. Let Leslie, who was later attached to an Underwater Demolition Team as Marine liaison officer, tell what happened:

"Our mission was to neutralize the L-shaped pier of all enemies but save it intact to handle plasma, ammo, supplies, and evacuate wounded Marines.

"We hit the pier fifteen or twenty minutes ahead of the first wave. The naval barrage had lifted. Then all hell broke loose. The Japs defended the sea wall fanatically against the alligators. Antiboat guns were fired on the long axis of the Marines who were shoulder deep in the lagoon, channeled by scullies and tetrahedrons into a fire zone."

During the assault, 90 out of the 125 amtracs were hit and destroyed. The survivors scrambled into the water, which put out their burning clothing but slowed them as they waded toward the beach. Many men were cut down and lay wounded or dead in that wide expanse of reddening shoals.

The wooden landing craft, unable to cross the shallow

reef, had to unload at the lagoon edge. Some Marines were given a lift in the surviving amtracs running a shuttle service across the reef; the rest had to wade.

By now the bad news about the reef was known, but there is no easy way of changing a complex ship-to-shore operation once commenced. The next wave, of tank lighters, had to drop their ramps at the reef's lagoon edge and let the tanks wallow across the shallows. Some tanks drowned in shell holes, others were knocked out by direct hits.

Many of the reinforcements never reached the shore, or were killed trying to push inland from the dangerously narrow beachhead. Nearly a third of the 5,000 Marines landing were killed or wounded on D-Day. The assault could not gain momentum because of the reef and its powerful shore defenses. During the blackest moments of that day, the Marine command at Tarawa made the unprecedented announcement: "Issue in doubt."

It was the only time in the Pacific that an American landing was in danger of being repulsed on D-Day. Underwater obstructions nearly tipped the balance.

At last the tide rose normally, however. Ramped landing craft brought reinforcements over the reef to insure victory. It was still a long and bloody fight, blasting and burning the enemy out of their unexpectedly solid and secure dugouts. American casualties had doubled—over 3,000 dead and wounded out of 16,800 Marines—by the fourth afternoon when the last literal die-hard had been dug out, and the battle of Tarawa was history.

Tarawa was the first time American troops had assaulted a blockaded coral reef against heavy fire. In the First World War, American and British troops had been able to land in friendly French ports before entraining to the front. The only attempt to land from ships onto an enemy shore was the disastrous defeat at Gallipoli, on the European shore of the Dardanelles. Many military experts had laid down the doctrine that troops could never land on a properly defended beach, any more than they believed that warships could fight a fort. Tarawa disproved this beach theory, but the four-day casualty cost almost matched the total Marine losses in all the months of bitter struggle in Guadalcanal's swamps and jungles.

This invasion of the Gilbert Islands was code-named "Operation Galvanic." It galvanized the public at home, who were shocked by the sudden, heavy casualties. Censorship did not hold back the grim photographs of dead Marines lying half in the water and half on the sand. The readily optimistic public had to be faced with the cruel cost of war. Shocked correspondents, politicians, and editors hunted scapegoats for Tarawa's "tragic mistakes," demanding that this must not happen again.

The Navy and Marine commanders knew that even bloodier battles lay ahead on the heavily fortified island road blocks on the direct ocean route to Japan. They determined to cut down the cost by learning every possible lesson from this fierce, hard-fought amphibious assault. A flood of reports, criticisms, and suggestions from admirals and generals down to junior landing officers poured into Admiral Nimitz's Pearl Harbor headquarters even before the victorious fleet returned from Tarawa and Makin in the Gilbert Islands.

Shortly before Tarawa, Admiral Chester W. Nimitz, Commander in Chief of the Pacific Fleet and the Pacific Ocean Area, had directed his own gunnery officer Captain Tom B. Hill to assemble a beach reconnaissance and demolition unit. But the time was too short to fit it into the Tarawa-Makin plans, although a few men did get assigned to Beach Parties at the last minute. After the landings at Makin and Abemama (a third, smaller, weakly defended atoll) these men tried to blast coral heads to make a channel for the big tank landing ships, but the job had to be finished with bulldozers.

Before Tarawa, when Admiral Turner was Commander of the Third Amphibious Force on his way from Guadalcanal up the Solomons, he had always been able to select landing sites on beaches without offshore obstacles. Turner had, however, faced a coral reef problem at Munda, where his Captain R. H. Rodgers had trained two Construction Battalions to blow a channel through a reef, for the supply of troops already ashore.

At Tarawa, the lack of accurate reef intelligence had nearly caused a military disaster. Photo-intelligence reports of water depths were not accurate and dependable enough. An unknown difference of one foot depth of water over a reef could endanger an entire assault. That fact was drilled into the minds of all those who saw the Marines struggling through hundreds of yards of waist-deep water while exposed to murderous enemy fire. It became apparent that estimates were not enough; men must go in ahead of the troops to measure the depths exactly, and to search under water for mines and obstructions.

Returning to Pearl Harbor, Admiral Turner and his staff wrote the Tarawa report, and simultaneously commenced preparation for the Marshall Operation, incorporating the lessons learned on the bloody reef.

Turner's Operational Readiness Officer, Captain Tom Hill, and the staff Gunnery Officer, Captain Jack Taylor, requested a conference on beach demolitions. Turner questioned the officers for two hours, and as their first proposals were, of course, still vague and visionary, he asked that they return the next day for a decision. The next day when Hill and Taylor arrived, Turner, having already given the problem hours of thought, immediately approved their proposals, spending further hours discussing ways and means. Captain Hill was given the responsibility of pushing the UDT plan through CINCPAC and the Commander in Chief, which he successfully did. He then was handed the task of providing men and material.

Throughout the war, the intense and continued interest and assistance of Admiral Turner bolstered the foundling UDT organization, and finally built it up to one of the Navy's hardest hitting units.

Halfway around the globe from Tarawa, and nearly a

year before, the Atlantic Fleet Amphibious Force stormed the shores of Africa. There, too, landing craft met a formidable barrier, an age-old defense technique created by man which would require the first use of underwater demolition in the European War.

2. The First Demolitioneers

DURING THE TOUGH FIRST YEAR OF WORLD WAR II, THE U.S. Navy was already planning to take the offensive in the Atlantic. By the summer of 1942, the Amphibious Force, Atlantic Fleet, gathered its strength for the first great amphibious assault landing, "Operation Torch," an attack on the North African coast.

Intelligence reported a boom and net blocking the Wadi Sebou River, the river highway to the Vichy-held Port Lyautey Airfield, on the west coast of French Morocco. Before assault ships could enter the river, the net's heavy cable would have to be cut by explosives, a job for demolition specialists.

In September 1942, a small detachment of sailors was picked for this first underwater demolition operation. Ten of them had helped raised ships at Pearl Harbor. They were led by salvage officers from two fleet tugs, Lieutenants Mark W. Starkweather and James W. Darroch. Seventeen men, all told, reported to the U.S. Naval Amphibious Base at Little Creek, Virginia, where they received a "cram course" in the art of demolition, cable cutting, and commando-type raiding techniques. One week later the first combat demolition unit was en route overseas to rendezvous with the assault force off the beaches of North Africa.

Just before H-Hour on November 8, 1942, while blacked-out transports behind them were spilling men down the cargo nets, the seventeen sailors in an open spoon-nosed Higgins boat wallowed over a heavy ground swell toward the darkly looming coast. Ashore, everything seemed quiet, and they were unaware that the Vichy garrison had been alerted in the big stone Kasbah fortress overlooking the river and its net.

When near the harbor entrance, a heavy rain squall hit the tossing boat, which was headed straight for the jetties flanking the river mouth. As one of the party, William R. Freeman, tells it:

"We were picked up by a breaking ground swell and went on like an express train. A red flare was fired when we passed the end of the jetty. Enemy fire began as we were hugging the south shore, proceeding slowly to the net. We were illuminated by searchlights from the Kasbah, and immediately kicked on full power and zigzagged in an effort to lose the light.

"We were taken under fire by 75's with no hits. An American destroyer took the Kasbah under fire, and the Kasbah countered with their main battery of coast artillery. Our game was up for the night as the operation was based on surprise. The order was given in the time-worn phrase: 'Let's get the hell out of here!'"

Going back through the heavy surf at the mouth of the Sebou, Lieutenant Starkweather was thrown against the coaming, nearly tearing his nose off, and a shipfitter stove in both ankles. Back on the transport, the demolition party braced for a second try another night.

For two days the American landing troops, new to war and learning the hard way, clawed through the heavy surf and fought a few miles inland, balked by the river looping protectively around the vital airport. The destroyer *Dallas*, loaded with U.S. Rangers scheduled to capture the airfield, lay useless offshore because of the river net blocking the passage.

Just after midnight of November 10, the net-cutting crew again boarded its landing craft, loaded with explosives, wire cutters, two inflated rubber boats, a huge underwater incendiary device which Gunner's Mate Freeman had built on shipboard, and two light machine guns.

Steering through a surf which was far worse than before, the men passed the jetties into quieter water without being discovered, and reached the net in pitch-darkness. A heavy one-and-a-half-inch cable held it up, buoyed by small craft anchored at intervals across the river. Above the cable boom was a smaller, taut wire.

Their explosive cable cutter, although it had rarely worked in practice, cut through the heavy wire boom on the first try. The smaller wire was easily sheared in two. The supporting boats began sagging downstream as the cable parted, and simultaneously the Kasbah opened fire with machine guns— evidently the smaller wire was an alarm.

The Higgins boat turned down river, firing back with both machine guns, the crew's tommy gun, and even Colt automatics. The Kasbah fired down relentlessly and machine-gun bullets plowed through the zigzagging wooden craft. The lieutenant ordered his men to stop firing back, hoping to hide their position. The Kasbah fire followed them all the way to the jetties, where an even worse danger threatened.

The incoming surf was monstrous—Army engineers later measured it at 30 feet where it boomed in between the jetties. Everything movable was thrown overboard to lighten the pitching, half-swamped boat. Explosives, Freeman's big incendiary device, the rubber boats, all were ditched, even one of the machine guns went overboard. But the boat arrived safely at the transport with thirteen holes through it. Not a man was wounded by enemy fire, although several were badly banged up and suffering from shock.

The demolition men had successfully accomplished their mission; the river highway was open. Before dawn the *Dallas* steamed up the Sebou, crashed through the broken boom and sagging net, and despite the Kasbah's fire, landed the Rangers on the vital airfield.

The first "Demolitioneers" returned to the United States to assist in the organization of other units, the need for which was apparent as the Navy raised its sights for the attack on both European and Pacific targets. Plans were being formulated for the massive cross-channel assault on Hitler's impregnable fortress, the "Western Wall." Intelligence reports streamed in regarding the formidable beach defenses designed to wreck or sink amphibious landing craft. Hitler was expending thousands of tons of precious iron, steel, and concrete in the construction of these underwater barriers.

As early as January 1943, U.S. Army engineers experimented at Fort Pierce, Florida, with procedures and equipment designed to clear these underwater obstacles. The development group of the Amphibious Forces, Atlantic Fleet, had been doing the same. These experiments showed that mechanical demolition methods would be inadequate to break through Hitler's growing channel defenses. Personnel hardy enough to encounter the variety of dangers to which they would be exposed must be organized into obstacle clearance units, trained to accomplish by hand tasks which modern mechanical weapons could not do.

On May 6, 1943, the first orders for the organization of clearance units were issued by Admiral Ernest J. King, who was both Commander in Chief, U.S. Fleet, and Chief of Naval Operations. His directive was in two parts: providing men for "a present urgent requirement" of the Amphibious Forces, Atlantic Fleet; and starting experimental work and training for permanent "Naval Demolition Units" for assignment to other amphibious forces.

The first job for the demolition men was to open channels through Sicily beaches which would be assaulted in July. The way to Sicily and Italy had been cleared by the successful North African invasion.

The first Naval Combat Demolition Unit started with thirteen volunteers who were near the end of their basic training in the Dynamiting and Demolition School at Camp Perry, Virginia. Selected to meet Admiral King's "urgent requirement," they were sent to the Naval Amphibious Training Base at Solomons Island, Maryland, in Chesapeake Bay. They were joined by other enlisted demolition men and eight officers. Lieutenant Fred Wise from the SeaBees (Construction Battalions) was designated Officer in Charge.

They were given a quick, intensive course in blowing channels through sandbars with explosive hose, and in working from rubber boats to place explosive charges on underwater obstacles which had been modeled by Army engineers. Then they sailed for the assault on Sicily.

Twenty-one men under Lieutenant Wise debarked from three attack cargo ships off Scoglitti, Sicily, on the morning of July 10, 1943. Loaded in ramped Higgins boats, with their explosives, the three Naval Combat Demolition Units waited patiently for orders that never came. The landing waves either found enough water over the sandbars or used alternative beaches. Lieutenant Wise went ashore and heard the anticlimactic news from the beachmaster that demolition would only delay the unloading.

By 1400 (2 P.M. on the military 24-hour clock) on D-Day, Scoglitti was captured. The demolition units came ashore with their explosives to blow up concrete road blocks in the water-front ends of the streets. With long, tubelike bangalore torpedoes they cleared off barbed-wire entanglements on the beach. There were no underwater obstructions, but for the next two days the men did useful work in salvaging stranded boats, buoying channels through the sandbars, and surveying the beaches. Then they shipped back to the States. Most of this first group stayed in Naval Combat Demolition as instructors, proceeding to the Naval Amphibious Training Base in Fort Pierce for the tougher training which was just getting under way in accordance with Admiral King's directive.

Another result of that directive was a telegram sent the same night to Lieutenant Commander Draper L. Kauffman, founder and head of the Navy Bomb Disposal School, recalling him to Washington.

Kauffman had started his honeymoon six days before, taking one of the few leaves he had enjoyed during more than three years of active warfare. He talked the hotel bellboy into taking back the telegram and delivering it to him the next morning instead.

Reporting to the Pentagon, Kauffman caught up with Captain Metzel of the Commander in Chief's Planning Staff, hurrying from one high-level conference to another. "Thought-a-minute" Metzel lived up to his nickname with his instructions to Kauffman. As exactly as Kauffman can remember, Metzel's orders were:

"During the next few years we will be making amphibious landings all over the world. If the enemy has any sense at all, he will protect his beaches with obstacles which will stop our landing craft offshore and force us to disembark our soldiers in water about six feet deep where they will either drown or lose their equipment. Your job is to put a stop to this. Get together some men and train them to get rid of these obstacles. Your orders will allow you to go anywhere you think best to set up a training base. You can have anyone you ask for, in or out of the naval service. This is an emergency and we don't have much time."

In tackling the uncharted task of launching Navy underwater demolition, Kauffman had unique background. He had followed in the footsteps of his father (Vice Admiral James L. Kauffman) by graduating from the Naval Academy, but since his eyesight was down to 15-20 on graduation he was not commissioned. Two years later he was retested, but again failed the eye examination. He stayed with the sea, however, and found a position in the U.S. Lines. Late in 1939, Kauffman, determined that poor eyesight wouldn't keep him out of the war, donned a French uniform and became a driver in the American Volunteers Ambulance Corps. He soon won a Croix de Guerre for braving machine-gun fire while picking up wounded. When the Germans smashed through the Maginot Line, they captured him and put him in Luneville prison camp.

As appeasement or propaganda, the Germans freed him and a handful of other American drivers. Kauffman reached England in September 1940 and talked his way into the Royal Navy Volunteer Reserve as a sublieutenant, just before London got its first heavy blitzing.

The British were glad to grab any warm body that would volunteer for the suicide assignment of Mine Disposal. Poor eyesight was no handicap in disarming enemy bombs, which required the fine touch of a safe-cracker. Since some of the "duds" turned out to be delayed action bombs, every unexploded bomb had to be defused. Kauffman volunteered for this duty.

Soon the Nazis started dropping naval mines by parachute onto England, with a bewildering variety of new mechanical, magnetic, or acoustic fuses. One slip or wrong guess on the part of the man disarming the bomb would start the little wheels inside buzzing harshly which meant explosion within one to a score of seconds.

At Christmastime, 1940, Kauffman was sent to work on a mine which had cracked through the ceiling of a bawdy house, entwining its parachute in the chandelier, and had finally lodged in the gentleman's sitting room. Christmas decorations were festooned around the 2,000 pounds of explosives when Kauffman examined it. Either his nonmagnetic wrench slipped as he turned the fuse guard, or his technique was errant. The mine began to buzz. Kauffman dove for the door. He had sprinted 40 yards when the mine detonated, hurling him through the air. Captain C. N. E. Curry, Royal Navy, of the British mine defense organization, noted in his official report:

"This would indicate that Lieutenant Kauffman did the equivalent of 100 yards in 8 seconds; it is possible that his extreme sense of urgency enabled him to do so."

Recuperating from an injured kidney, Kauffman was glum about the rule that nobody could go back to mine disposal after one had blown up on him. Then a mine landed on a nearby airfield—and the nearest other mine disposal officer was eight hours away. Kauffman phoned for and was granted permission to disarm it. He sat staring at the mine from a discreet distance while he finished one whole cigarette, before he closed in to tackle the fuse—successfully.

That November he was on leave in Washington when Rear Admiral William H. P. Blandy, then Chief of the Bureau of Ordnance, foresightedly asked him to set up a U.S. bomb-disposal organization. The Navy was now willing to waive 20-20 eyesight to get an explosive expert. The British released Kauffman and he was at last commissioned in the U.S. Naval Reserve. A month later, Pearl Harbor was attacked. Kauffman flew out to help dispose of unexploded Jap bombs. They proved simple compared to German mechanisms—no booby traps.

After heading the Bomb Disposal School for a year and a half Kauffman was handed the problem of forming underwater demolition teams. The first thing to do was to locate a site for the new school. After scouting other amphibious training bases at Solomons, Maryland, and Little Creek, Virginia, Kauffman chose Fort Pierce, Florida, because of its year-round warm water and because of the enthusiasm of Captain Clarence Gulbranson, USN, the Base Commander, for the new organization. Kauffman began lining up junior officers from the Mine and Bomb Disposal Schools, and explosive experts. His early efforts and continuing enthusiasm won him the tag of "The Father of Demolition," by which he is still known in Underwater Demolition Team circles.

The project started from scratch, without program, doctrine, materials, or trainees. All it had was a home in the still-building Naval Amphibious Training Base. There, on narrow Causeway Island between the ocean and the Indian River opposite Fort Pierce, four men moved into a tent in the first week of June. These were Kauffman; his executive officer, Lieutenant (jg) James Warnock from the Bomb Disposal School staff; Lieutenant (jg) James Wetzel, specially commissioned from a big powder company to furnish technical advice; and Ensign John Francis, also "stolen" from Bomb Disposal.

More training officers were recruited with promises of early action, which some of them—"Bert" Hawks and "Lew"

Luehrs, for instance—got half a year later at Kwajalein. Almost all the early group were assigned overseas demolition duty as soon as they could be spared and replaced.

The next problem was to get men to train. By June 16 Kauffman requested five SeaBee (Construction Battalion) officers, five SeaBee petty officers, and thirty men. All had to volunteer for "hazardous, prolonged, distant duty."

Other requirements, which haven't changed very much to the present day, were youth—twenty to thirty-five; strength and endurance; swimming ability (only 200 yards, at first); and no fear of explosives. Men and officers were to be volunteers, since it was believed that only a man with self-confidence and courage would volunteer for extra-hazardous duty. Many of the first trainees were older, higher-rated men, eager and overdue to leave the muddy grind of Camp Perry for overseas combat.

Volunteers were challenged by a growing rumor that the new organization would be a "75 per cent casualty outfit"—a theory which seemed thoroughly plausible both to men and officers. All other details were secret—strict military security proved amazingly effective throughout the war. That secrecy not only preserved hundreds of demolition men's lives but resulted in the success of many amphibious operations and the prevention of countless thousands of casualties to American soldiers and Marines.

As the volunteers trickled into Fort Pierce in June and early July, they found little in the way of housing, equipment, or training program. The intense Florida summer heat, oversize mosquitoes and prolific sand fleas presented built-in beach defenses. But from the start, the trainees had a far from secret weapon—their fighting spirit.

In preparing the training program, Kauffman asked an existing amphibious group at the base, the Scouts-and-Raiders, to compress the highlights of their own eight-week physical training program into a single week's schedule. The rival Scouts-and-Raiders were more than willing. The result was officially named "Indoctrination Week," but it has never been called anything but "Hell Week." This first week started training in high gear.

Kauffman and his officers went through "Hell Week" along with the first trainees; this established a precedent in UDT, which requires that officers and men demonstrate the same capabilities and endure the same hardships.

Since everyone expected demolition operations to be conducted from rubber boats or in shallow water, the trainees worked in full combat gear—heavy field shoes, fatigues or green combat uniforms, helmets, and Mae Wests (bulky, inflatable vest-harness lifebelts). Every day of "Hell Week" started with an hour of hard physical training, topped off by a three-mile double-time march. Then came hours in inflated black, bulbous-rimmed rubber boats. The six-man units paddled the loaded boats (explosives filled the seventh man's space) against tides and surf and wind. They portaged them over rocks and reefs and dunes and jetties, by day and night. They landed and launched them through surf, and paddled through muddy, weed-tangled inlets, working against a time schedule. For twelve to sixteen hours a day they had to meet increasingly tough physical tests.

"Hell Week" was climaxed by the appropriately named "So Solly Day." Before dawn, the volunteers embarked in landing craft, which were driven through the surf to a beach. Just as the ramps were dropped to permit the trainees to land, the beach erupted in a thundering sheet of flame as heavy demolition charges were detonated. For the rest of the day they were driven through swamps, mud, surf, and jungle growth, always harried by unseen booby traps. When they feared to move, the ground was blown up from under them. The instruction staff tossed improvised half-pound TNT hand grenades close (supposedly not closer than ten feet) to the bruised, shaken trainees. Booby traps lined the jungle trails, to catch the unwary. As they plowed waist-deep through the muck and water of mangrove swamps, heavy 20-pound charges blew columns of water high above them, raining down showers of mud and debris.

The day culminated with the trainees confined in a small perimeter, crouching in foxholes. For a solid hour, charge after charge was detonated around them. At first the shock of unexpected explosives was startling, then it became something of a game, but a full day of exposure to continuous shattering concussion would try the fiber of any man. The purpose of "So Solly Day" was to weed out anyone with an "inherent fear" of explosives, a weakness which would imperil both himself and his teammates in combat. Survivors of this training seldom knew such fear again. "Hell Week" washed out 30 to 40 per cent of the volunteers, separating "the men from the boys." Those who qualified had confidence that they could carry on against the toughest conditions. It also taught men a safeguarding respect for the power of explosives.

In this first week of training, the men learned the value of friendship in war. All through training and later in combat, men were paired off together in the UDT buddy system, which particularly applied to swimming. Where the buddy system has been observed, not a single UDT man has been lost through accidental drowning. Friendship and close teamwork became the maxim of the UDT organization.

The first months at Fort Pierce meant a constant struggle with procurement. Naturally, both good men and good steel were in demand throughout the Armed Forces. The training commands developed good men; it was up to the research scientists to equip them properly.

At first civilian scientists were enlisted as idea men in the DOLO Committee (Demolition of Obstacles to Landing Operations) established in August 1943. This was replaced by the Joint Army-Navy Experimental and Testing Board (JANET), proposed by General Marshall and organized by Admiral King on November 2, 1943. JANET, of which Kauffman was a member, was assisted in its evaluation and experimentation by the Naval Demolition Research Unit (DRU). This support from the Chief of Naval Operations speeded the organization and equipage of UDT, and resulted in the development of many techniques. To this day, UDT has enjoyed the support and encouragement of the highest naval officers.

The location of all these activities at North Island, across the channel from the Amphibious Base at Fort Pierce, was ideal. The demolition training, JANET, Demolition Research Unit and the Army engineering activities were all within a short distance of one another. The research units were set up to develop equipment for the coming invasion of Europe, but Normandy was stormed before any marked assistance came from JANET. In fact, the scientists have never developed mechanical clearance methods superior to the tactics of underwater swimmers hand-placing explosives. Half a Construction Battalion spent the war on North Island in a thankless race, trying to build obstacles faster than the trainees could demolish them.

In the early days of training at Fort Pierce, swimming was only a test and a method of physical training, rather than a part of scouting or demolition work. All training concentrated on the demolition of obstacles. The lesson of Tarawa and need for beach reconnaissance had yet to be learned. Therefore, trainees were taught to wade through the surf, carrying explosives in to the obstacles in rubber boats. Men were not allowed off the boats in deep water without life belt and life line attached. As with the Scouts-and-Raiders, planning was based on sailors approaching the enemy beach stealthily at night. The same advice from British experience was given by Major Richard Fairbairn, of the Royal Engineers, loaned by Combined Operations to impart commando and hand-to-hand fighting techniques to the demolition trainees.

An "experimental and research" detail was formed among the instructors, to try any device that might be of use in combat. Sportsmen had already pioneered the use of flexible rubber swim fins, and the Fort Pierce staff tried them. Unluckily, however, the swimming experts were used to a hard-kicking crawl, and the heavy fins quickly gave them

leg cramps. Besides, fins seemed likely to become handicaps
in surf or on coral reefs, so they were promptly discarded as
unsuited to military use. The glass-fronted rubber face mask
was also tried out, with its amazing effect of clarifying and
magnifying underwater vision; but men in boats would
have little use for it.

The size of the original rubber boats determined the organization of the trainees into permanent units of five men
and one petty or commissioned officer. Each six-man "Naval
Combat Demolition Unit" was given a consecutive number,
starting with NCDU Number 1. To encourage unit rivalry,
each was given a nickname—Kaine's Killers, Heideman's
Hurricanes, Jeter's Mosquitoes.

The Naval Combat Demolition Units were expected to
remain independent, each under its own officer. They com-
peted with intense rivalry as they tackled the real training
problems, such as hand-placing demolition charges on obstacles, or onto reefs to level them off, timing the fuses for
detonation. They learned communications, using radio sets
from the hand-carried cracker-box walkie-talkie up to the
larger transceivers (sending and receiving sets) in landing
craft. They practiced operating the ramped landing craft,
recognizing coastal silhouettes by day and night, making
stealthy approaches through rocks and surf, and mapping
depths offshore with sounding lines.

During the summer of 1943 it was a struggle to get even
the minimum of equipment. The first rubber boats arrived
with only two paddles apiece, instead of the six required for
the units. Such then-fantastic requirements as underwater
watches (for timing blasts or pickups) and swim-diving apparatus, faced months of delay and a discouragingly high
rate of equipment failure.

Kauffman asked for self-contained diving equipment but
was warned that the Allies still had developed nothing safe
enough to use. The Italians were well ahead in that field,
with their masks and self-contained oxygen rebreathing
units. Nevertheless, some of the Italian two-man submersible

boat crews and "Gamma" swimmers towing limpet mines in raids on British Mediterranean harbors had died or blacked out to surface as helpless casualties because either their oxygen had failed, or they had suffered oxygen poisoning from working too hard and too deep. Many months later, commercial invention and Navy testing developed the early model "Jack Brown" oxygen breathing unit and mask, and the "Lambertson Lung." Some Fort Pierce trainees learned to use them in time for the invasion of France, but a change in the landing plan canceled the combat tryout of this apparatus.

New military explosives were being tested. A major achievement was the development of primacord, the almost instantaneous waterproof explosive detonator. Primacord, which looked like yellow clothesline, became one of the mainstays of military demolition.

The greatest headache was getting waterproof fuse igniters to touch off the primacord and the explosive packs. Time and again the man assigned to pull a fuse would shout the traditional dynamiter's warning: "Fire in the hole!" The trainees would take cover, counting the seconds and watching the underwater obstacle which had been packed with explosive. Nothing would happen. Another wet fuse. Another misfire. Successive models of waterproof fuse igniters were developed by the Navy during the war, and continued to give trouble in the water despite the best efforts of inventors and testing boards.

Kauffman's men themselves hit upon a "field expedient" which worked well enough to become standard practice. Just as the GI used similar rubber devices to keep mud and snow out of his rifle muzzle, the demolition men sheathed their underwater fuses in prophylactics. A supply officer, looking disapprovingly at the fantastic consumption of condoms by the demolition teams throughout the war, might well have suspected they had found the mermaids' undersea lair.

In more mechanical directions, naval ingenuity was working overtime on the problems of beach clearance. A fantastic series of secret devices were invented to push, tow, or shoot explosives into position to clear natural or man-made obstructions. But experience on beach after beach was to prove that the most versatile and effective of all the weapons was man himself, braving and conquering enemy defenses.

Attrition during training was high. Only a handful of men graduated from Fort Pierce in the first training class. The six men of Naval Combat Demolition Unit No. 1 left late that summer before the other teams had finished training. The unit reached San Francisco under secret orders for the reoccupation of the Aleutians, but because of a foul-up on orders and transportation for the little, unknown unit, they literally missed the boat. Deserted Kiska was taken without benefit of naval underwater demolition. The men were ordered to the Central Pacific and were merged in later demolition teams.

The next two units, under Lieutenants (jg) Frank Kaine and Lloyd Anderson, were shipped to the Southwest Pacific. They formed the nucleus of a half-dozen similar six-man units which served through the war with the Seventh Amphibious Force, helping the SeaBees and General MacArthur's Engineer Special Brigades clear boat channels after the landing waves had taken beaches from Biak to Borneo. Because of their small numbers, and the theater commander's reliance on the large and well-equipped Army Engineer Brigades, these naval combat demolition units based in the Southwest Pacific were never used ahead of the troops.

In the first "class" at Fort Pierce, eleven units graduated and went overseas. Besides the three already mentioned, two went to North Africa where they trained succeeding units and saw action in the invasion of Southern France many months later. One went to England. Two units were sent to Rear Admiral Wilkinson in the South Pacific. Three went to Rear Admiral Turner in Hawaii, in time for use in the temporarily organized Underwater Demolition Teams, first used in the Kwajalein operation.

3. Baptism in an Atoll

As one direct result of the lessons of Tarawa and conferences with Captain Hill, Admiral Turner recommended the reorganization of the six-man Naval Combat Demolition Units into Underwater Demolition Teams (UDT). The new teams were to have a strength of 100 officers and men, formed into a headquarters and four operating platoons.

Admiral Nimitz quickly obtained Navy Department approval of this new policy and the establishment of a tactical school in Hawaii for UDT training and underwater experiments, which was given top priority. Two Underwater Demolition Teams were urgently required for the prospective attacks on Kwajalein and Roi-Namur. One month was available for obtaining volunteers, and for organizing and training the men who became UDT 1 and UDT 2.

A SeaBee officer, Commander Edward D. Brewster, was reassigned to command UDT 1. Another SeaBee, a tall Texan, Lieutenant Thomas C. Crist, was placed in temporary command of Team 2.

From Fort Pierce came Naval Combat Demolition Units in charge of Ensigns Hawks, Luehrs, King and Chief Carpenters Harris and Gordon. They were swept into Admiral Turner's personnel dragnet which was assembling other volunteers from all the Services who might qualify for demolition training. From the Marines came officers and men with Tarawa experience; and from the Army, land demolition experts.

Training in reconnaissance, landing craft seamanship, and the detonation of explosives began at the Waimanolo Amphibious Base, across the end of the Island from Honolulu.

25

The Fort Pierce men and the Pacific veterans alike had to learn new techniques. Obstacles and mines modeled on the defenses of Tarawa were used as drill targets.

To reduce the hazard of sending men into an enemy beach for obstacle clearance, a promising secret weapon was devised. The "Stingray" was an ordinary low-ramped wooden landing craft, filled with several tons of explosive. Its steering and firing gear were radio-controlled, and its gasoline motor specially fitted with hydraulic shift. It could be re-mote-controlled to a reef or man-made obstacle and then scuttled by one signal and exploded by another. It was designed to blow a sizable gap, through which landing craft could proceed to the beach.

As soon as Lieutenant Crist and a few others learned to operate the remote controls, they were called on to give a demonstration for Captain Hill. Somebody got the bright idea of adding rocket launchers to the drone craft for extra fireworks.

Lieutenant Crist started the floating bomb toward a small deserted island. It cruised straight and true. The first signal fired the rockets perfectly. But their flaming backlash set the boatload of dynamite afire. Brewster ordered the main charge fired, but Crist pointed out that it would explode all right as soon as the fire reached a detonator fuse. He hardly got the words out when a most spectacular explosion duly impressed all observers. The blast also killed several hundred pounds of prime tuna fish, which Chief Roeder loaded into a weapons carrier and traded ashore for two cases of Stateside whiskey.

Chief Howard L. Roeder, naturally known as "Red" for his fierce red bushy beard, was one of the SeaBees recruited for demolition. He was a soldier of fortune, an "Old China Hand" who claimed to have fought there. He was due for a greater adventure on a secret UDT mission at a later date.

Just before Christmas, Underwater Demolition Team Two was sufficiently manned and organized to be sent to San Diego, where the team reported to Rear Admiral Richard L. Conolly, Group Commander of the 5th Amphibious Force. Team Two was ordered to pick up more Stingrays, and a complete load of scarce equipment from the mainland, including 50 tons of dynamite, yards of bangalore torpedoes (explosives in sectional tube form), 25 tons of the superior military explosive tetrytol in packs, miles of primacord, and 40 inflatable rubber boats.

Admiral Conolly requested line officers with combat experience for the team which would be a small part of his Task Force, and placed two Sicily veterans in charge.

Lieutenant Commander John T. Koehler, who would play an important role in the future development of UDT, became commanding officer. As executive officer of an "advance base unit" in Gela, Sicily, he had been thrown into the lines with other Navy personnel when the Hermann Goering Panzer Division broke through, only to have its tanks routed by counterattack and Navy gunfire.

Lieutenant William G. Carberry was at another Sicilian landing point, Licata. Now he became executive officer of Koehler's UDT 2.

Admiral Conolly's task force included a newly developed and very important amphibious weapon—infantry landing craft converted to gunboats, LCI(G)s, which had recently been tried out in the South and Southwest Pacific, employed for close-to-shore gunfire support in landings. On Admiral Turner's demand, the California Institute of Technology supplied quantities of rockets and rocket launchers. Conolly equipped the gunboats with batteries of rockets set to fire ten at a time onto the beach, in addition to their regular rapid-fire 40mm and 20mm "pompom" cannon, and heavy .50 caliber machine guns.

The new gunboats were divided between the Conolly and Turner task forces in Hawaii. The admirals themselves sailed in new specially designed command ships with vastly improved communications systems which couldn't be blacked out by the concussion of battleship salvos as had happened in the Gilberts.

The two task forces, plus the Majuro and the Reserve Groups, staged from Hawaii and proceeded separately on "Operation Flintlock." This assault on the Marshall Islands was the first invasion of territory which had been Japanese before Pearl Harbor. The task group under Rear Admiral Harry Hill (who had commanded the Tarawa Attack Force) followed one day later to seize undefended Majuro Atoll as a supply and refueling base and fleet anchorage.

Also at Majuro, but at that time unaware of the existence of UDT, was "Red" Fane who later was to command another UDT 1. Fane was First Lieutenant and Cargo Officer of the *Mauna Loa*, an ammunition ship. While transferring shells to the flagship *Pennsylvania*, a 14-inch powder can caught fire on her deck, flames roared masthead high. While the crew of the *Pennsylvania* stood frozen, Fane's damage control crew turned hoses on the can, as he leaped across to the deck of the *Pennsylvania* and kicked the burning can over the side. A year later, tiring of carrying ammunition for other ships to fire, Fane volunteered for "extra-hazardous duty" and found himself in UDT.

Meantime Admiral Spruance's Fifth Fleet had been pounding the Marshall Archipelago for days. Rear Admiral Mark A. Mitscher's Fast Carrier Task Force smashed Japanese air power based on Kwajalein and other Marshall strongholds. As Commander of the Fifth Amphibious Force, Admiral "Kelly" Turner was in tactical command of the assault on Kwajalein. Admiral Spruance would only take over if the Japanese Fleet came out to fight for its island bases.

Kwajalein, the world's largest atoll, offered a double target. Its islet-studded barrier reef outlines a 66-mile-long deep-water lagoon shaped like a thin shark diving to the southeast. The largest islands on the narrow border reef are Kwajalein Island at the sharp-pointed snout, and the twin islands of Roi-Namur at the north tip of the triangular fin. Each would receive the full attention of one task force.

Turner's Task Force 52, carrying the Army 7th Division

which had recaptured the Aleutians, reached Kwajalein Island before dawn of D-Day, January 31, 1944.

The reef isles nearer Kwajalein had been softened up by battleship bombardment the day before. Now, around dawn of D-Day, ships and carrier planes pounded them deafeningly.

This was the signal for Underwater Demolition Team One to test its secret weapon against the mile-long islet of Enubuj, just west of Kwajalein. Although the islet's modest reef didn't require any demolition, Admiral Turner wanted a combat test of the Stingray drones. Each drone was loaded with three tons of cratering explosive intended to blow a sizable gap in coral or man-made obstacles. UDT 1 must complete its mission on the reef and get out of the way half an hour before the troops left their line of departure at sea and headed in to the beach.

The test began. Two drone craft started toward the beach, each temporarily manned with a mechanic and coxswain to set its controls. The two-man crew then threw a rubber boat overboard and jumped into it, waiting for the following control boat to pick them up. One master craft controlled the two slave boats. A spare team, consisting of another control boat and a third drone, stood by.

One of the two drones heading for the beach slowed without orders, getting deeper in the choppy water, then abruptly went under while still 600 yards from shore. Something had gone wrong with its pumps. Its robot partner sputtered, the motor stopped, and it drifted to a halt, rocking in the waves. The reserve team started the third drone toward the shore, but after its crew left it, the motor conked out. The crews paddled back to their drifting drones and frantically tried to get the motors working. Time was running short. The landing waves were already starting toward shore. The Stingray operation was quickly abandoned, and the drones limped or were towed out of the way to avoid blowing up the approaching troops. This early test of push-button warfare was a total failure.

Later investigation revealed that officers who were skeptical of the untried UDT operation had thriftily relegated old, worn, badly repaired landing craft as sacrifice drones—"inexcusably and without the knowledge of the Force Commander," Admiral Turner officially commented. Anyone who has been chewed out by "Kelly" Turner would not envy the responsible officers.

Fortunately this fiasco did not delay the landing on gun-fire-plastered Enubuj. Its coconut palms were already reduced to the crew-cut stubble which was getting the nickname of a "Spruance haircut" in honor of the Fifth Fleet's commander.

Meantime, members of Team One had another mission of greater importance than the drone test. Although Admiral Turner later noted that he had not expected the new underwater demolition teams to be of any great value at Kwajalein, he had prepared five different plans for their use in exploring the beaches. The original schedule for UDT 1 was a midnight reconnaissance of the reef stretching from occupied Enubuj to the squarish western end of Kwajalein, the chosen landing beaches.

Air photos taken before the fleet left Hawaii showed the Japanese working hard on a wall across those western beaches, similar to the fatal barricade at Tarawa. Photos taken two days before the landing and air-dropped to Turner's flagship on "D minus one" (a day before D-Day) had not revealed any obstacles or mines on the reef; but the wall was clearly shown, a heavy barrier of concreted rocks with seasoned hardwood posts slating seaward to oppose amtracs or tanks. The reefs might offer other hidden tricks.

Therefore, Admiral Turner switched to one of his alternate UDT plans—two daylight reconnaissance missions on the reef before landing, one at high tide and the other at low tide. Sending demolition men to work literally under the noses of the enemy in daylight appeared extremely hazardous, but he was confident that the fleet's fire power could keep the Japanese buttoned down. At ten that morning of

January 31, 1944, the battleships *Pennsylvania* from 4,000 yards and *Mississippi* from 2,000 yards, assisted by several destroyers, began bombarding Kwajalein Island.

Turner's plan called for four ramped landing craft to approach on the morning high tide, manned by UDT men, photographers, leadsmen, radiomen and machine gunners.

Ahead of the boats lay the reef which the landing troops must cross tomorrow, a wide ribbon of coral stretching from Kwajalein to Enubuj. Across the sawed-off western end of Kwajalein's low crescent, the stone-and-log wall stretched forbiddingly. Behind the wall Japanese riflemen and machine gunners crouched in their dugouts, taking a beating from the ships' guns. As Turner had surmised, only a few sniper shots and one or two widely missing mortar bursts greeted the landing craft.

In the leading boat which ventured up to the reef within a quarter mile from shore were Ensign Lewis F. "Lew" Luehrs, trained in Fort Pierce demolition and scouting, and SeaBee Chief "Bill" Acheson. As Luehrs tells it:

"When the Chief and I found out we were about to make a recon on the island of Kwajalein, we decided that if we came within range of too many coral heads, we would take off our fatigues, and with our trunks hidden carefully below (others aboard might think we were crazy) swim in onto the reef for a closer view.

"The transport gave us a royal send-off, a last meal and farewell, and let us over the side for the big event. We approached the beach to within about 500 yards in the boat. When the coxswain became squeamish and the coral heads thicker, we dove over the side of the boat and proceeded in toward the beach. We were in the water about 45 minutes, and were able to see gun emplacements, and a large log barricade on the entire tip of the island. We found that the reef was covered with coral heads, which would prevent the landing of small boats, but no mines.

"When we returned to the ship, we were whisked off to the flagship *Monrovia*, still dripping wet, for a very impressive staff meeting, and to tell our story to Vice Admiral Turner, Rear Admiral Griffin, and Captain Knowles. We advised the use of amtracs instead of boats."

The landing took place in amtracs.

Underwater demolition had taken a first tentative step—from the boats into the water. Ensign Luehrs and Chief Acheson measured the depths by wading on the deeply covered reef, and swimming about the coral heads in order to estimate their size and number. They had stripped to their swim trunks. They had no dive masks, just underwater goggles. The two men went far ahead of their boat, much closer to shore than the 500-yard mark.

Meanwhile heavy showers in the early afternoon stopped the air strike and ended air photography. Attack schedules can't be called off for rain, however, and the low-tide reconnaissance teams set out at four that afternoon (1600, on the 24-hour clock by then adopted by Army and Navy). The scouts, in slow-moving steel-armored amtracs armed with machine guns, gave the low-tide reef a practical test in the vehicles which would carry the troops ashore the next dawn.

Both morning and afternoon groups gave a favorable enough report, no man-made obstacles on the reef, only scattered coral heads, and enough high-tide water over the reef. There was no need for underwater demolition or further reconnaissance.

The most important UDT report, however, struck Admiral Turner so forcefully that he remembered it when interviewed ten years later. The naval gunfire, although much heavier than at Tarawa, had not breached tank passages through that wall across the western beach above high-water mark. A similar unbreached wall had helped bring disaster to the British and Canadians at Dieppe, France, and had nearly done so at Tarawa. On D plus one, Turner ordered far heavier naval gunfire from closer inshore on it, and a block-buster air bombing just before the morning landing helped make several wide breaches in the wall.

On the morning of February 1, D plus one, two Army

regimental combat teams crossed the reef and poured ashore, riding the rising tide in their newly armor-plated amtracs with three machine guns apiece, led by a wave of "amphibian tanks," each of which was an armored amtrac with tank turret and cannon. The mechanized waves swept through the breached wall to drive inland, where dismounted Army troops dug the defenders out of their holes. Later waves of landing craft rode the high tide most of the way across the reef without grounding. Tarawa's mistake was not repeated.

Team One stood by with its landing craft, but was not needed until the next day. The transports were scheduled to leave, and the team was unceremoniously marooned ashore on the already captured west end of the island. The team's training with explosives paid off, as they blasted channels through the reef inside the lagoon for the tank landing ships and supply ships. They also blew up several battle-wrecked Japanese barges blocking the shore. Soon the big tank landing ships nosed into the newly cleared channels, and opened their bow doors to drop ramps and unload vehicles onto the beach.

At least once during the four days while the Army was plowing its way up the island, a UDT demolition squad was called to the heart of the battle zone. While troop fire kept Japanese defenders pinned inside a thick-walled pillbox, the UDT men ran up to its blind side. Hastily they packed their haversacks of tetrytol against the heavily reinforced concrete, tied the load together with primacord fuse, and ran back to take cover from the explosion. With the side of the pillbox crumbled, the troops finished the job and the Japanese—perfect Army-Navy teamwork.

Team One moved up the beach after the Army, the length of Kwajalein, and then onto the next sizable island of Ebeye which had a strongly defended seaplane base. On both islands they received valuable training and plenty of hard underwater work while making channels and ramps.

This was only half the battle of Kwajalein Atoll. The

Northern Attack Force meanwhile was striking the Siamese twin islands of Roi and Namur, two squarish reef-bound islands connected by a strip of beach and a man-made causeway, located at the north tip of the shark's fin. Admiral Conolly's schedule was the same as Turner's—take the flanking islands on D-Day, January 31, then strike the main target the next day.

Soon after dawn, landing teams in amtracs seized two small islands on the west side of the triangular fin nearest the waiting fleet. The islands guarding two passes into the lagoon were code-named "Jacob" and "Ivan," easier to remember than Ennuebing and Mellu.

In a landing craft, Lieutenant Tom Crist scouted "Jacob" passage, and reported to Commander Koehler that the island appeared to be a good base for the team. By noon, the skipper of their cargo ship was eagerly dumping drone boats and the team's unwelcome explosives over the side. Koehler and Lieutenant Carberry led their men and boats onto the island which became their headquarters.

Battleships and cruisers were pounding Roi and Namur. Minesweepers cleared the passes into the lagoon. Infantry landing craft and a destroyer followed them, preparing to strike the target from within. Amtracs crossed the choppy lagoon during intermittent rain squalls, landing new assault teams on the lagoon shore of the eastern islands. Artillery followed onto the islands just east and west of Roi-Namur, to add to the hammering the big islands were receiving from the fleet gunfire.

Lieutenant Crist unloaded additional drones from the transport *Callaway*, which also carried the team's explosives, as well as part of the team. The transport's skipper filled the drones with the team's touchy cargo of nitrodynamite, and later wrote a blistering report about loading such dangerous, low-priority stuff aboard a transport with 1,300 troops and key officers.

At one hour before midnight, the fire-support ships offshore and in the lagoon stepped up their bombardment of

Roi-Namur in order to cover a night survey of the chosen landing beaches. Aboard an infantry landing craft in the lagoon, the Marine officer in charge organized his scouts and the UDT men who would do the job together.

The reconnaissance crews started the outboard motors on their rubber boats and headed for the southern beaches of Roi and Namur facing the lagoon. Marine scouts and UDT men were in full combat uniform with life belts, under strict orders that if a swimmer went over the side for observation, he must be on a life line which would be carefully paid out as he swam to the beach. This had been standard Fort Pierce training doctrine also.

Under cover of the heavy fire from ships carefully sited so that their gun flames wouldn't silhouette the rubber boats, the scouts made their quick survey and soundings offshore. The reefs on the lagoon shore seemed sloping and clear of mines and obstacles. As well as the observers could tell at night, landings were possible anywhere along the beaches. The rubber boats pitched and tossed too much in the rough water for a complete survey in the dark, but the favorable report brought to the flagship later proved correct.

As soon as it was light on the morning of D plus one, Team Two launched its drone boats into the lagoon, followed by amtracs used as controls. The plan was to test the drones against the reefs just before the troops landed.

The sea outside was so rough that Admiral Conolly sent tank landing ships (LST) inside the lagoon to unload Marines into the assault craft. The turbulent lagoon held several hundred milling craft, already somewhat disorganized by bad weather, motor failures, and imperfectly rehearsed amtrac crews. They were trying to form into waves, near the gunboats which would back them up and the turreted amtrac "tanks" which would lead them, for close-up fire support. Out in the ocean, the battleships were closing the range to pound the islands continuously from a mere mile offshore and earning the Amphibious Force Admiral the nickname of "Close-in-Conolly."

Lieutenant Commander Koehler had been favored with drone boats in good running condition. Carberry and Crist were in the amtrac, with Lieutenant William Lambert "Bert" Hawks handling the controls.

They aimed the first drone toward the pier at the center of the enemy beach. The landing craft, loaded with five tons of 60 per cent dynamite, vanished into the smoke and haze of the bombarded beach. Crist told Hawks to push the "arming" switch (to get the drone's charge ready to fire). The lagoon chop was sending dollops of spray into the low amtracs, wetting the men and the radio. Crist waited a few minutes, then gave the order: "Fire!"

Hawks pushed the firing switch on the remote-control radio.

Nothing happened. Even amid the din of the ships' bombardment they should hear the 10,000-pound dynamite blast. Suddenly, out of the thick, low, brown battle haze hiding the beaches, the drone boat reappeared. They tried to regain control; somebody guessed wildly that the Japs were jamming the radio signals. The drone went into a tight circle, turning endlessly, only a few hundred yards from the beach. Realizing they couldn't leave the runaway boat circling there, squarely in the way of the first landing waves already forming to head for the beach, Hawks hailed a stand-by craft and boarded it with Coxswain Johnson and another UDT man. As their landing craft headed for the armed and triggered drone, Jap machine-gun fire from the beach rattled across the water at them. They came alongside the runaway drone, and Hawks and Johnson jumped in, moving gingerly but fast. They cut out four fuses, just in time—the remote arming device had worked, and the circuits were ready to fire! They brought the drone under manual control, and steered away from the machine-gun fire.

Crist and Carberry decided to try another drone. This one started toward the beach, got a few feet away from their amtrac and promptly circled and rammed them. As Crist comments, "Being rammed by 10,000 pounds of dynamite is not a pleasant experience."

One of the men was knocked overboard, but the drone didn't explode. They placed it under manual control again, and, deciding to get the whole dangerous operation out of the way of the oncoming Marines, hand-steered the drones and control craft back to the home islands.

Japanese electronic genius was given undue credit for jamming the Stingrays. Later check-ups indicated that salt spray did the job, short-circuiting the delicate remote-control transmitters and receivers. Push-button warfare had drawn another blank.

Luckily the beaches proved accessible without any underwater demolition. The Fourth Marine Division earned its first battle honors by taking little more than a day to overrun the battered twin islands, digging out the dazed but bitterly fighting Japanese garrison. As soon as the beachheads were secured, Lieutenant Commander Koehler took a party of UDT men ashore with explosives, to lend a hand in blasting Japanese out of culverts and blockhouses.

On Namur, Koehler and his UDT men came close to the fighting which raged around a blockhouse where the Japanese were holding out, hidden deep in a concrete storage vault. The Marines used a flame thrower—and found out too late that it was an underground ammunition dump. Several Marines were killed by the explosion, along with all the Japanese. The UDT men were shaken but not hurt. Getting back to their special duties, the team blasted out a sloping edge on the reef to let the tank landing ships nose up onto the coral.

Kwajalein Atoll was secured, north and south. Turner and Conolly had written a brave new page in the growing book of amphibious warfare. Kwajalein was no pushover; the two assaults cost almost 2,000 casualties, compared to Tarawa's 3,000-odd and barely over 200 at Makin. But Kwajalein had proven to be a real advance in assault technique.

In his report on this "Flintlock Operation," Admiral Turner commented: "Overemphasis of certain problems which experience at Tarawa had exaggerated in the minds of those concerned . . . caused general doubt regarding the effectiveness of our weapons and tactics, and much time and effort was expended on dubious and fruitless schemes."

One such scheme was the tricky Stingrays. Although they were brought along on the next amphibious invasion, they were never used again during the war in the Pacific. As Turner reported to Admiral Nimitz:

"Probably the only effective method of destroying beach mines and obstacles is to send men in to perform individual demolitions in advance of landings."

During the Kwajalein operation, Turner received his promotion to Vice Admiral, and the added duty of Commander, Amphibious Forces, Pacific Fleet (as well as Commander of the Fifth Amphibious Force). The speedy occupation won approval for another seven-league stride toward Japan, aimed at the westernmost atoll in the Marshalls, which later won a different kind of fame in the Atomic Age—Eniwetok, close to Bikini.

Rear Admiral Harry Hill's Eniwetok Expeditionary Force included ships and craft from both Roi-Namur and Kwajalein, and the reserve Marines and soldiers under Brigadier General T. E. Watson, USMC. In an infantry landing craft, UDT 1 embarked from Kwajalein as part of the reconnaissance party.

Eniwetok Atoll is roughly ring-shaped, with Engebi Island as its northern jewel, and Eniwetok and Parry Islands thickening the southern rim. Engebi was the first target because of its airfield. A 400-yard-wide coral shelf stretching from Engebi into the lagoon caused some concern, so UDT men were ordered to reconnoiter it.

The assault followed the Roi-Namur pattern. Using captured Japanese charts, minesweepers led the assault ships right inside the lagoon.

At five that afternoon, UDT scouting parties boarded two

Marine-manned amtracs, and headed for the Engebi coral shelf under cover of naval gunfire. Lieutenant Luehrs led one of the UDT groups; this time, all of them wore trunks under their combat greens. As the two amtracs approached the reef, Japanese mortars and machine guns began sniping at the scout craft. The amtracs answered with their machine guns, and called for ship gunfire to be directed on the trouble spots.

As the UDT men spotted underwater coral heads in the clear water over the reef, they stripped to their trunks and sheath knives, donned goggles, and dove overboard to check the depth. A coral head can tear the bottom out of a landing craft, or disable the screws and rudder. The dangerous coral heads were marked with yellow buoys. For two long hours, the amtracs cruised the area within 50 yards of the shore under scattered fire, then pulled back to place red and black buoys to mark the boundaries of the 400-yard-wide boat lanes which they had explored. Luehrs and his fellow swimmers dove in again and again to make sure the buoys were solidly fastened. The UDT men in their staff meeting that evening reported enemy pillboxes ashore which had so far been missed by naval gunfire. Those targets were duly "creamed" before the next day's landings.

The next morning, three of the UDT reconnaissance party boarded the first wave of landing craft to act as guides to the beach. A naval lieutenant was in the right flank guide craft, Luehrs and Chief Acheson were on the left. Due to the battle haze, the landing wave began slanting out of the channel too far to the left.

Taking command of the guide boat, Luehrs raced into the defenders' rifle and mortar fire to catch up to the landing craft, crowding them back into the channel he had helped buoy. The amtracs then headed straight for the beach, narrowly escaping shipwreck on a mass of underwater coral heads the UDT men had spotted the day before. Luehrs' initiative earned a Silver Star medal.

The UDT operation did not get off scot-free. Team One's

leader, Commander Brewster, was wounded by Japanese gunfire.

The Marines landed despite enemy fire from the beach and the flanks, fighting their way across the island, wiping out resistance by sundown. It was now discovered that Eniwetok and Parry were held by strong, dug-in garrisons which had played possum under their camouflage while Admiral Hill's ships cruised past them into the lagoon.

The next day, therefore, without time for as much naval gunfire preparation as Engebi received, the Army hit Eniwetok. The reserve Marines were added to the attack force, which took four days to dig out every underground strong point, and another day for weary Marines from Engebi to wipe out the garrison of nearby Parry Island.

Those beaches offered no problems to the amtrac landings, but the UDT men were called upon to clear up the lagoon channels and anchorages, and make ramps ashore for the tank landing ships. Finally Eniwetok Atoll was a secure American forward base. Leaving a garrison in occupation, the assault forces returned to Hawaii, transporting the weary demolitioneers.

While Team One was still at Eniwetok, Lieutenant Commander John Koehler was already busy establishing a new base and a training program for UDT in Hawaii. During March, Vice Admiral Turner requisitioned all of the demolition-trained personnel available from Fort Pierce, which was turning out increasingly large classes of trainees. The Amphibious Force Commander intended to use five Underwater Demolition Teams in the next westward advance. UDT had received its baptism of fire, and had proven worthy of greater responsibilities.

4. Demolition Drill

Six men arrived in England on November 1, 1943, as the entering wedge to break Hitler's Atlantic Wall. They were the eleventh Naval Combat Demolition Unit to be qualified from the "First Class" at Fort Pierce. Lieutenant (jg) Heideman and his unit reported to Plymouth, and were attached to Commander Naval Forces Europe, who had no idea who they were, what they were sent for, and what their future mission might be. Such was the secrecy which shrouded the build-up for the Normandy Invasion.

In December, nine more units from the second Fort Pierce class arrived and were shipped from one end of England to another without finding anyone responsible for housing and training them. Lieutenant Robert C. Smith, who had been in the Sicily landing, became Officer in Charge of all the Naval Combat Demolition Units. He kept the men busy in their spare time, scavenging the countryside for demolition drill. Road blocks and obstacles, which had been placed as counterinvasion barriers along the English coast, were hauled to a beach eight miles from the Falmouth Base. Under the supervision of Heideman, who had taken a quick course in British explosives techniques, the Naval Combat Demolition Units blasted away at every spare moment.

Very few ranking officers knew of the existence of the "demolitioneers." However, Lieutenant (jg) Lane Blackwell, technical liaison man on the staff of the U.S. Naval Attaché, and Major Richard Fairbairn, British Liaison Officer of the Eleventh Amphibious Force, both of whom had visited Fort Pierce, gave them such assistance and intelligence information as was available. But the top-secret invasion plan was so closely guarded that it could not be given to the units' junior officers. They were discouraged by the lack of interest of anyone in high authority in their problems, and morale became so low that when the news of the UDT success in Kwajalein arrived in February, Lieutenant (jg) Walter "Scotty" Cooper wrote seriously to Fort Pierce, requesting a transfer to the Pacific in order to see action.

The young officers thought the British were no farther advanced than themselves in demolition methods, but they did pick up valuable hints about new types of Nazi beach and harbor obstacles. Besides the limited British instruction, Larry Heideman was flown to Fort Pierce in February to witness tests the Army Engineer Board was making with JANET and the Navy training staff against Jap and Nazi obstacles. Lieutenant Colonel John T. O'Neill, who attended the tests, became Commanding Officer of the Fifth Corps Special Engineer Task Force to which the Navy demolition units in England were later attached.

Unit officers attending the British school "COXE" (Combined Operations Experimental Establishment) obtained pictures and literature about obstacles already placed on the coast of France, the most difficult of which was called Element "C," or the Belgian Gate. This was a lattice-faced steel gate propped up on the landward side by 14-foot steel bracings. The grilled face was 10 feet high and 10 feet wide, the whole structure made of six-inch angle iron, one half inch in thickness, welded and bolted together and having a gross weight of about three tons. These monsters could be rolled onto the beach at low tide and were strong enough to withstand any surf. Large numbers had been discovered back of the dune line along the entire coast of France, and were expected to be placed on the beaches at a later date by forced French labor. The Belgian Gate provided an entirely new problem to Naval Combat Demolition.

Although steel was a high priority item in blitzed England, the demolition wanglers soon constructed two complete bays of Element "C" on the practice beach. Their problem was to flatten the obstacle with the least possible amount of bursting shrapnel to endanger the demolition men and nearby troops, and without leaving a high tangle of steel which would itself be an obstacle to landing craft.

No military explosive pack for the purpose had ever been invented. Lieutenant (jg) Carl P. Hagensen, a Pennsylvanian who had graduated from the University of Maine the summer before Pearl Harbor, studied the problem. He filled sausagelike waterproof canvas bags with a newly developed plastic explosive, Composition C-2. A cord on one end of the small canvas sausage and a hook on the other end solved the problem of speedy attachment to the iron girder. A lead of fast-detonating primacord led out for tie-in to a common center.

The "Hagensen Pack" was tried—and worked! With sixteen packs tied at vital spots and exploded simultaneously by a connecting "ring main" of primacord, the steel gate fell flat. Before the end of the war, the improvised Hagensen Pack would get an official Navy "Mark" designation, and would be extensively used in the Pacific.

A majority of the Naval Combat Demolition Unit's personnel were old "powdermen" from the SeaBees. The officers were construction engineers. As such they were well experienced in the commercial methods of handling high explosives. There is, however, a vast difference between commercial and combat demolition. In commercial practice, safety rubber-soled shoes are worn, nonsparking tools used, explosives are stowed in special containers, temperatures kept cool, cigarettes, matches or other source of fire are taboo in an explosive area; the "kid glove" treatment applies to all handling and movement. In combat, the demolitioneers slung their deadly load over their shoulders in canvas sacks, were jostled about in pitching craft, towed their powder through plunging surf in the face of enemy fire, and were required to thrust tubes of explosive (Bangalore Torpedoes) through enemy minefields and barbed-wire entanglements. In combat every safety precaution in the book was of necessity violated, and the teams drilled for hours to perfect themselves to meet these conditions. In the final plan, the demolitioneers were allotted 20 minutes in which to place approximately 20 tons of explosives in 2- to 20-pound individual loads on rugged steel barriers, tie it all together with a primacord main trunk "line," and detonate it! All this while struggling through rough surf, a fast-rising swirling tide, and with thousands of enemy guns pouring a shattering barrage on them! Last but not least, a majority of the enemy obstacles had "Teller" mines placed on them triggered to detonate on contact.

In February, the ten demolition units were split into three groups and sent to Fowey, Swansea, and Salcombe. There they practiced landings with the Second, Sixth, and Seventh Beach Battalions who would organize the beach after the landings. The three groups were scheduled for Utah Beach and the right and left flanks of Omaha Beach, but neither men nor officers knew this till just before D-Day.

Lieutenant Hagensen was with the group destined for Utah, and pushed the testing of his packs on Belgian Gates newly built on a Fowey beach, where a forgotten anti-invasion land mine was occasionally discovered the hard way, when someone would accidentally set it off.

The Swansea group built road blocks, posts and rails on the long flat beaches, and ran time tests on loading and destroying obstructions. These demolition drills later proved invaluable when the operation plans for the actual invasion were being written. Meanwhile eight more Naval Combat Demolition Units arrived from the United States and were divided among the three groups.

By March, the Beach Battalions were ready to go to the marshaling area to await orders to invade. In the absence of official word as to what part the Naval Combat Demolition Units would play, Lieutenant (jg) Walter Cooper, as officer in charge of one group, wrote a desperate request describing the demolition units and proposing plans for

their use on the unknown beaches ahead, which Commander
Eugene Carusi, of the Sixth Beach Battalion, took to the top.

At the same time, the Army and Navy invasion high command were studying intelligence reports and air photos
showing that obstacles were suddenly sprouting on those
wide tidal flats charted as Omaha and Utah beaches on their
top-secret plans for invasion. The Germans had previously
concentrated on fortifying the more obvious Pas de Calais
beaches opposite Dover. But by the end of February, they
had started placing obstacles farther west, where it could
hurt—on the chosen Allied invasion beaches toward Cher-
bourg. Only then, when the need for their services became
critical, did the high command give the Naval Demolition
Units the support and assistance they required to conduct
what appeared to be a suicidal mission.

Since the method of attack would involve assault demo-
lition, it became necessary to reinforce the Naval Combat
Demolition Units. Fort Pierce flew all its available men to
England, a total of sixteen units. Personnel from the Army
Combat Engineers were assigned for training by the Naval
Combat Demolition Unit.

The Eleventh Amphibious Force and the Fifth Army
Corps commands early in April ordered a joint conference
of the Naval Combat Demolition officers and the Army
Combat Engineer officers who would share responsibility
for beach clearance. The conferring officers were told to
prepare a "hypothetical" operation plan for clearing a long,
wide, gradual sand beach with a 25-foot-high tide change,
rising a foot every eight minutes! They should figure on
clearing gaps from sea to shore through rows of steel Belgian
Gates, through heavy steel-and-cement-based pyramids (tetrahedrons) and X-shaped "hedgehogs," through deeply embedded steel rails and slanting wooden ramps, all liberally
salted with contact mines—the most formidable defensive
beach blockade ever devised.

For their four-day conference with the high-ranking Army
Engineer officers, Lieutenant Smith requested British Major

Fairbairn to act as senior U.S. Navy representative to lend them some rank in the discussions. Both Army and Navy groups finally prepared separate plans, which had the common feature of working on the obstacles in daylight at low tide, and combining both services' demolition men, as neither had enough personnel to accomplish such a huge task alone.

The program was modified and adopted by the top planners of Operation Neptune (code name for the Navy phase of General Eisenhower's over-all Operation Overlord). The demolition men's requirement of low tide changed the date of D-Day itself, since the hour of landing would depend on the tide and must be very close to the time of the British landings under General Montgomery farther east, which presented their own different tide and obstacle problems.

Because of their great number, it was decided to attack the obstacles dry-shod, ahead of the incoming tide. The idea of employing experimental water-borne devices, among them the numerous drone boats which had arrived for remote-controlled demolition, had to be scrapped. Success would be dependent on the courage of each individual man, placing explosives by hand while under enemy fire.

On Utah and each of the two halves of Omaha, eight gaps would be blown by a combined Army-Navy team. Each team must clear a gap 50 yards wide for landing craft from the low-water mark across 300 yards of sand to the high-water line of shingle on the beach, blasting through three or four lines of obstructions.

The Naval Combat Demolition Units were expanded to "gap assault teams" numbering an unsuperstitious thirteen. These would be joint Army-Navy teams led by the Navy Demolition Unit officers: five Naval Combat Demolition Unit men, three U.S. Navy seamen sent from a pool in Scotland, and five Army combat engineer noncoms and privates.

In addition, each gap would get a separate 26-man team of Army engineer troops under an Army lieutenant, charged with clearing the landward obstacles while the Navy team took care of the seaward obstructions. Each engineer team would be aided by two tanks and a bulldozer or tankdozer (a tank fitted with a bulldozer blade in front).

In mid-April all the Navy groups assembled at Appledore. With a clear blueprint of their task finally available, they pushed final training.

The Navy command now recognized that the demolition operation needed commanders of rank and line experience. Under the supervision of Captain T. F. Wellings, USN, Gunnery Officer of Task Force 122, two lieutenant commanders in the United States were assigned to the job. Lieutenant Commander Joseph H. Gibbons, a soft-spoken Southerner, but a pug-nosed fighting bantam, had graduated from the Naval Academy in 1924. Instead of going into the Navy he entered the Coast Artillery and later joined the New York Telephone Company. Getting a wartime USNR commission in 1942, he ran an advanced amphibious training base, then served as executive officer of an assault cargo ship at the invasion of Salerno. He was convalescing in the St. Albans Naval Hospital when his new orders arrived. After a week's intensive briefing by a demolition chief in Fort Pierce, he flew to England, taking command of the Omaha groups on May 4. Lieutenant Commander Herbert A. Peterson, a New Englander, had a similar lack of demolition experience before his equally short briefing at Fort Pierce. Peterson had commanded a destroyer escort; now he would command the demolition units at Utah Beach. Once in England, the two commanders quickly organized their units, using their two-and-a-half-stripe rank to get vital last-minute intelligence information. This resulted in Lieutenant General T. R. Roosevelt, Jr., arriving at the training camp. He gave the men an impressive and heartening talk on the vital nature of their mission.

The hasty draft of "boot" seamen to fill the teams arrived from a replacement pool in Scotland. The chiefs and other demolition experts worked overtime drilling the soldiers and sailors into fast-loading teams. Training ended May 22, and the gap assault teams moved en masse to Salcombe, where the making of Hagensen packs was given top priority.

Ten thousand canvas sausages of explosive were ready by D-Day. Nearly all of the canvas packs were sewn by hand by "sailmakers" in lofts throughout England. Mortar ammunition bags were used to hold the 40-pound load each man would carry ashore. Waterproof fuses would be carried in ammunition bags or strung around the fuse pullers' helmets.

On June 1, 1944, the group which was to attack on Utah Beach left Salcombe for the marshaling area. On June 3, the remaining Naval Combat Demolition Units, who were to attack Omaha Beach, went to Portland for embarkation. The invasion of France was on its way.

5. The Bloody Sands of Normandy

When Thou Passest Through
The Waters,
I Will Be With Thee.
ISAIAH 43:2

HITLER'S ATLANTIC WALL WAS IN SIGHT AT LAST. THE FIRST waves of troops in their bobbing assault craft could dimly make out the French hills through the overcast dawn and the smoke of shellfire. Omaha Beach was marked by a crescent of dark hills five miles long, its horns formed by sheer cliffs. Directly ahead of the approaching boats were five narrow ravines which could be used as exits from the beach, if German strong points and minefields didn't block them. In front of the central slopes was a short stretch of marsh and high grass. A few battered beach villas dotted the shore line.

Along the shallow curve of the beach in front of the villas a bank of shingle rock eight or ten feet high—bare, rounded, water-worn stones banked solidly against dune and sea wall— formed an impassable barrier to tanks and vehicles. Before the sea wall, facing the boats, stretched three hundred yards or more of tidal sands still exposed by the ebb tide just turning flood. The beach, wide open to gunfire from the overlooking hills, was closed to boats and vehicles by continuous rows of man-made traps. Three, four, sometimes five rows deep, a hundred yards from front to rear, the obstructions ran parallel to the shore line, out to where they would be just covered at highest tide. Every obstacle was topped with Teller mines, deadly pancakes ready to shatter a boat's hull or men's bodies on contact.

49

Inland, every available bomber had dropped thundering bombloads intended to smash the beach defenses which were now being pounded by naval shellfire. Ahead of the landing craft, lines of British rocket ships closed the beach, turned parallel to it and fired a thousand rockets apiece onto the shore target before turning back to sea. The demolition men in the "Gap Assault Teams," up with the first waves, straining to spot their particular landing point in the hell ashore, could readily believe the good word: "There will be nothing alive on the beach when you land."

Many officers had passed on the assurance they had received in a briefing aboard the flagship *Ancon* that all the German strong points, 75mm to 155mm artillery and heavy machine-gun nests would be knocked out by naval gunfire and saturation bombing. The officers who didn't raise the hopes of their men, however, were wise. For trouble lay ahead.

The bomber waves, using the "Pathfinder" method, with the first bellwether plane signaling when to drop, asked and received a thirty-second delay to make sure the bombloads did not hit incoming troops—which resulted in their bombs landing well inland from the beach defenses. The saturation bombing disrupted enemy communication and later reinforcement to the beaches, but the immediate defenses looking down on the landing troops were unharmed.

Naval shell and rocket fire could not knock them all out. The Nazis were ready at Omaha, even though they knew (they thought) that no beachhead could be established or supplied over those open, storm-swept, heavily mined beaches.

The five possible exits through the hills (charted from right to left, from west to east, as D-1, D-3, E-1, E-3, and F-1 on Dog, Easy, and Fox beaches) were guarded by twelve German strong points. Concrete casements sheltered from ships' gunfire held antitank and antiboat guns, French 75s and the highly efficient German 88s. Pillboxes hid machine guns. Open positions and fire trenches for lighter guns and snipers were connected underground and surrounded by minefields and thick concertina barbed wire. The guns were slanted to crisscross the beaches, zeroed-in to points reaching a mile offshore. Back of the bluffs along the shore were rocket pits and concrete mortar positions. On the walls of the mortar pits, German thoroughness had painted detailed oil pictures of each beach target area, with its exact deflection and range clearly marked.

The emplacements were known to be manned by the defensive 726th Infantry Regiment. Intelligence had unfortunately not discovered that the crack offensive 352d Infantry Division had recently moved for maneuvers into a position close inland.

The attacking forces had their surprise weapons too. In addition to the demolition teams, the attackers were led by DD (Duplex Drive) tanks which had propellers for use in water, and caterpillar tracks for land. When disgorged into the water by the tank landing ships, they wore accordionlike sheaths of watertight canvas, which let them swim like boats till they grounded, shed their canvas, and crawled ashore.

The DD tanks would lead the way at H-Hour (set for 0630, 6:30 A.M.), followed a minute later by a company of infantry landing on each beach to clean up snipers. Only then would the Navy demolition men and the Army engineer troops hit the beach to blow the obstructions. At least, that was the plan. . . .

The demolition men were embarked in tank landing craft barely over 100 feet long, filled with the 13-man Navy unit, the 26-man engineer team, and the craft's own crew, plus two tanks, tankdozer, gear and packs of explosives. Each armored tank landing craft, LCT(A), towed a 50-foot mechanized landing craft (LCM) deep-loaded with explosives.

During the exhausting channel crossing tows broke loose and had to be recovered. Three of the larger tank landing craft broke down or swamped, forcing their teams to finish the trip in the overcrowded 50-foot LCMs, drenched and seasick. Many men in the larger craft were also soaked, battered, and sick. When the bigger craft reached the transport area miles off the French coast in overcast pitch-darkness around 2 A.M., there were mishaps while transferring men to the fifty-footers in heavy sea and wind. Some of the demolition craft were delayed precious minutes, causing later confusion with infantry waves in the tight landing schedule. More often, however, the infantry's landing craft were late or hit the wrong beach—with the result that the lightly manned gap assault teams led the way into enemy gunfire on several beaches, ahead of tanks and infantry!

At last, loaded into 50-foot mechanized landing craft, the demolition crews and their explosives reached the line of departure for the last lap to shore. The men wore gas-impregnated coveralls over khaki shirts and trousers and heavy underwear; field shoes, a web belt with wire cutters, banana-like crimpers for mine horns, cartridges, gas mask, inflatable life belt, canteen, first-aid packet, helmet, fur-lined M-2 coat —and a bulky 40-pound load of canvas Hagensen packs. Some carried carbines. Some had heavy signal reels wound with 800 feet of primacord. The chiefs or ratings picked as fuse pullers, carried bags of waterproofed two-minute-delay fuse assemblies easily exploded by bullet or shrapnel but essential to firing the primacord network.

The Channel chop, after making everybody miserable, now dealt a more serious blow. The tank landing craft on the left half of Omaha Beach disgorged their secret DD tanks three discreet miles from the bombarded shore line. Wind and waves ripped the canvas tops loose and buckled the framework, filling the deep-laden shells with water. Most of the DD tanks scheduled to lead the assault on the left flank drowned out before they got beyond the line of departure.

Men floundered in the water, but the demolition craft had to pass them by, proceeding on their mission. On the right flank, the landing craft skippers drove inshore until the DD tanks could almost touch bottom. The DD tanks and the regular tanks made the shore to offer some cover for the troop landing waves; however, most of the tanks were trapped by the shingle barrier and knocked out by German artillery and mines.

After half an hour of steady bombardment, the gunfire from battleships, cruisers, and gunboats screaming over the men's heads moved farther inland.

The bombardment was not one-sided. The first waves of landing craft came under fire while still more than half a mile from shore. German 88s hit floating targets with deadly accuracy. Machine-gun bullets drummed on the steel sides and ramps of the landing craft carrying the first waves of infantry and demolition men. There was definitely somebody alive on that beach!

Close to H-Hour, 0630, the first waves of landing craft grounded, dropped ramps, and poured troops into waist-deep water under some of the heaviest enemy fire ever known. Beyond the surf lay a 300-yard dash inland across the sand between obstacles, to the dubious shelter of the sea wall.

Two or three minutes behind the first infantry, and in some spots *ahead* of *anybody*, came the demolition teams, spilling out of a ragged wave of sixteen 50-foot craft strung along three miles of beach. An unusually strong tidal current of several knots ran east along the shore, drifting all the boats a hundred yards or more to the left of their intended beaches, eastward of their destinations.

The right-hand gap assault team in Boat Number One, scheduled to land on the westernmost beach sector, drifted more than one sector to the east. The rest of the sixteen-boat wave was strung across the sea still farther east of them. When the first boat's commander, Lieutenant Larry Heideman, was promoted to supervise the right flank of Omaha Beach demolitions, the unit was placed in charge of Chief Bill Freeman, veteran of the first North African underwater clearance. Take this unit's experience as a sample:

The wave of demolition boats, strung some three hundred yards apart, came under fire when they were still half a mile from the shore. As Freeman's landing craft scrunched onto the sloping, sandy bottom and the ramp dropped, the chief checked his watch—0633, a proper three minutes after H-Hour.

The men, loaded with 40-pound packs and combat gear, leaped into the waist-deep water and splashed toward the line of 10-foot steel gates on the sand ahead. Sniper fire increased after the ramp dropped, and the men wasted no time getting to the dubious shelter of the mined steel-latticed wall on the dry sand.

On the cross-Channel trip, Chief Freeman and the Army Engineer lieutenant had revised their tactics, and now engineers took some of the team's Hagensen packs to work on the seaward line of gates. Freeman and his Navy crew filtered through the gates into the gunfire to work on the next rows, mixed ramps and posts. They were the first men on their beach. Behind them, nearer the steadily approaching surf, some DD tanks were cruising up and down the sand, firing toward the shore. "Friendly" fire was threatening the demolition men, until Freeman profanely waved them away.

German 88s were booming in salvos of three, searching for boats and men coming ashore. Shrapnel and bullets started taking their toll.

At the landing craft, the two green seamen fresh out of boot camp worked like veterans, hauling their heavily loaded rubber boat off the ramp into the water. When it was hit and sunk, losing the reserve explosives, the seamen salvaged the green can buoys to mark the future gap, but the marker flags were lost. One after the other, the two seamen were hit coming through the water. The Army first-aid man tried to help them to shore, and was himself instantly killed by a sniper's bullet, leaving the two teams without trained medical aid.

Men were falling among the obstacles. A gunner's mate who, sick in bed two days before, had got up for the long-awaited day, was riddled with bullets. His buddy was hit in the leg, and an Army private with the team was fatally wounded. But the survivors only worked harder to load the obstacles. The surf was advancing across the sand as fast as a man would walk. When the water reached the obstacles, it would rise among them a foot deeper every eight minutes.

The larger engineer team finished loading its line of gates

first, and lit the purple smoke signal as warning of a detonation. The Navy team dropped flat, and the blast hurled smoke, sand, and shrapnel skyward. Then the engineers started working toward Freeman's men, who were loading rows of ramps, posts, and hedgehogs, despite constant fire and increasing casualties.

Inshore of the gates was a line of ramps and posts. Each ramp was a heavy timber, its seaward end buried in the sand, sloping up toward the shore, braced on stout vertical or inverted V-shaped posts, an inclined plane which would overturn and sink an incoming boat or let it slide up the ramp to explode the mine at the tip. The posts were deeply buried in the sand, leaning to seaward with a mine for a cap. Farther inshore was another line of steel or wooden posts, each with its Teller mine. Nearest the enemy beach was a line of steel hedgehogs.

The hedgehogs offered some thin protection from sniper fire. Four-foot-high steel obstacles, they were made of three straight, heavy angle-irons, joined and crossing in the middle in an X, their feet firmly set in a steel-and-concrete base. Their projecting points were of course decorated with mines.

Besides loading the obstacles, the demolition men had to place a pack gingerly around each mine. Merely blowing a wooden ramp or post in two would leave a mine-tipped log to be picked up by the tide and possibly torpedo an approaching landing craft.

The loading was completed in record time. Five minutes ahead of the advancing surf, Gunner's Mate Bob Bass raced from obstacle to obstacle unreeling the heavy drum of primacord, tying the main fuse to each of those on the obstacles. After he attached the waterproofed detonating assembly that would touch off all the charges in one big "shot," he looked to Freeman for the signal to fire. But the chief couldn't give the word.

A new obstacle, a living one, had just blocked the area. The demolition men had landed on schedule, but an infantry-filled landing craft, delayed and drifted off course, arrived

ten minutes late. Instead of being already on the beach
driving off snipers, the infantrymen wading from their assault
craft dropped flat among the explosive-loaded obstacles,
pinned down by the terrific fire.

Grimly Chief Freeman and the Army lieutenant drove
them away, even kicking the frozen-scared men. They had a
chance running ashore, but not staying here; the gap was
going to be blown.

Some of the infantrymen, so new to battle, now showed
true courage, helping wounded demolition men along on
the long trek toward shore.

The signal was given at last—twenty minutes after the
team had landed—and Bass pulled the fuse. The purple
warning signal smoked skyward.

"Hit the deck!" Freeman yelled.

A heavy roar drowned out the battle's din for the prone
men. The whole gap area spouted water, smoke, wood, sand,
and steel high into the air. It was 0655, only 22 minutes after
the team's boat touched bottom. The gap was blown clean,
a 50-yard-wide lane open from sea to shore. In tribute to
his men's letter-perfect performance, Chief Freeman gasped:
"God, it was right out of the damned book!"

Freeman anchored a green can buoy by an unblown steel
gate at one side of the gap's seaward entrance; somebody tried
to put one on the other side. Then they headed for shore. An
Army engineer helping one of the wounded "boot" seamen
ashore was fatally wounded; the sailor survived. Bob Bass,
who had done two men's work laying and blowing the gap,
helped the other wounded seaman ashore. An 88mm shell
burst nearby and shrapnel ripped Bass's shoulder, but he
kept going; he lived to get the Navy Cross. One of the Navy
unit was killed going ashore, as were two of the Army privates
with the unit. The survivors scuttled from obstacle to obstacle, then hurried as fast as exhausted and wounded men
could, across the naked bullet-swept sand, to reach the rocky
shingle bank. There, partly sheltered from sniper fire, they
dug a trench in the rubble and sand. which Freeman ordered

THE BLOODY SANDS OF NORMANDY

lined with inflated life belts for the wounded. He himself was slightly wounded, though he didn't include the fact in his later reports.

There was no plasma here. The regular medics were scattered, and desperately overworked. Many were themselves casualties when their infantry landing craft was wrecked on its way in to the beach.

Two of the Coast Guard infantry landing craft were hit by shellfire trying to get through the newly blown gap. They burned and sank, nearly blocking the passage.

All that morning and afternoon, the beach and the men pinned down on it were pounded incessantly by mortars, artillery, and small-arms fire. But at low tide in the late afternoon, Freeman rounded up the uninjured men, salvaged explosives from engineer outfits and wrecks drifted ashore, commandeered a bulldozer and a couple of still-operating DD tanks, and led his men back onto the sand to double the width of the gap they had cleared in the morning half hour.

Because of the shortage of boats, the wounded men were not evacuated to the fleet until seven that evening. Out of the dozen men in Freeman's unit, four died and four others were wounded. An official report would note simply, "67 per cent casualties."

In the official questionnaire after the operation, Freeman gave a somewhat surprising answer to one query: "What difficulties did you encounter in blowing obstacles?"

"*None.*"

So ran the report of a *successful* gap clearance. Not many teams were so lucky. Of the sixteen channels to be blown, only five were cleared along the entire front of Omaha Beach that morning.

The four boats scheduled to land just east of Freeman's crew had four different kinds of trouble. A sinking tank landing ship forced one team to make most of the channel crossing in its 50-foot auxiliary boat. Arriving when the obstacles were completely covered at eight o'clock, the men had to wade ashore under fire. They were far luckier than the third boat, which dropped its ramp just as a salvo of shells landed squarely in it, touching off its explosives, killing the Navy lieutenant and killing or wounding all but one of the men.

The next boat crew was shot to pieces while trying to load explosives onto their obstacles. One man was killed, and all but one of the other Navy men were wounded. One soldier in the crew nearly made it safely, crawling to the sea wall before he was hit. The seat of his pants had a sizable hole in it, and he turned to his sergeant saying, "Now I know why they told me to keep both ends down."

The fifth boat headed straight for the beach with its machine gunners standing boldly upright to answer the fire from shore. The ramp dropped and the men hit the beach ahead of infantry or tanks. By the time they had all their obstacles loaded, fifteen minutes later, the area was full of infantry. The crew waited helplessly until the advancing tide drove the green troops onto the beach. Trying to fire the flooded explosives, they were badly disappointed when only part of the gap blew up.

The sixth boat crew was more fortunate and blew a wide gap on Easy Green, two beaches east of Freeman's area. Here the Nazis had not yet placed steel gates. Only two lines of ramps and a line of steel hedgehogs blocked the path to shore. Pinned down among the obstacles were infantrymen of the first wave, stopped by the heavy fire on the open beach.

Lieutenant (jg) William M. Jenkins improvised a scheme for dealing with this human problem. He and Chief Jacobson went among the troops, pulling fuse igniters one at a time and yelling at the men to move out or be blown up in two minutes. They moved. The engineers with the crew froze at first under the machine-gun crossfire and the shock of four waves of German rockets from the beach. But the Army lieutenant quickly recovered, spurred his men to work toward the beach, and loaded half the exposed landward hedgehogs himself. Chief Jacobson and a seaman were killed, but the rest carried on.

A gap varying from fifty to a hundred yards was blown clear, and traffic moved through. Later, two tank landing craft came in with the tide, missing the markers, and hit mines. They sank, half-closing the gap.

The next two crews had similar troubles. Troops scheduled to land with the first wave arrived late and filtered slowly through the obstacles. Jeeps and bulldozers with crawler-trailers moved in ahead of the tide, ripping through the primacord fuses which the demolitioneers had just placed. One crew managed to blow the seaward ramps, but the engineers inshore were shot to pieces before they could clear the hedgehogs.

The widest section of Omaha, named Easy Red on the war charts, marked the beginning of the left flank. Here three out of the four boat crews landed on the correct beach and blew their gaps, speeding the troops' first big push inland.

"Easy" was the wrong name for anything around Omaha. The Nazi strong points guarding E-1 ravine covered the area where the demolition crews came ashore. A Nazi shell hit Boat Nine before it dropped its ramp, killing one of the Navy crew and wounding its officer, Carpenter William H. Raymor, and two others. Despite his wound, Raymor led his men to the the barricades, joining forces with the engineers. The first blast blew half the obstacles; a second series of charges cleared a fifty-yard gap in the middle of Easy Red. The demolition men had no troop problem—they were all alone except for the Nazi gunners.

The next boat team blew an even wider gap than the prescribed fifty yards. Ensign Lawrence S. Karnowski of Kansas landed along with the first infantry waves in his area of Easy Red beach. Five of his men hurried to the obstacles with part of Lieutenant Gregory's engineers, while the others got their overloaded rubber boats off the landing craft into the water, under increasing fire.

Karnowski and his men loaded the line of ramps nearest

the surf while the engineers worked inshore. The Army troops moved inshore, but another wave arrived before the charges could be fired, so the Navy team spread out to load a hundred-yard gap. Finally they cleared the area enough to touch off the blast, twenty minutes after landing. Then they went back to the job on the pilings, despite the converging fire from two German strong points. Gregory's engineers were still loading their packs on the steel hedgehogs. Man after man was killed, soldier and sailor alike. The Navy chief petty officer fell, and Machinist Lester Meyers took over his job with the primacord main trunk line. The tide was already among the obstacles when they fired their second shot. Ten minutes later everybody hit the deck again as the engineers blasted their line of steel hedgehogs, fifty yards wide. Then the demolition men waded ashore, Karnowski carrying a wounded man so that he wouldn't drown among the obstacles.

In the dubious lee of the shingle sea wall the two officers made sure that first aid was given. Then Karnowski and Gregory grabbed packs and igniters and went back into the choppy sea, wading and swimming, to load and blow up the scattered obstacles which had not been destroyed by the main blasts. They cleared everything but a few scattered hedgehogs near the dune line.

Karnowski came through without a scratch, although Gregory was killed at his side by shrapnel on the beach later. Five of the original seven-man Navy unit were casualties, and Meyers was missing. (It later turned out that he had gone up the ravine with the Army as it advanced inland, a favorite sport of sailors during invasions!)

Out of the six remaining boats farther east, only one managed to blow a gap, on the left side of Easy Red Beach. Loran Barbour, Chief Aviation Ordnanceman, and his men tied their packs and fuses on the obstacles. The gunner's mate running the primacord line between two groups of obstacles was shot and instantly killed, but a buddy grabbed the primacord reel and finished the job.

Chief Barbour was just about to light the warning purple

smoke signal when a Nazi shell struck a pack and fired the "shot." Five of the Navy crew were killed, Barbour and all but two of the others were wounded, and the Army engineer crew was badly shattered with fifteen casualties; but the gap was open. Despite his wounds, Barbour directed marking the gap and evacuating the wounded, until he himself collapsed and was carried to shore. A wounded gunner's mate, John Line, stayed in the gap with the two unwounded men and the Army survivors to finish clearing it. Afterwards, he stayed on alone to direct the first boat traffic through.

A variety of disasters overtook the other five boats. A Nazi mortar touched off the fuse in one team's rubber-boatload of explosives, killing the officer and three men, wounding the others. Chief Markham rallied the survivors and blew a partial gap before helping the wounded to the beach, where four men crouched in a shallow trench until a German shell buried them. Markham dug them out alive.

Whatever superstition may say, Gap Assault Team Thirteen was one of the worst victims. A salvo of 88 mm shells among the obstacles killed every man but one.

The next boat never reached the obstacles—a shell hit its rubber boats as the ramp dropped, leaving more men dead than wounded.

The fifteenth boat faced a line of steel gates. German artillery, having gotten the range while shooting at the rocket ships, now hit the engineer crew unloading explosives for the demolition boat. The Navy men got their packs on the steel gates, but their last fuse assemblies were shot away by shrapnel, which also cut off the fuseman's fingers. The tide was coming in, men were pouring through the gap, and a mortar shell hit the rubber-boatload of extra supplies. All the men could do was help each other ashore.

The last of the sixteen landing craft in the assault wave grounded on a sandbar a thousand yards out from its left flank beach. Let Lieutenant Alfred Sears, then a chief electrician's mate, tell what happened:

"Ensign Stocking showed us on an intelligence chart the

locations of all the German strong points. He was assured that they would be knocked out by the time we hit the beach. We were so confident of this, that on the way in to the beach on D-Day, most of my men and I were sitting on top of the engine room decking of the landing craft, enjoying the show, fascinated by the barrage from the English rocket ships. About one thousand rockets shattered the beach directly where we were to land. It looked pretty good.

"Two minutes later the picture completely changed. About 1,200 yards from the high-water mark, an Army sergeant tapped me on the shoulder and pointed out a German pillbox up on the hills which was directing heavy machine-gun fire on us. The slugs were drumming on the sides of the landing craft—we hit the deck. One bullet ricocheted around inside the well deck, hitting the back of the helmet of an Army boy, knocking him flat on his face but not wounding him.

"We hit the sandbar, dropped the ramp, and then all hell poured loose on us. The soldiers in the bow received a hail of machine-gun bullets. The Army lieutenant was immediately killed, shot through the head.

"The other Army men were killed or wounded and it took all hands to get the explosive-laden rubber boats off. The landing craft was hit in the engine room by an 88 shell, and was burning. Our explosives against the engine room bulkhead were set on fire. We took all the explosives we could carry and went off the ramp.

"I went under, with forty pounds of explosive and a carbine, wire cutters, canteens, shoes, helmet. I inflated my life belt and it caught on the gas mask. I went under again, head-first. I was topheavy. Finally I got the life belt up under my arms. A shell burst in the water, but I didn't know I was hurt, until I started swelling afterwards and they had to cut my clothes off. They were throwing everything at us.

"I heard Stocking holler, 'I'm hit,' he had taken one through the shoulder. I moved over to him and just as I reached him he jumped and said, 'I'm hit again.' This time it was through the leg. I stripped off his gear, inflated his life jacket and towed him in to the beach. The landing craft blew up behind us. I was in so bad a state that I did not realize that the concussion had hit me from the waist down.

"On the way in, I came across one of our boot seamen; he was suffering from shock and said, 'What will I do, I'm scared!' I told him to help me with Ensign Stocking. Helping the other man snapped him out of it, and we made it in without being hit again.

"We were pinned down on the beach all morning by machine guns and mortar fire, continually taking casualties. We had only the bed of a narrow-gauge railroad track for protection. [This was a temporary track used by the Nazis to move obstacles onto the beach.]

"A couple of tanks came in. They were immediately knocked out and their surviving crew members joined us. We tended our wounded all day, and at night dug foxholes on the side of a hill up from the beach. I then found out that I had taken a large piece of shrapnel in my right knee and other smaller wounds on both legs, also I was suffering concussion from the underwater burst. We were strafed and bombed during the night. At daylight I could not move, my lower body and legs having swollen up. We found out that we had dug our foxholes in the middle of a field of German land mines."

At this time one of the support teams under Lieutenant Commander (then Ensign) Duquette crashed into an obstacle. Duquette states:

"We were hung up on a tetrahedron which had been driven through the bottom of the boat, held fast 500 yards from the beach, point-blank range for German gunners. I ordered all hands to inflate their life belts, then carrying forty pounds of TNT apiece we swam for the beach. Machine-gun bullets lashed the water around us, the tide scattered us up and down the beach. Only seven of my men made it in."

With the eight-boat support wave (which found the tide so high they could do little clearance) came three control

craft, carrying Lieutenant Commander Gibbons and his
deputies for the two flanks of Omaha Beach, Lieutenants
(jg) Larry Heideman and Walter Cooper. Each rode with
his opposite number of the Army Engineer Combat Battalions, Lieutenant Colonel O'Neill and Majors Isley and
Jewett.

On the way into the beach, Gibbons' boat hit a mined stake,
which luckily failed to explode. When the craft finally
grounded in waist-deep water among the obstacles, Gibbons
ordered the troops ashore, and followed. After wading a few
yards, he unexpectedly stepped into a tide-scoured runnel and
went under. When he inflated his life belt, it knocked his belt,
pistol, knife and first-aid pack off, and popped him up above
water into a sleet of bullets. He shucked off the life belt, and
swam in, keeping under water as much as possible.

All was confusion on the beach. Gibbons spotted two of
his men who said they were the only survivors of their
crew. He moved down the beach where he found another
crew more nearly intact and detailed a man to bring the
lost pair to join them.

Commander Gibbons vividly remembers his journey down
that beach:

"The 88s fired in salvos of three. We'd wait till the third
burst, then run for the next mound or shellhole. I jumped
into one foxhole, and a second later another body came
hurtling in on top of me, yelling, 'Get the hell out of my
foxhole!'

"I got, asking no questions. I never knew till later that it
was one of my own seamen."

There was no rank in foxholes, and no safety on the beach
that day. It was win or die.

The story has been too often told to need repeating, how
little groups of brave infantrymen fought their way across
the shingle wall and up the slopes, crawling through minefields, wiping out machine-gun posts and concrete strong
points as they fought up the mined ravines or over the
crests, pushing the Germans off the bluff, fighting all that

morning and afternoon, until finally the beach was threatened only by long-range shelling.

Enemy fire was still heavy from surviving strong points on the hills and behind them, that afternoon when the tide slackened and the surviving demolition men went back to their dangerous task among the obstacles.

Only six of the engineers' first wave of sixteen bulldozers and tankdozers had got ashore without drowning out or being smashed by shells. Three of them were hit soon afterwards, but more bulldozers landed with high tide. The Navy crews, and any engineers who hadn't gone inland to the minefields, followed the receding tide, destroying obstacles. New and tragic obstructions were strewn throughout the area—wrecked tanks and landing craft, broken bulldozers, and shattered, drowned bodies.

The demolition men scrounged dynamite and machines from the SeaBees, and engineers and beach parties, and salvaged whatever explosives had been boated or washed ashore. Bulldozers and commandeered tanks sheared through the wooden ramps and pilings. The Navy men countermined the obstacles, augmenting their scanty stock of explosives with the Nazis' own Teller mines. The support teams did yeoman work. By the time the tide poured back over the beach that evening, thirteen clean and plainly buoyed gaps had been blown, some of them 100 to 150 yards wide. The demolition crews that day cleared one-third of all the tidewater obstacles which the Nazis had emplaced during the previous four months.

The net results? Troops and supplies poured through the breach in Hitler's vaunted Atlantic Wall, securing the beachhead farther inland for the final break-through. Of the little band of Navy and Army demolition men who played their important role in breaching that wall, however, more than half were casualties.

It has often been printed that the Navy demolition men suffered 41 per cent casualties, and the Army engineers much the same, at Omaha Beach. This was the immediate battle-

field report, before all the wounded were listed. A careful
check of the roster, however, shows 31 killed, 60 wounded,
and 84 noncasualties among the Navy personnel, a casualty
figure of 52 per cent.

Fifteen Distinguished Service Crosses were awarded by the
Army to its combat demolition men, including the three
officers who, with their Navy opposite numbers, directed
their craft up and down the beach supervising the clearance
and then went ashore under fire to complete it.

Among the Navy force, Navy Crosses were awarded to
Freeman, Bass, Line, Markham, Barbour, Jenkins, and
Karnowski, in addition to a number of Silver Stars and
Bronze Stars to others who were especially outstanding in a
day of widespread heroism. The entire Navy Combat Demo-
lition Unit of the Omaha force received one of the three
Presidential Unit Citations awarded to the Navy for the
Normandy landings. It read as follows:

For outstanding performance in combat during the invasion of
Normandy, June 6, 1944. Determined and zealous in the fulfill-
ment of an extremely hazardous mission, the Navy Combat
Demolition Unit of Force "O" landed on the "Omaha Beach"
with the first wave under devastating enemy artillery, machine-
gun and sniper fire. With practically all explosives lost and with
their force seriously depleted by heavy casualties, the remaining
officers and men carried on gallantly, salvaging explosives as
they were swept ashore and in some instances commandeering
bulldozers to remove obstacles. In spite of these grave handicaps,
the Demolition Crews succeeded initially in blasting five gaps
through enemy obstacles for the passage of assault forces to the
Normandy shore and within two days had sapped over eighty-
five percent of the "Omaha Beach" area of German-placed
traps. Valiant in the face of grave danger and persistently aggressive against fierce resistance, the Navy Combat Demolition
Unit rendered daring and self-sacrificing service in the performance of a vital mission, thereby sustaining the high traditions
of the United States Naval Service.

6. Fire in the Hole!

UNLIKE THE MEN AT OMAHA BEACH FIFTEEN OR TWENTY miles east, the Utah Beach assault troops were lucky from the start. But even though their mishaps often turned into blessings, it was still no beach picnic!

The right flank control boat was shelled and sunk more than two miles at sea. In the smoke of the naval bombardment and air strikes ashore, the first landing waves missed their landmarks. The strong southeast tide carried them 2,000 yards to the left of the charted "Utah Beach." The beaches where they actually landed had fewer offshore obstacles than the intended ones, and fewer guns among the low dunes, since the Germans did not expect a landing attempt so near the river mouth.

The first waves of the 8th Infantry Regiment landed promptly at 0630, H-Hour. Five minutes later, the second wave of landing craft dropped ramps in hip-deep water facing a 1,500-yard-long strip of sand a mile southeast of the charted landing place. Two thirds of the twenty-four landing craft disgorged heavily armed infantrymen who hurried across the sand through shells and machine-gun fire.

From the remaining craft, eleven heavily burdened demolition teams, averaging eight Navy men and five Army engineers, ran to the first line of obstacles on the still-dry beach. Swiftly they went to work, wrapping their Hagensen packs around the ramps, pilings, and hedgehogs. Lieutenant Hagensen, the inventor of the packs, led one of the units.

Following the teams came their support boats. Lieutenant Commander Herbert Peterson, in charge of the Naval Combat Demolition Force "U," had made a quick decision back

at the transport area. He and his support boats with added
men and explosives were supposed to accompany the wave
of Army engineer teams who would clear the landward
obstacles. Those 26-man Army teams hadn't arrived on time.
Weather, convoy confusion, engine trouble—no matter why,
they were vital minutes behind schedule. So Peterson
rounded up his circling boats and headed immediately for
the beach.

He found his first-wave men hard and successfully at
work. Enemy shelling was finding some targets. Scattered
German firing crossed the beach from strong points which
hadn't yet been cleaned out by the infantry. A quarter of an
hour after the demolition men landed, DD tanks crawled
out of their canvas cocoons and lumbered up the beach
to hammer the sniper nests.

The Atlantic Wall was unfinished here. Only eight bays
of unconnected steel gates faced the eight-boat demolition
wave. Often a single boat at Omaha had encountered as
many. Between and behind the steel gates were wooden
ramps with firmly braced timbers. Behind these, rows of
reinforced concrete and wooden posts slanted ominously
seaward to skewer incoming boats. Last came a row of four-
foot-high concrete tetrahedrons—triangular pyramids of
solid concrete. The obstacles had not yet been mined and
would have been easy targets but for the fast-flooding tide.

Some of the belated Army engineer teams were beaching
now, hurrying across the sands to tackle the obstacles. But
in many cases the small thirteen-man Navy-led teams loaded
their entire 50-yard-wide areas from sea to shore, all alone.
In record time they finished tying the primacord lines, then
twisted the cranks of their "Hell Boxes" to fire their "shot"
electrically.

The tide crept in at a fast walk. Over the din of battle,
"Fire in the Hole!" resounded. Eight gaps were blown, but
there was still time for more. Peterson and his "exec," Lieutenant Robert C. Smith, passed the word to keep clearing
all possible obstacles, starting with those which would be

flooded first. Working in 50-yard stretches, the teams blew new gaps. The last obstacles were waist-deep when they were blown. Seven hundred yards of beach opposite La Grande Dune were completely cleared for boat traffic on the flooding tide by 0800—an hour and a half of fast, dangerous, and brilliantly successful work.

The teams "secured" in foxholes on the dune line, and at the afternoon low tide went back to work, clearing another 900 yards of beach. Almost a mile was opened to reinforce and supply the growing Utah beachhead.

The commander of Assault Force "U," Rear Admiral Don P. Moon, reported officially right after the landing:

"Obstacles on Utah Beach presented no problems. Detailed information of the experiences of the demolition parties is not at hand. . . ."

The unofficial diary of Jackson "Tex" Modesett, who served as Gunner's Mate First Class in Lieutenant Bohne's unit, gives a little of that detailed information:

At 2 A.M. we went over the side into the landing craft. The worst boat ride I ever had. It was dark and we were crowded, with all our explosives, rubber boat, etc. Pete was the first to get seasick. It was rather cold and we were soaking wet in no time. Buck got sick until he was so weak he couldn't stand up. Pretty soon I stuck my head over the gunwale and threw up a bit.

It took us about four and a half hours to get to the beach. Just after daybreak, it seemed like all hell had busted loose. Our bombers started going over the German strong points dropping bombs and the enemy was really pouring the antiaircraft fire into them. We saw a big U.S. bomber pull out of formation just a few seconds before it burst into a million flaming pieces.

Shells were hitting all around us, and several boats, including the control boat of the first wave, were hit and sunk. Around 6:30 A.M. we hit the largest, flattest beach I've ever seen. The landing craft had to let us off in water about hip deep and we had better than 200 yards to wade before we hit our first obstacles. . . . We started toward our obstacles under very heavy shell and machine-gun fire. Bullets were kicking up the water all around and some shells came so close over our heads that you could actually feel the wind from them. I guess I was scared plenty, but was so busy I didn't realize it.

When we got our first obstacles ready to blast, we found we didn't have a smoke grenade to warn the incoming troops. . . . I told Lieutenant Bohne I was going up the beach and borrow a grenade from the next crew. He said: "O.K., Tex, go ahead!"

I had run about 30 yards when I heard an 88 shell hit behind me. I felt like it got some of the boys so I didn't even look back. I found the next crew, borrowed a grenade, and started back.

When I got close to where I had left the gang, I saw a couple of tops of human heads lying in the sand a few yards apart and almost a whole backbone with all the flesh and ribs torn away from it, and a string of guts about 25 or 30 feet long strung out in a straight line, and a few hunks of bloody meat that would weigh about a pound. That was all that was left of two of the soldiers in my crew.

The other fellows were lying down flat and Bohne was grinning up at me with blood all over his face. He had shrapnel plumb through his helmet and pieces of the two men sticking to him. He had a piece of shrapnel in the back of his right shoulder and a bad cut on his right arm. But he never blacked out, and I took his canteen and cleaned him up the best I could. "Georgia" came over and got his whiskey canteen and we all had a big slug of it to warm us up and stimulate us. . . .

I went over to Janowicz and his eyes were about half open. He was dying with a hole as big as your fist in the left side of his chest. He only lived about five minutes, but wasn't conscious then. . . . Our signalman was splattered in several places with shrapnel, but I don't believe he had any serious wounds.

Three men were about fifty yards up the beach loading a section of steel gate so they weren't affected by that shell. God was kind to me when he sent me away from there to go after that grenade. I had figured I was in greater danger running around in the open amongst shell and machine-gun fire than the other fellows, as they were down flat and had the big wooden ramp between them and the sea wall.

Dead soldiers were lying everywhere, and it gave me a funny feeling when I had to walk right by some poor fellow with a leg or arm torn away and begging me to do something. There was moaning and crying all over the beach, mostly from mortally wounded men, but some from the shell-shocked ones who were just hysterical over what they were seeing.

We worked like hell, and cleared our beach of obstacles all right, plumb up to the sea wall, but it cost me half my crew.

So much for the "detailed information" behind the cold statistics that four naval personnel were killed and eleven wounded while clearing obstacles. As Ernie Pyle once said, no engagement is a minor one to the man who gets killed in it.

Utah Beach was no minor engagement; it was just a highly successful one. It was major in both size and importance.

On D plus one, the Navy demolition units stood by with no duties except to dispose of a few unexploded rockets and shells. Some of the men whiled away the tedium by souvenir hunting. Chief Leland A. Prewitt and a sailor were inspecting a deserted-looking enemy concrete blockhouse above the beach. When the chief started toward an open window slit to peer inside, a steel shutter quietly slid across it.

The chief ran back down to the beach and, coming upon an Army lieutenant, told him there were Germans in the strong point.

"There aren't any Krauts on *my* beach," the lieutenant scoffed. Prewitt bet him five dollars that there were.

Running into "Weary" Wirwohn and "Tex" Modesett, Prewitt told what he'd seen and asked if they wanted to come along. They did.

The three petty officers went back, armed only with pistols. The blockhouse was buttoned up tight. Another concrete stronghold dug into the hillside nearby was invitingly open, however, and the demolitioneers thought it might be connected underground with the blockhouse. It proved to be a generator room for a searchlight. Lockers contained German officers' clothes and gear. Watching carefully for booby traps, the three men found a sack full of explosives. They tested a piece of fuse to see how fast it would burn; then . . .

Sneaking down the trench that led to the closed blockhouse, they put six blocks of explosive against the door, and strung a fuse. Tex started around the corner of the trench to pull the fuse lighter—and saw the little steel shutter just sliding shut again.

He pulled back, "so weak and shaky he could hardly talk"; then he poked his pistol around the trench corner and peeked after it. The little shutter was closed. Hurrying to the big steel door, he pulled the fuse. The three men took cover and waited. A very short wait.

There was a heavy explosion. After a few seconds, a German came running out of the dust and smoke where the door had been, his hands stretched high, yelling, "Kamerad! Kamerad!"

The Americans made signs for him to call the rest of the men outside, but he didn't seem to understand until Tex poked him in the belly with the .45. He understood that, and yelled to the dugout in German. Four or five more soldiers staggered out, hands high. Possibly remembering the empty taxi in the circus from which an endless procession emerges, Tex poked him twice as hard. The prisoner yelled again. It seemed as if the blockhouse would never stop erupting concussion-dazed Germans. There were fifteen of them, including an officer.

The three startled petty officers herded their rich catch to the MP stockade. Their next stop was the Army lieutenant, who paid Chief Prewitt his five dollars without an argument. Then back to the strong point to inspect their capture. It turned out to be a spotting point for the gunfire still intermittently shelling the beach.

They were interested in a new discovery—seven intact German "doodlebug" tanks. This ingenious push-button demolition weapon was a tiny radio-controlled robot tank, loaded with 250 pounds of explosive, to be guided against Allied vehicles or ammunition dumps on the beach. These hadn't been used. Two of the petty officers disarmed the tanks and unloaded the explosive.

There was work to do the next few days. With their own and borrowed engineer explosives, the demolition men cleared a mile of beaches packed with obstacles. Then, on June 13, they sailed back to England, where a new assignment awaited them; they had a date on the Riviera. Meantime, just as the Omaha unit received the Presidential Unit Citation, the Utah demolition units received the only Navy Unit Commendation awarded for the Normandy landing.

7. Push-Button Warfare

A MONTH AFTER THE NORMANDY INVASION, LIEUTENANT Commanders Gibbons and Peterson met again in England. A Naval Demolition detachment was being ordered to the Mediterranean for a newly scheduled operation.

"I'll take Force 'U.' We weren't as badly shot up as your force was," Peterson offered. "Besides, there won't be too much action."

"No," said Gibbons, who was senior officer. "We'll flip for it."

Gibbons can't remember whether the coin came heads or tails, but he won—or lost, as one prefers to look at it. Fate decided that his large but battered Omaha group could go back to the States instead. It was a good thing; all too many of the men were still in hospitals, and some had not been located since their evacuation from France.

A few battle-happy demolition men had "accidentally" attached themselves to the troops moving inland from the beach. Chief Freeman was one of these. He found his way back from the hedgerows of Normandy just in time for the storm of June 20 which wrecked the artificial harbor at Omaha and piled shipping everywhere, threatening the overburdened supply lines. Freeman was promptly spotted by the harbormaster and drafted for clearance and demolition. Expert powdermen were at a premium during those few crucial days. Released at last, Freeman got back to England with a properly edited account of his interim activities. He found he was being commissioned an ensign.

"What a blow!" he commented, as a true chief petty officer would.

Commander Gibbons gave newly commissioned Ensign Freeman and Chief Al Sears a special assignment—to take all personal gear that the demolition men had not claimed, load it in a truck, add a lot of extra, useful loot, and tour the military hospitals of England to locate all the widely scattered men and give them their personal effects or needed clothing. Forwarding their gear through channels would have taken another war's duration. The pair were welcomed as Santa Claus in uniform.

Commander Peterson, meantime, with ten veteran Utah units, embarked in a Mediterranean-bound convoy in mid-July. At Salerno, a large group of Fort Pierce trained men were waiting for them.

Demolition practice for the coming invasion of Southern France was held on the beaches of Naples and Salerno. Units were beefed up with five Army combat engineers, and a three-man small boat crew from the Navy.

Push-button warfare was scheduled for a full-scale test. The demolition men got three flotillas of "Apex Boats"— another name for the drone and control landing craft. Fortunately their ramped drone craft were in much better shape than the Stingrays which had failed at Kwajalein.

Added proofs that American ingenuity tried to clear beaches with the minimum risk to the men were the unsuccessful "Woofus" boats—demolition craft whose rockets were supposed to blast underwater obstructions—and "Reddy Fox" torpedo-driven explosive tubes intended for the same purpose.

The invasion of Southern France was called the war's worst-kept secret, with the time and place being common gossip ashore. Demolition was no exception. The open-cockpit drone craft lay at Salerno in full view of the Italians while the Navy men equipped them with radio controls, explosives, and scuttling devices. While the task force was assembling, the demolition boat teams ran a full-scale rehearsal, radio-operating the drone boats into the Italian beach in broad daylight for the benefit of anyone interested.

By three o'clock on the morning of D-Day, August 15, the attack force had reached the coast of France. The target area was a beautiful stretch of Riviera coast between Toulon and Cannes. Hill villas provided ideal sniper nests and artillery observation posts. Obstacles were reported in two of the three beach areas. Mines, concrete tetrahedrons and jetted posts of steel or concrete had been placed offshore.

In the darkness, a dock landing ship on each flank flooded its well decks and regurgitated a swarm of small boats—a dozen Apex drones, a score of other landing craft full of demolition men with packs to be hand-placed. In the central area, the boats were gingerly lowered from davits.

Well before dawn the demolition landing craft started for the beaches. Heavy naval shelling and plane bombing started at 0600. H-Hour was set two hours later, after three waves of demolition drones had exploded their charges.

The day was perfect. Fluffy clouds drifted across a beautiful blue sky, above the fleet's barrage balloons and the plumes of smoke rising from the bombarded shore. It was different in every way from the gray, threatening overcast of Omaha and Utah.

On the left flank Rear Admiral Frank J. Lowry's Alpha Attack Force faced obstacles on both its beaches. In Cavalaire Bay concrete tetrahedrons reared their pointed heads just under the surface. The obstacles were mined with German thoroughness.

The electronic robots were launched. Six "male" drones led the way toward the beaches, carrying a ton of explosives to enlarge the gaps the deadlier females should open. The control craft cruised abreast, two hundred yards apart, each followed by three deeply laden robot "females" in single file. As each female came alongside its male boat about a mile from the beach, its crew set the craft on radio operation and scrambled into the control craft.

All eighteen of the female Apex drones started for the beaches; fifteen of them exploded in the general target area, with a series of impressive geysers of water, smoke, and debris. Two of the lethal craft conked out, failing to fire. A third went completely haywire, running away, and exploding near a sub-chaser. The "friendly" blast was so effective that the sub-chaser was severely damaged and put out of action.

Despite their comparative success, the drones did not clear the way sufficiently. The control boat crews hurried in under fire to place demolition packs on the obstacles by hand.

In the central area near St. Maxime, scout boats reported there were no underwater obstacles other than mines. Rear Admiral Bertram J. Rodgers called off the Apex boat wave.

On the eastern beaches, in Agay cove, a submarine net blocked the entrance. Two units under Lieutenant Edward P. Clayton, a Utah veteran, sped toward the net in their landing crafts, and despite small-arms fire from the shore, blew it up with their hand-placed charges.

The beach in front of the town of St. Raphael was the most heavily fortified in all the Southern France landings. Its 1,400-foot length was strongly barricaded under water with 240 six-foot concrete pyramids topped by barely submerged box-type waterproofed mines as powerful as three Teller mines. At five-foot intervals, these underwater dragon's-teeth formed an impassable barrier.

Four male Apex boats approached the beach, each trailed by three females at 50-yard intervals. A line of rocket ships also approached to shellac the beach, topping off the naval bombardment. Out of range at sea, troop landing craft circled to keep their stations on the line of departure.

The female drone crews were to jump into the control boats at the 1,000-yard line, sending the drones ahead under radio control. Unfortunately the powerful German batteries ashore had zeroed in that same line. When the rocket ships and the male drone boats reached that 1,000-yard deadline, the hidden German 88mm cannon fired salvos at them in a neat grid pattern. The shellfire was so accurate, and closed

the range so fast, that all the landing craft and rocket ships
had to turn tail.

The troop landing waves at sea continued treadmilling.
The drone squadron turned back toward the beach to make
another pass. It was holding up the invasion.

This time the drones reached the 1,000-yard starting line
despite the shelling. The deeply loaded female Trilbys came
alongside their Svengali controls, dumped their crew, and
continued toward shore under radio control.

Suddenly the radio operators aboard the control craft
realized their Trilbys weren't behaving according to orders.
The females moving inshore yawed crazily off course. One
drone performed a neat 180° turn and headed back to sea
toward the landing waves.

There was no time to ponder whether the Germans were
jamming the radio control frequencies or whether the treachery was just female-robot perversity. The nearest control
craft went high-tailing at top speed after the female carrying her lethal load toward the troops. As the control craft
came alongside, A. W. Foster and another Navy enlisted man
jumped into the drone, hastily disconnected the firing assembly, and with a gasp of relief brought it back under hand
steering.

Frantic messages went back and forth between command
ships trying to figure out how to control the drones. Every
three minutes, with horrible regularity, another salvo of
88s probed for the demolition craft and the zigzagging rocket
ships. Some of the drones were weaving toward the beach,
though far from their target areas. The control boats desperately sent signals to fire the scuttling charges on their drones.

Three of them exploded in the general target area. One
blew up squarely in the line of concrete dragon's-teeth, but
incredibly, the four-ton blast did not breach the obstacles,
or even set off the mines a few yards away. Two drones ran
onto the beach harmlessly without detonating. One went
far off to the left flank and then exploded. Another ran
in close circles near the shore, neglected, too near the Ger-

man guns to be recaptured. Still another started back to sea toward the troops, as if with idiot malice. Ensign Clark Magill took off after it in his control craft, although it was almost surely radio-triggered to explode at any moment. Running alongside, he jumped aboard the drone, cut off the fuses and radio controls, and grabbed the wheel. Only two of the drones could be successfully held back by their crews.

Meantime the German pyramids and mines were waiting in full strength under water to wreck the landing waves. Every three minutes brought a salvo of 88s. The water in front of the beach swarmed with drones, yawing madly in all directions out of control.

Rear Admiral Spencer S. Lewis made a quick but difficult decision. He canceled the St. Raphael landing, and shifted the whole assault force several miles eastward, to land on a narrow beach which had already been opened without need for demolition. The troops would fight their way on land back to St. Raphael, taking it from the rear. This was probably the only American amphibious assault ever repulsed by its own forces.

The snafu had a happy ending. The Army general ashore approved the Navy decision to change its landing plans. The demolition crews ran down their berserk drones, bulldogged and tamed them, and returned to safe anchorage in the Agay cove.

Early the next day the demolition crews returned to St. Raphael, which had been taken by land attack. In the old-fashioned way, those remarkable thinking machines called "men" ingeniously fastened explosive packs against the pyramids and box mines, and blew them up.

While the boat crews were clearing the harbor, Lieutenant Clayton and Ensign Blumberg placed packs in some wrecks off the beach's right flank. Blumberg, in trunks and completely unarmed, was wading close to shore when a pillbox opposite him suddenly opened and twenty-seven Germans stepped out, one carrying a tommy gun in the crook of his arm. There was one badly worried demolition officer until the Nazis made it clear that they were anxious to surrender.

One other postassault episode is worth recording. When the Germans retreated from St. Tropez, they hastily wrecked the harbor installation, blew up a pier, and scuttled all boats and small ships in port.

The next morning a naval demolition crew was ordered to clear out the sunken craft, so that ships could unload in the harbor.

A diver donned his Jack Brown oxygen lung and mask and dove to place a 20-pound pack in the first wreck, a large sailboat whose mast projected in the center of the harbor.

When the diver returned, Carpenter Byram connected the pack's electric cable to the "Hell Box," and shouted: "Fire in the hole!"

Some hundreds of French kibitzers around the port didn't understand, and the busy Army troops ashore couldn't have cared less. Byram cranked the generator handle.

When the whole harbor splashed back into its basin and the civilians crept out again, Carpenter Byram turned to the officer-in-charge and commented unnecessarily: "It was mined."

The innocent little pack had triggered all the mines in the well-loaded harbor. The unit never produced such a spectacular result in the course of clearing out other wrecks, but its warning war cry received prompt and respectful attention for the next two days in St. Tropez harbor.

With the beaches and harbors duly cleared for the swift flow of supplies to the army marching up the Rhone valley, the demolition men were released. They had polished off the last naval combat demolition task of the war in Europe, with men accomplishing what machines couldn't. From north and south, the rising tide of American war power was flowing inland through France to drown Hitler's empire.

8. Swimmer Search at Saipan

"A man who is not afraid of the sea will soon be drownded, for he will be going out on a day he should not. But we do be afraid of the sea, and we do only be drownded now and again."

—*The Aran Islands*,
JOHN MILLINGTON SYNGE

HALF A WORLD AWAY, ONLY EIGHT DAYS AFTER THE NORmandy landings, a few score unarmed demolition men swam during broad daylight, up to entrenched Japanese snipers and mortars. Saipan was the first major test of the newly organized Underwater Demolition Teams; the first full-scale swimmer reconnaissance, a radical change in UDT technique; and the first time that naval gunfire had been specifically assigned to UDT.

Saipan was a major objective in the Amphibious Force advance across the Pacific towards Japan, a 1,300-mile stride westward from Kwajalein. The Mariana Islands stretched 100 miles from Guam north to Saipan, whose Aslito Airfield was only 1,400 miles southeast of Tokyo, within round-trip range of the new B-29 bombers.

Immediately following Kwajalein, Admiral Turner directed the skipper of UDT 2, Lieutenant Commander John Koehler, to establish an advanced Pacific UDT base. Koehler set up the first tents of the "Naval Combat Demolition Training and Experimental Base" on a beach near the ocean pier of the small Kamaole Amphibious Training Base, a hundred miles southeast of Pearl Harbor, on the Hawaiian island of Maui. He worked out a practical train-

81

ing program, based on the experimental Marshall Islands' operation. At first he stressed boat handling, coordination with gunfire support ships, surf drills, coral blasting, and hand-placing demolition charges.

Captain Hill and Captain Taylor, gunnery officers for Admirals Nimitz and Turner, understood the importance of demolition, for logical if not obvious reasons. Gunfire, bombing, and rockets had not been able to channel through underwater reefs, or to clear mines and man-made obstructions. In fact, the explosion craters, and the "dud" rockets left from "Woofus" boat barrages, created new obstacles. The fiasco of the "Stingrays" at Kwajalein, and the drone boats and "Reddy Fish" torpedo-driven warheads in Southern France, was followed by failure of other remote-controlled devices under development at JANET, such as "Corrigan's Shillalah," an automatic-controlled craft which would go up on land from the sea and detonate against sea walls or pillboxes; the "Cutteroo Grapnel," a projectile to snare barbed-wire entanglements; and the "Hellion," designed to project demolition charges into underwater obstacle patterns. It appeared that no mechanical or push-button weapon could reach the efficiency of the naked warriors.

Already Koehler realized that complete dependence must be placed on the swimmer, and that the development of individual equipment such as face masks, swim fins, compasses, and mine-detecting devices deserved priority.

A few men had tried goggles for underwater vision at Kwajalein. Lieutenant Crist and training instructor Roeder later asked for dive masks covering eyes and nose. Spearfishing was not yet a common sport, and the glass-windowed green rubber masks were rare. Only a few could be found in Hawaii sport stores. Just in time, an officer saw an ad in a Stateside magazine. An urgent radio dispatch appropriated the sporting goods company's entire stock, which was secretly flown out.

Above all, Koehler improved team training and organization. He was going full steam ahead, organizing and equip-

ping teams for the June Saipan invasion. He set the pattern
for training and the development of combat tactics. Koehler
was acting commanding officer of the base during two inter-
ludes between Regular Navy commanders of sufficient rank.
The rest of the time he was executive officer, and training
officer as well. He was in constant touch with Admiral
Turner concerning the speedy development of UDT.

The teams from the Marshalls were broken up, releasing
their temporarily borrowed Marine and Army men. SeaBees
and sailors served as a veteran nucleus. Carefully selected
volunteers from the Fleet and six-man units from Fort
Pierce were combined. Two new 100-man teams were
formed, each including 14 officers and 86 men.

Lieutenant Thomas C. Crist and Lieutenant William
Gordon Carberry, with Roi-Namur experience, took charge
of the new Teams Three and Four. They were soon joined
by Team Five, a shipment of Fort Pierce men who were full
of tall tales of sun-bathing and romance aboard their transport, a converted Matson liner. (The ship had also carried
the first detachment of WACs, the Women's Army Corps,
from San Francisco to Pearl Harbor.)

They all pitched in to complete the Maui base. Enlisted
men were six to a tent, officers three. The men's quarters
had neither hot water nor lights. The only recreation areas
were a lava-studded ball field, and a bare hall which lost
its popularity as soon as a newly appointed base commander
banned smoking. Fire was a constant hazard in that explo-
sive-crowded area. The mess hall burned down in May,
forcing the trainees to eat outdoors amid flies and sand and
heat. But they were able to make full use of the ocean for
recreation as well as for training.

The newly formed UDTs quickly built up an *esprit de
corps* which, in excess of high spirits, led to occasional off-
duty brushes with Air and Marine groups. The men were
proud of their organization, Underwater Demolition Teams,
intensely proud of their individual platoons within the

teams, and the boat crews in the platoons. Last and strongest was the devotion and friendship of the swimmer pairs—the "swim buddies." UDT men were taught to appreciate the meaning and value of friendship in war. It has been said that "friendship between two men engaged in the business of war is as old as war itself."

This intense pride and competitive spirit became so violent, however, that when two UDTs were in a port together, liberty was seldom granted both teams at the same time. The competitive spirit would soon result in personal challenge, and pity the man or men, including Shore Patrol, who ever tried to stop such a set-to. Trained to the peak of physical condition and keyed up for combat, the UDT man was best let alone. He seldom would look for trouble and never with an "outsider" who was just no match. A close relationship and strong mutual confidence developed between UDT officers and men. The men were particularly proud of their "skippers" and platoon officers. Moulding the men into strong operating teams was no problem; discipline and morale came from within.

Somehow the unit never acquired a nickname. The original units referred to themselves as "demolitioneers" or "demo" for short. If asked what outfit they belonged to, they'd say, "I am in demolition." The term "frogmen" is seldom used or heard in UDT, unless half-jokingly about a spearfisherman. "I am in UDT" is the phrase most often, and always proudly used.

At some point in the early history of UDT, the men gave birth to a ballad to the tune of the Georgia Tech engineer song. The printable verses are:

SONG OF THE DEMOLITIONEERS

When the Navy gets into a jam
They always call on me
To pack a case of dynamite
And put right out to sea.

Like every honest sailor
I drink my whiskey clear.
I'm a shootin', fightin', dynamitin'
De-mo-li-tion-eer.

Out in front of Navy
Where you really get the heat,
There's a bunch of crazy blasters
Pulling off some crazy feat.
With their pockets full of powder
And caps stuck in their ears,
They're shootin', fightin', dynamitin'
De-mo-li-tion-eers.

They sent me out to Italy
To clean the Fascist up.
I put a case of TNT
Beneath the dirty pup;
And now they're rushing madly
Straight up into the air.
I'm a shootin', fightin', dynamitin'
De-mo-li-tion-eer.

Some day we'll hit the coast of France,
Put "Jerry" on the run.
We'll wrap a roll of primacord
'Round every goddamn Hun,
Goebbels and Herr Goering
Can blow it out their rears.
We're the shootin', fightin', dynamitin'
De-mo-li-tion-eers.

When our Marines reach To-ky-o
And the "Rising Sun" is done
They'll head right for some Geisha house
To have a little fun.

> *But they'll find the gates are guarded*
> *And the girls are in the care*
> *Of the shootin', fightin', dynamitin'*
> *De-mo-li-tion-eers.*
>
> *When the war is over,*
> *And the Wacs and Waves are home,*
> *We'll swim back to the U.S.A.*
> *And never more shall roam.*
> *All the local maidens*
> *Will get the best of care,*
> *And we'll raise a bunch of squallin', bawlin'*
> *De-mo-li-tion-eers.*

Assigning ships to UDT was another Admiral Turner innovation in amphibious warfare. There had been confusion and foul-ups in the Marshalls, with demolition men and equipment scattered among half a dozen cargo ships and troop transports, exposing other vital units to the hazard of the teams' explosives. Admiral Turner decided to assign a high-speed transport (APD) to each team.

The early "Assault Personnel Destroyers" were four-stack destroyers from World War I, remodeled for troop transport by removing two stacks and one fireroom to give additional bunk space. They were fast but uncomfortable, designed for carrying troops on a quick trip to a landing beach. It was not foreseen that some teams would stay aboard such crowded transports almost continuously for eight months.

Maui was busy that April of 1944. Lieutenants Crist and Carberry took Teams Three and Four across the Equator to Florida (the South Pacific island next to Guadalcanal). There each team drilled with its own private destroyer transport during maneuvers with the Marine Fifth Amphibious Corps.

Newly arrived from Fort Pierce for the Saipan invasion were Teams Six and Seven. Team Five was getting used to its new and very active commanding officer—none other than the Fort Pierce training commander, Lieutenant Commander Draper L. Kauffman.

Kauffman had been firmly and frequently told that his greatest usefulness was in Fort Pierce, training men for France and the Pacific. He had, however, recruited too many officers with promises of early action, to accept this order tamely in his own case. One winter day early in 1944, he was called on the carpet in Washington to explain why he had been requested simultaneously by two Amphibious Force commanders, Admiral Kirk in England and Admiral Turner in Pearl Harbor.

"You made one mistake," Kauffman's superior told him. "Both dispatches have identical wording."

When Kauffman's request had reached Hawaii, demolition-minded Admiral Turner (an old friend of the Kauffman family) had already heard about the young officer's experience from his father, Rear Admiral James Kauffman, who was then in Pearl Harbor as "ComCruDesPac," Commander of Cruisers and Destroyers, Pacific Fleet. Turner required the services of a demolition expert, and Lieutenant Commander Kauffman was ordered to Hawaii and put in command of Team Five. Many of his officers and men had served with him on the Fort Pierce training staff. In April 1944, a month before the departure for Saipan, Kauffman was designated senior UDT officer on the operation, and summoned to Pearl Harbor for briefing.

Admiral Turner showed him a chart of Saipan's west coast, with a shallow barrier reef eighteen hundred yards off the chosen beaches, zeroed-in by mortars and lined with fire trenches full of machine guns and snipers.

"I want you people to swim in to the beach about nine on D minus one Day," Turner said. "Make a detailed survey of the depths of the water, the obstacles, antiboat mines, the gun positions ashore, surf conditions, and other details. I also want you to blow out all obstacles in the area."

"Will it be dark of the moon or full moon?" Kauffman replied.

"Moon? What's that got to do with it?" Turner asked blankly. Then he caught on. "You've been in the Navy long enough to know that zero nine hundred is daylight. If I meant night I'd say twenty-one hundred!"

Kauffman soberly estimated 50 per cent casualties, with loss of vital information, and protested, "You don't swim in to somebody's beach in board daylight, sir!"

"You do," the Admiral said in effect, concluding the discussion.

Admiral Turner was certain that most of the men would return. He would provide battleships, cruisers, destroyers, and airplanes to keep the Japanese buttoned down. Turner knew from Kwajalein that men could not complete an accurate reconnaissance at night, and he was ready to assume the calculated risk. This he had told Admiral Nimitz a few days earlier in a conference attended by Kauffman's concerned father.

Team Five's commander returned to Maui with a sudden passion for swimming. Until now the swimming requirement had been 600 yards. The barrier reef at Saipan extended from 900 to 1,800 yards off the landing beaches. A new training rule was announced. No man could go on the coming operation unless he could swim a mile. The staff concluded if he could swim the mile in to the beach, he'd manage to get back, somehow.

Long-distance swimming developed a great respect for the sea in the hearts of the men, particularly when a heavy surf thundered over the coral reefs. Only through developing outstanding strength and skill in the sea could they hope to survive.

In the officers' club at nearby Puunene Air Base one night, a seemingly impromptu brag session started between Kauffman and Team Seven's commander, Lieutenant Richard Burke, a former Mine Disposal School officer. The two commanders wagered case after case of beer on the comparative swimming abilities of themselves and their team officers. This was publicly put to the test the next day before the cheering teams. The whole thing was a put-up job, but it spurred similar overtime competition among the men of the three teams, Five, Six, and Seven. All but three men finally passed the mile-swim test, and these were brought along anyway.

Another shock was Admiral Turner's insistence on a complete, detailed survey of reef and lagoon depths. Such hydrographic surveys normally required boats, transits, and elaborate methods which the Japanese gunners certainly would not permit. The inventive Kauffman devised a "string reconnaissance" method by which a swimmer would head for the beach, unreeling fishline marked with cloth knots at 25-yard intervals, where soundings would be taken.

When a UDT officer asked for 150 miles of fishline, the Pearl Harbor supply officer did a double take and asked how long he'd been in the Pacific.

"About two months, sir. Why?"

The supply man shrugged. "Thought you were suffering from combat fatigue."

The demolition teams gave Navy supply a rough time. When the supply officer refused to issue scarce binoculars, the top command told him in effect to give the teams anything they asked. Hawaii was looted of all the light canvas sneakers in the islands, for climbing over coral reefs. The too-white sneakers were dyed for water camouflage, and came out a lovely baby blue.

Never bashful, the UDTs asked for a fire-support ship to practice with. The Admiral supplied battleships, cruisers, and eight destroyers to fire over the swimmers' heads off the Hawaiian target island of Kahoolawe. Lieutenant Commander Koehler and the other training officers, supervising the swimmers from a small craft halfway between the team and the battlewagons, watched the 16-inch guns lower to fire point-blank over their heads. Koehler observed: "Those guns swing down till you're looking right down their muzzles!"

It was useful training for swimmers and for the fire-support ships as well. A heavy barrage would be needed to cover the UDTs during the swim up to enemy beaches.

When Major General Thomas Watson of the Second Marine Division listed twenty-five questions about the Saipan reef and lagoon, he added skeptically that he didn't expect UDT to be able to get 5 per cent of the needed information. Kauffman disagreed, and requested a Marine liaison officer to help evaluate what they discovered. General Watson announced with typical Marine Corps esprit: "I'll give you a better man than anybody on your team—Gordon Leslie."

First Lieutenant Alan Gordon Leslie, USMCR, had some claim to the billing. He had hit the Tarawa pier with his flame thrower many minutes ahead of the first troop landing wave. Lieutenant Leslie emphasized to UDT that the Marines wanted to know where their amphibian tractors could land. He took to his new assignment like a UDT to water. Kauffman wanted another good platoon leader, and asked Leslie if he'd swim in with the team. The Marine officer agreed enthusiastically.

To command Team Six, Koehler picked Lieutenant De-Earle M. Logsdon, engineering training officer of Admiral Kauffman's destroyer command.

Team Seven's commanding officer, Dick Burke, had not been an original UDT enthusiast. Trying to get back to overseas duty from his job as instructor at the Mine Disposal School, he had attended a UDT demonstration at Fort Pierce. He returned to Washington with the conviction that he wanted no part of "that suicide unit." Instead he was assigned to a harbor clearance battalion in Hawaii.

His first orders were to go to the Maui UDT base and learn about coral blasting. As he reports it:

"I flew to Maui and again met UDT. Kauffman was Commanding Officer of Team Five, and John Koehler was Executive Officer of the base. That night I went out with Team Five as an observer on a beach reconnaissance, and at five the next morning met in Kauffman's tent for a critique. All his team officers said what a fine operation it had been. I was asked for a few words, and none of them were any good. It seemed to me that there was no organization, and I said so.

"The next day Kauffman and Koehler offered me the job as Commanding Officer of Team Seven. I said I had a nice soft job waiting for me and I couldn't see giving it up for something like UDT. That afternoon they flew to Pearl and came back the next morning with my orders to Team Seven.

"It was the best thing that happened to me in my six years in the Navy. From that moment I was at home. I have never met a finer group of officers and men. After having suffered the rigors of Fort Pierce together, the team resented an outsider coming in to take command, but that didn't last very long."

Koehler and the three team commanders completed the training for Saipan. Swimmers were qualified in the mile swim, and practiced surveying techniques. Radio communication was still ragged. The coxswains had improved their handling of small boats, although this was gravely doubted on the day of high surf and confusion late in May when the three teams loaded their gear aboard the waiting high-speed transports.

Small boats could not beach in the surf without broaching, so some equipment was carried in an amtrac which smashed against Team Five's destroyer transport *Gilmer*. The *Gilmer's* officer of the deck was frantic, and the amtrac driver was amazed at such friendly solicitude for fear his low open craft would swamp—until he was profanely ordered to keep off or he'd hole the destroyer's thin hull.

On the dock a crate of binoculars and waterproof watches being lowered into a wave-tossed landing craft smashed against the dock, littering the ocean floor with the last watches and binoculars in the Hawaiian area. Team Five's executive officer, Lieutenant John DeBold, luckily was an expert and enthusiast with the self-contained Jack Brown diving outfit, and promptly dove "on oxygen" to search fish-like under water. Fortunately all the waterproof watches were recovered in one package, and he fished out most of the binoculars only a little the worse for sea water.

At last all the teams' gear except explosives was lashed down on the decks of their destroyer transports. The sensitive explosive detonators were stowed in special magazines. The overflow of tetrytol was packed solidly between the deck and the bottom tier of UDT bunks. Tetrytol was supposedly stable enough to withstand shock and not explode unless directly hit, but it would burn easily. The smoking lamp was permanently out in the men's quarters.

Eighty bunks were jammed four deep into the space of a hotel double room, with explosives stacked against the bulkhead. The smaller bunks near the ship's bow were allotted to shorter men. Chief petty officers shared similar quarters on the next deck with the ship's enlisted men. Team officers crowded in with ship's officers. As one transport commander commented: "To have twenty-seven officers live in a 1917 destroyer wardroom is not at all satisfactory. Fortunately, relationship between ship and team personnel was very good."

The tough demolition men found it difficult to conform to ship duties and discipline, so foreign to their own type of regulations. One Fleet admiral described them with grudging admiration as: "Half fish and half nut."

Ventilation below decks was not adequate for such crowded conditions. Most officers and men slept topside, even in rain or rough weather, whenever they could find room enough.

Dick Burke tells how one problem was solved on his team's first cruise:

"The *Brooks* was a dirty old four-stacker with a tired crew. They had just come from the Guadalcanal area where they had been ferrying Marine 'Recon' companies, and they thought us a pretty tame bunch of guys. They didn't like having thirty tons of tetrytol stored all over the ship—under the bunks, in the mess hall, any place there was a bit of spare room.

"Our Marine Corps observer, First Lieutenant Edward

Ryan, was a tremendous giant of a man who never got enough to eat. Naturally the officers' steward would keep the best and the most for the ship's officers. This riled all hands.

"Our Marine took over. Three days out, he arrived at the wardroom table with full battle gear—offensive weapons most in evidence. He called all the mess stewards to his place, pulled out his large knife, showed it to them, his bayonet, and his .45 pistol. Each one he passed under their respective noses, and demanded food, large quantities of it. Never again did the passenger officers leave the table hungry."

The crowded, uncomfortable trip was broken by a short rehearsal in Roi, then on to Saipan.

Saipan's central mountain loomed in the dawn as the advance group approached on June 14, keeping 5,000 yards off the western shore. The fast carrier force and its battleships had pounded the island, wiping out all Japanese air power in the Marianas. The sun shone bright in a blue sky with cotton-ball clouds drifting in the trade winds. A spine of green hills, running north and south from the 1,500-foot central mountain, was dotted by terraced farms and camouflaged artillery caves.

There was just enough breeze to kick up a two-foot surf over the broad strip of coral reef, one to two hundred feet wide, that ran north and south paralleling the shore. Between the reef and island lay a long open lagoon, nearly a mile wide at the north end of the chosen beaches, narrowing to a hundred yards or so at its southwest corner. Halfway down the target area, the line of brown sand beaches bulged seaward at rocky Susupe Point. This headland (also called Afetna Point) was strongly held by Japanese mortar and machine-gun dugouts. It would mark the dividing point between the two Marine divisions' beaches.

On the day before, antiaircraft had knocked down a Navy Avenger, flying 3,000 feet over the lagoon. Two crewmen were killed, but the pilot, Lieutenant William Martin, was blasted free. He pulled the ripcord and found his parachute shredded. He pointed his feet down, hit at an angle in four feet of water, and sat with a thud on the bottom. He was a hundred yards from the beach and a hundred yards north of Susupe Point. Jap snipers from both areas fired at him as he grabbed his chute together and porpoised seaward toward the reef. He reached the reef unhit, splashed across it in a crouching run, and dove into the ocean beyond. He inflated his seat lifeboat, rigged his torn chute as a sail, and got to sea, where a plane picked him up. Back aboard ship, he reported that the lagoon was four to six feet deep, and the reef one and a half to two feet under water, with colored pennants marking it every 300 yards (presumably range markers for mortars).

Martin's report was radioed to the demolition teams with orders to check it and locate the sunken plane.

Roger Hour, when Teams Five and Seven would start their reconnaissance, was 0900. Kauffman still expected over 50 per cent casualties. He made every officer and enlisted man in his team memorize the chain of command—a numbered list of fifteen officers who would take charge, one after another, as their seniors were knocked out. Quick promotions seemed probable, but they must not confuse or stop the mission.

As the men boarded their landing craft, now only a mile from the reef, the destroyers, cruisers, and battleships fired over their heads at the shore. Patches of hazy smoke rose from the beaches and green hillsides.

Hidden Japanese batteries suddenly answered, confident in their camouflage and smokeless powder. Team Five's transport *Gilmer* was straddled on all sides by bursts. Hastily, with two men wounded, it retired to a safer station. The battleship *California* took a direct hit in the control tower, and had to pull out to 5,000 yards, reducing the effectiveness of the northern area's support fire.

North of Susupe, four landing craft fanned out toward their respective beach areas. Japanese mortars concentrated on the audacious little targets. Luckily the Japanese fire was only accurate where it was "registered" on the flagged buoys.

The mortar bursts followed the landing craft instead of leading them. One zigzagging boat was trailed by 26 shots, all falling the same number of yards behind. The shellfire was so intense near the reef that the boat crews stayed 50 yards to seaward.

The swimmers crouched down in the open cockpits. They looked fantastic, clad in blue sneakers, kneepads for crawling on coral, swim trunks, canvas work gloves to protect their hands from poisonous coral scratches, glass-fronted face masks, and helmets. They dangled balsa wood floats to mark mines, oblong plastic slates to record the water depth, and spare pencils for writing under water. One man in each swimming pair carried a big reel of measured fishline. Four officers carried waterproofed handy-talkie radios.

Adding a final surrealistic touch, each man was camouflaged blue and was painted from toe to chin, and down each arm, with horizontal stripes of ordinary black paint a foot apart, with shorter lines between. This war paint was not in imitation of the Indian naked warriors; it was Kauffman's idea for quick measurement of lagoon and reef depths. The swimmers could touch their feet or hands to the bottom in shallow water to check its depth against their bodies.

On command, each pair of "buddies" jumped into the rubber boat lashed alongside, flopped into the water and swam toward the reef. Seven pairs of swimmers covered each boat's 700-yard beach.

Near Susupe Point, when the pairs got halfway in, one swimmer turned back to make sure that at least half the information got back; the other swimmer was ordered to swim within fifty yards of shore before returning, although Kauffman didn't believe many could get that close.

Chief Davis was nearest Susupe Point, where the sniper fire was heaviest. He hung his face mask on a Jap marker thirty yards from the beach as absolute proof that "Kilroy was there." The swimmers in that area located Martin's plane, confirmed his one-man survey, and came back with added information that changed the Marine battle plan.

On the northern half of the team's beaches, the reef was 200 yards wide, and the lagoon stretched almost a mile to shore. Figuring that swimmers wouldn't make the whole distance, an advance party started across the reef's two-foot surf on "flying mattresses." These small inflated rubber rafts have an electric motor for silent propulsion—and for the shocking torment of the rider if the waterproofing leaks!

Six "flying mattresses" carrying two swimmers apiece headed into the lagoon. Ensign Marshall's mattress was overturned on the reef by a near mortar burst. Unable to right it, he started the mile swim across the lagoon. "Red" Davenport got well into the lagoon when a Jap sniper punctured his mattress and he took to the comparative safety of swimming. Kauffman and the others anchored their mattresses in the lagoon 300 yards from shore, swimming the rest of the way.

Following the harried mattress teams, pairs of swimmers swam steadily toward the beach, the lineman unreeling his fishline and taking soundings every 25 yards while the "searcher" zigzagged, looking for mines or coral heads to mark with his balsa floats.

Jap mortars and snipers concentrated on the landing craft and the rubber mattresses, but didn't neglect the swimmers. Machine-gun bursts swiftly taught them to take evasive action; they porpoised, staying under as long as they could, coming up for air at a different spot. A couple of men, looking through their face masks under water, saw spent, sinking bullets which they caught as very personal souvenirs.

The swimming officers found the handy-talkie radios were too unhandy to carry on a long swim under fire and had to abandon them.

On each of Kauffman's four beaches, he had an officer on a flying mattress with a roving commission to steer the linemen and encourage or rescue them. He himself was on one of the rafts with a farsighted enlisted man as his "seeing eye." Kauffman had poor vision, his buddy was color blind! So the "seeing eye" would point out an object to Kauffman who would tell him what color it was. The blind leading the blind! He reported later:

"Every single man was calmly and slowly continuing his search and marking his slate, with stuff dropping all around. They didn't appear one tenth as scared as I was. I would not have been so amazed if 90 per cent of the men had done so well, but to have a cold 100 per cent go in through the rain of fire was almost unbelievable."

As Kauffman got well into the lagoon, he saw a series of heavy splashes not far behind his mattress. Thinking the support ships were firing short among his swimmers, he extended the aerial of his cracker-box radio to call his executive officer, Jack DeBold, who was protestingly relegated to a landing craft outside the reef, relaying messages to the gunfire support ships. Kauffman snapped: "Tell those damned ships to knock off the shorts!"

From DeBold came a cool reply: "Those are not shorts, they are overs. They are not ours."

Japanese were getting the range, their mortar shells bursting near and even under the swimmers. Harold Hall was blown clear out of the water by an undersea burst—and survived. Five other swimmers suffered internal injuries from blast concussion before that hour-long swim was completed.

An air strike was timed to strafe the beaches with low-level bombing and machine-gunning when the swimmers got half-way ashore. At 1000, the ships lifted their fire in order to miss the planes. The battleship put its fire 500 yards inland to avoid the swimmers. The destroyers were standing far out, away from the zeroed-in reef.

But the planes didn't come. When the fire lifted off the beaches, the Japanese stood up in their trenches ten yards back of the water line and fired point-blank at the approaching swimmers. This, a dead-pan ensign commented later, was "detrimental to morale." As Kauffman wrote his father the next night:

The mattresses were the main targets. I got no mortar bursts nearer than 15 yards, but four other mattresses were sunk without scratching the men on them. Only one man was killed—Christensen, one of my very best men.

I anchored my mattress 300 yards from the beach and started in at 1000, expecting heavy air support as promised during the half hour while we were attempting to get in to the water line. Not one plane appeared. I got to about 100 yards from the beach, and even with my bad eyes I could see Japs moving around, manning their bloody machine guns. I set up my radio and called for the damned aviators, but quickly closed it up after that one transmission as it secured me too much fire.

Kauffman tried to signal his men to turn back at the 100-yard mark because of the lack of air support, but most of them went in to the 50-yard line. Going back, they kept under water as much as possible as they zigzagged to the reef, scrambled over it, and swam toward the cruising pickup boats. Kauffman, nearing the reef on his flying mattress, headed for swimmer "Red" Davenport to offer him a tow.

"Get that damned thing out of here!" yelled the normally courteous UDT man. His commander understood when he remembered that "Red" had already had one mattress shot out from under him.

The landing craft ran back into the mortar fire near the reef to pick up each swimmer, reversing engines and coming to a dead stop while the exhausted man scrambled aboard or was yanked up by helping arms.

Finally the count was complete. Besides the dead Christensen, only two swimmers were missing—Root and Heil. They were from Ensign Jack Adams' boat, and he cruised off the reef for half an hour looking for them while the other boats went to the *Gilmer*. At last Kauffman had to make the hard command decision; he radioed Adams to leave the men rather than risk the swimmers in his boat with their badly needed information.

At 1230, a cruiser reported seeing what might be two men clinging to a buoy a mile and a half south of where they had swum in. Kauffman headed toward there in a landing craft with a crew of four. En route in the lagoon they saw what looked like a man's head. Kauffman dove off the landing craft and crossed the reef; with his bad eyesight he had to swim really close before he saw that it was just a coral rock. Meantime the landing craft had cruised out of mortar range.

Kauffman waited, hanging onto the reef while the boat returned, its crew standing up like victorious boxers with hands clasped overhead. He couldn't understand why, until he saw six men in the boat. He climbed onto the reef and waved back. A couple of sniper bullets reminded him he was a good target. Scrambling across the reef, he swam to the boat, and was helped up the Jacob's ladder, exhausted. Then he got the story.

Heil's leg had been injured going in. His buddy bandaged it, and left him to swim in to the beach and make his survey as ordered. He picked Heil up on his return, and towed him to a Japanese buoy several hundred yards at sea to get out of the reef zone of fire.

Meanwhile Lieutenant Dick Burke's Team Seven had rough going on the four beaches south of Susupe Point. He had not followed Kauffman's inventions of the string reconnaissance or the painted human yardsticks, but otherwise the plan was similar—pairs of "swim buddies" to measure the reef and lagoon depths.

A battered sugar refinery stood at the north end of the tree-shaded town of Charan Kanoa. One of its tall stacks, surviving the bombardment, served as a landmark for the narrow channel cutting through the reef. A dozen Japanese barges were anchored in the lagoon just south of the channel in front of the town. To the rear of the beaches were woods full of Japanese snipers and pillboxes which stretched all the way down to the gun emplacements in rocky cliffs at Saipan's southwest corner.

Four landing craft set out for the reef under the ships' covering gunfire. The survey craft, in charge of the team's executive officer, Lieutenant (jg) Bruce Onderdonk, had to survey the Charan Kanoa boat channel. His boat made a preliminary pass parallel to the reef's outer edge, dropping buoys to guide the swimmers and drawing mortar fire (and Lieutenant Burke in the next boat farther south raised hell on the radio intercom about the ships' poor aim— until, like Kauffman, he realized his boats were under Jap fire).

Onderdonk's boat circled for a second run. Six swimmers flopped over the side to start into the channel. Suddenly a mortar shell burst squarely under the ramped bow of the boat, lifting it high into the air.

"Over the side!" someone shouted.

Seven men jumped out of the boat, including the coxswain from the ship's crew (the *Brooks* had insisted on manning the boats with its own crews, although Burke wisely insisted on carrying the regular UDT coxswains as well). One member of the ship's crew, however, redeemed its reputation by grabbing the wheel until the UDT coxswain could take over the yawing craft. Circling under fire, they picked up the startled seven who had abandoned ship.

Onderdonk had all he could do to rescue the boat crew; fortunately, they were using a new technique for picking up swimmers. This scheme was invented by another Team Seven boat officer, Lieutenant (jg) Sidney Robbins. A life ring was trailed behind the boat, which the swimmer could grasp and be dragged in to where he could be hauled aboard, without stopping the craft while under fire.

Meantime the six reconnaissance swimmers, wearing inflatable life belts and dangling slates around their necks, headed steadily toward Charan Kanoa, into the heart of the gunfire. The Japanese barges were packed with mortars and light machine guns, forming a deadly trap waiting for the landing waves. The trap was unexpectedly sprung by the Underwater Demolition Teams when the Japanese revealed their positions by shooting at the swimmers.

Two of the six men were wounded while in the water, but all of them kept swimming to within fifty or a hundred yards of shore, diving and dodging while sounding the depths. The ships' guns began to fire at the barges. Lieutenant Burke had called for that gunfire, and for white phosphorus shells to spread a smoke screen along the beach to cover the swimmers' escape. All six men got back to the boats with their information.

Burke's own boat had a more tragic mishap. It was equally within range of the barges and the town's snipers. The boat, having dropped its swimmers, was zigzagging away, when a Japanese mortar burst squarely aboard, hitting the UDT coxswain, Albert Weidner, in the chest, blowing him from the wheel. The ship's gunner was instantly killed, and another man from the ship's crew was wounded. Burke ordered the boat back to the Cruiser *Indianapolis* to evacuate the casualties. Then the landing craft returned to pick up its swimmers who had completed their reconnaissance, although one man had been hit by shrapnel while in the water.

The third boat was so badly shot up that its skipper did not attempt to drop swimmers. The coxswain was hit in the spine before reaching the reef, and another man took a bullet through his stomach. The petty officer in charge of the boat zigzagged along the reef to discover as much as possible; they saw no mines or obstacles.

The last boat, under Lieutenant Robbins, dropped its swimmers on the southernmost beach despite fire which wounded one unlucky man twice in fifteen minutes. The swimmers penetrated the lagoon and returned without a scratch. Robbins then cruised north to pick up the swimmers from Charan Kanoa and a rubber-boatload of would-be rescuers.

Lieutenant Burke ordered a phosphorus smoke screen and recalled all swimmers to the *Brooks* for blankets, coffee, medicinal brandy, and a pooling of their information.

The two team captains, Kauffman and Burke, met aboard the *Gilmer*, ready to report "mission accomplished" with a loss of three men—one from each team and one from the *Brooks*. It had been found that there was no need for demolition before the landings—the Marines' amtracs could land unimpeded. They took their report to the advance group commander, Rear Admiral Oldendorf, on the cruiser *Louisville*. He dispatched the good news by coded radio to Rear Admiral Hill's attack force, which was steaming toward Saipan scheduled to arrive before morning.

All the team officers stayed up most of the night, preparing charts of reefs and lagoons for distribution to the arriving Amphibious Force. At dawn the junior officers of the two teams stepped aboard the flagship *Rocky Mount*, expecting to deliver their information and charts to some equally junior officer. They were immediately haled before Vice Admiral Turner and Lieutenant General Holland Smith, who questioned them steadily for most of an hour, and congratulated the teams heartily on their work.

Ensign Adams reported to the Second Marine Division tank commander that the Operation Plan's scheduled tank route (chosen on the basis of air photo intelligence) at the extreme north of the beaches just wouldn't work. The swimmers had found the water was two feet deeper than estimated and would drown out the tanks. But the UDT had charted a previously unsuspected diagonal route farther south, just north of Susupe Point, where the swimmers were sure that tanks could get across. It didn't disturb the team a bit that this would involve a major tactical change in the Second Division's landing and battle plan, switching the tank force from the Marines' left flank to the right. . . .

After Kauffman reported to Rear Admiral Hill, he was summoned by the Second Division commander, Major General Watson, to discuss the reconnaissance.

"Don't ever try that again, you'll lose half your men!" the Marine general roared. "Even the Japs can get a hit at thirty yards." Then, brandishing the changed tank plan which had been properly delivered to him by the team's Marine liaison officer, he became genuinely angry. "Are you the man who's been ordering my tanks around? Whose tanks do you think they are?"

General Watson finally agreed to the changed plan, but he warned that if every tank wasn't ashore by noon, or if any tank drowned out on the UDT route, a certain UDT lieutenant commander would either be court-martialed or shot!

At H-Hour that morning, 0830, UDT officers were in more literal danger of being shot. Because of their close-up knowledge of the beaches, they rode in the control landing craft to mark the outer boundaries of each beach and guide the waves of Marine amtracs into their allotted lanes—a UDT contribution to this and future landings in the Central Pacific. They watched the turreted "amphibious tanks" and amtracs crawl over the reefs as the UDT had predicted.

The thundering barrage of the naval armada pounded the beaches. The gunfire "walked" inland as the amtracs paddled across the lagoons and crawled up on the sand through every bit of fire the Japanese could pour down from the hills.

On the beaches south of Susupe Point, Team Seven officers guided fifty-foot tank lighters onto a shelving reef which their southernmost crew had explored. The lighters dropped their ramps, and tanks rolled out, splashing through the lagoon shallows to smash into the Jap defenses.

Farther north, on the disputed new tank route north of Susupe, Ensign Adams led the way for the tanks in an open, unarmored amtrac, followed by Lieutenant Commander Kauffman in another filled with buoys and anchors to mark the tank path across the lagoon.

The coxswain following them in the first tank lighter was skeptical about getting far enough on the surf-pounded reef to drop his ramp.

Marine Liaison Officer Lieutenant Leslie, who was aboard, told him, "Full speed ahead."

He obeyed all too well, and rammed his steel craft high and dry 25 yards on the reef. The ramp dropped and the tank crawled out to follow the two amtracs along the slanting underwater path across the lagoon. Japanese mortars opened up on them, but the tank ran the gauntlet success-fully.

Adams' amtrac was hit by shrapnel several times before it turned back and got across the reef to seaward. Kauffman's amtrac, dropping buoys to mark the route, took a near burst. There was a scuffling in the cockpit, and the com-mander turned to see who was hit. The crew were only scrambling to pick up still-hot pieces of shrapnel for souve-nirs.

Two of the stranded tank lighter's crew, scared of the surf, clung to the dubious shelter of their craft despite Jap-anese fire. Finally a UDT man swam onto the reef with a line, which he firmly tied around the protesting refugees. They were duly dragged through the surf to a boat, rescued in spite of themselves.

Meantime the other tank lighters nosed more carefully up to the reef and spilled their tanks, which trailed across the buoyed lagoon path like half-submerged dinosaurs.

Kauffman, learning by radio that the shore party com-mander wished to give him instructions for blowing a small boat channel through the middle of the reef, hailed an in-bound amtrac, and boarded it with Lieutenant Leslie.

On the beach, the Leathernecks were dug in under con-stant shell and mortar fire from the hills. Their advance lines were halted in many places.

When the amtrac grounded, Kauffman and Leslie jumped out. They were clad in blue trunks, light blue canvas shoes; the stripes were only partly scrubbed off their bare torsos. A sweaty Marine looked around from his foxhole, blinked, spat, and said, "By God, I've seen everything now! The tourists are here and we ain't even *got* the damned beach yet!"

Suddenly realizing that they were "out of uniform," and also being shot at, Kauffman and Leslie dove for foxholes. They kept low as they hunted up the shore party com-mander, got his requirements for the channel, and boarded the first available amtrac to get away from that uncomfort-able beach.

That D-Day was no time for underwater demolition. The reef was too busy a shuttle station, with ships unloading supplies onto the amtracs and the DUKWs, the amphibious trucks that looked like barges on wheels and proved invaluable in ferrying the "beans and bullets" ashore.

That night, Lieutenant Burke and seven of his team put flashing buoys at the entrance of the natural Charan Kanoa boat channel which his team had surveyed. Despite enemy fire, the channel was constantly jammed with small boat traffic, day and night.

Team Five was aboard the *Gilmer*, which served as part of the destroyer screen around the fleet that night, when it intercepted a group of five small Japanese ships heading down to reinforce the north end of the island. General quarters sounded, and the demolition men went to their explosive-packed bunk rooms.

With the *Gilmer* firing heavily and taking an occasional hit, curiosity led some of the team to sneak a look at the battle from the well deck. The Japanese ships fired several streams of tracers at the *Gilmer*, which cured the sight-seers' curiosity in a hurry.

Luckily none of the Japanese shells touched off the team's stored tons of explosives. Commander "Jack" Horner laid his 3-inch guns so accurately on the Jap ships that the *Gilmer* set four of them afire; a screening destroyer joined the party and made the fifth kill. But the *Gilmer* was the undisputed victor of the Battle of Marpi Point.

Spotting Japanese survivors in the water at dawn, the *Gilmer* swung its landing craft over the side. Some of the UDT men joined the transport's crew in the small boats. The first Jap survivor fought against rescue, but a boat hook solved the problem, first tapping his skull and then hauling him aboard. The other survivors then decided they could follow him aboard without losing face. They were taken aboard the *Gilmer* and put under the care of the ship's doctor.

The UDT teams were now under the orders of the Force

Beachmaster, Captain Carl E. Anderson, USNR, for demolition and clearance work. "Squeaky" Anderson, so named from his high-pitched voice launching a continuous and amazing stream of invective, was barely over five feet, but every inch solid Scandinavian, a "Mr. Five by Five" if there ever was one. A dirty baseball cap was pulled down over his round and furiously red face. A Marine shirt hung open over his bare chest, with the buttons and sleeves ripped off. His green combat trousers were torn off (not cut) several inches above the knees, as shorts. He wore carefully shined black shoes, and black socks with garters. Easily as much out of uniform as any UDT man ever managed to be, he had adopted a general's privilege of prescribing his own uniform.

He sounded like a shrill and angry tiger, and rigged bull horns on the beaches to make sure the unloading crews jumped when he squeaked. Nearly sixty, he did more work than three officers in their twenties. He was an Alaska sourdough who had run fish canneries and operated coastwise steamers. Called to active duty in the Aleutian campaign, he promptly proved his ability to organize a beach and get the stuff ashore fast. Rear Admiral Harry Hill kept him along when the fleet went south for the Gilbert and Marshall invasions, then on across the Pacific.

"I'm Squeaky Anderson, the Force Beachmaster," he told the three Underwater Demolition Teams at Saipan, and proceeded to drive them like Simon Legree. He ended by proudly calling them his All-American football team.

Their chief task was to blow channels through the barrier reefs for small craft and amphibious trucks. Day and night they laid explosive packs and fired blasts, cutting a boat channel through the tough coral reef north of Susupe and the shallows inside, permitting a constant stream of boats and DUKWs to rush ammunition, food, and plasma to the Marines and the Army 27th Division, busy forcing more than twenty thousand Japanese out of their caves and dugouts.

Saipan, the first mountainous island tackled in the Central Pacific, proved far more difficult than had been expected.

In addition, the Carrier Force and other units of the fleet had to speed westward to meet and rout the Japanese Fleet which had sortied from the Philippines to relieve Saipan. The scheduled assault on Guam, for which the Crist and Carberry teams were standing by, on screening duty off Saipan, was postponed a month.

Lieutenant Logsdon's Team Six had also been standing by, impatiently. The morning swim at Saipan had luckily not lived up to Kauffman's expectation that they would need this team as mass replacements for his team and Burke's. Team Six, griping at being sidetracked, finally got some action. The southern shore of the island was sufficiently cleared of enemies by June 20 (D plus five) to permit Beachmaster Anderson to build ramps for the tank landing ships. It was a four-day job for Logsdon's men, and they received some sniper fire from the Japs.

The UDT crew found piles of Japanese boat and personnel mines—ready to be planted under water. The landing date just barely beat the defenders to the punch. The Japanese had already mined and obstructed the natural harbor of Magicienne Bay on the east coast, but the Americans were too uncooperative to land in their trap.

Clearing beaches was too unexciting for some demolition men. Team Five discovered four men missing. They *might* have sneaked ashore to joint the fighting.

The word was passed, and two days later a Marine major returned the four men with the comment: "These men have done an excellent job with my battalion, but I'm sending them back. Either I'll get in trouble or they will."

The Underwater Demolition Teams had only one major disciplinary measure—dropping a man from the team. The four begged to be kept in UDT. They were among the best swimmers and were needed for the coming invasion of the nearby island of Tinian. So their commander, Kauffman, gave the men a choice—be dropped, or spend five days on war's worst assignment, the burial detail. They chose the latter.

After three days of burying Marines who had fallen in the bloody struggle up the island, the men couldn't take it; they said they'd rather be dropped from the team. But the skipper decided they had learned their lesson, and took them back.

Meanwhile the Marines and the Army fought their bitter way up Saipan's bristling spine, suffering many times the casualties of "bloody Tarawa" with considerably less public concern. France was filling the headlines, and most people had no idea where or what Saipan was.

The UDT job at Saipan was finished after twelve days of laboring for "Squeaky" Anderson. Team Six was assigned to join Teams Three and Four for the delayed assault on Guam, now set for July 21.

The men of UDT had reason to be proud of their performance at Saipan. Though at first apprehensive of swimming toward an enemy beach in daylight, they had learned to use the sea as their protector. The drills in long-distance swimming, swimming under water and through heavy surf, had paid off. Rather than "we do be afraid of the sea," it could be said that they gained a great respect for the sea. The phrase "and we do only be drownded now and again" has been an infrequent term in Underwater Demolition Teams.

9. "Welcome, Marines!"

GUAM HAD FLOWN THE STARS AND STRIPES AS A NAVY BASE
until the Japanese imperial tide of conquest flowed over it
on December 10, 1941. Two and one-half years later, the
Rising Sun was being belted off its flagstaff by the circling
battleships, cruisers, and destroyers of Rear Admiral L. Conolly's advance force.

The Guam invasion plan, code-named "Stevedore," called
for a pincers movement, landing troops on reef-guarded
beaches on the north shore and west shore separated by Apra
Harbor and its heavily fortified guardian Orote Peninsula,
which bulged from the middle of the narrow, banana-shaped
island.

The "Battle Against the Island Defenses," as Admiral Conolly styled it, began in mid-June 1944 while Admiral Turner's
task force was launching an assault on Saipan a hundred miles
farther north. A systematic ship and air bombardment commenced on July 8. The bombardment of Guam was one of
the heaviest in all history.

UDT 3 arrived with the advance group on July 14. They
could see from their transport decks the flat fringing reef,
heavily barricaded. Obviously no landing craft or amtrac
could pass the obstructions. On board the old-style destroyer
Dickerson, Lieutenant Tom Crist gave his swimmers their
final briefing. They had seven days to clear the reefs before
W-Day, "William" Day in Navy voice code. (D-Day, incidentally, is not a uniform designation for landing dates,
although it was used for both Normandy and Saipan.)

Admiral Conolly was furnishing heavy fire support, from
the battleship *Idaho,* the cruiser *Honolulu,* two destroyers,
and four gunboats. These LCI(G)s, infantry landing craft

converted to gunboats, had already proved their fire-power value at Kwajalein and more recently at Saipan. Now they were assigned as close-in cover for UDT work. Long and narrow, with a round command tower amidships, the gunboats were floating platforms with gun tubs forward for the rapid-fire pairs of 20mm and 40mm guns, and batteries of slanting rocket tubes backed by heavy metal shields to absorb the flaming backlash. They could fire off a tremendous barrage of rockets when most needed by the swimmers.

A UDT officer boarded each gunboat to assist in gunfire control. Then the flotilla headed for the northern "preferred" beaches in front of the small village of Asan. The gunboats cruised between 500 and 1,000 yards off the shelf-like reef, backed up by two destroyers and the team's transport. The cruiser and battleship watched for any heavy Japanese battery to unmask.

At 1430 in the bright tropic afternoon sunlight, four ramped landing craft swept toward the Asan beaches, their telltale wakes streaming in the blue water. The only planes watching overhead wore stars instead of round red "meatballs."

The boats dropped a few swimmers opposite the beaches. Only a few snipers harassed them. The Japanese did not dare reveal themselves. Although they were amazed to see naked men swimming in to the beach, they did not feel in any danger from such an attack.

On Asan Point, commanding the beach area, a Japanese 47mm antitank gun was camouflaged from air observation. Its gunners tensely watched the boats and swimmers swarming toward their beaches, then returning in safety. One gunner, captured after the Marines landed, reported bitterly that he had kept his gun trained on them: "I could have wiped them out, but I was ordered not to shoot till the troops tried to land."

Then it was too late.

Under the muzzles of Japanese guns, the swimmers coolly studied the task that lay ahead of them.

A flat hard apron of reef, like Tarawa's, extended from 200 to 350 yards out in front of the mile-long shallow crescent of shore line. It was a "drying" reef, exposed at low tide and covered by two feet of water at high tide. The seaward edge sloped gradually down to deep water, an invitation to ramped landing craft with their slanted V-bottoms just fitted for the beach contour. The invitation stopped right there, however. The entire length of the beach was blocked by continuous lines of four-foot, rock-filled wire cribs.

On completing the swim, the team and the task unit cruised farther northeast to the beaches opposite Guam's capital, Agana. There they went through the same landing craft maneuver, but no swimmers were risked in the water—this was a feint to fool the enemy as to the actual landing place. The little flotilla was ostensibly window-shopping. This time the Japanese management ashore objected strenuously. Mortar fire blazed out at the landing craft as they neared range markers set at the reef's seaward edge. It was a hot midsummer hour's work.

A Marine liaison officer accompanied the team on its reconnaissances. In Maui, Second Lieutenant Frank F. Lahr, USMCR, had joined Team Three to explain the troops' landing needs and to coordinate the team's reports to the troops. Lahr was so immediately enthusiastic about the UDT work that he insisted on going along on every possible occasion. He soon won the universal nickname of "The Marine." Team Three and The Marine adopted each other for the duration.

Again that evening at nine, the team's four craft crept in to the landing beaches at Asan. Each boat dropped men in rubber boats, paddling to the reef edge. The men wore jungle-green fatigues, kneepads, coral sneakers, and work gloves—the reef was almost dry at low tide, and they had to crawl over the rough coral, trying not to show a silhouette against the starlit horizon.

Ashore the enemy were busy. Men were shouting high-pitched orders in Japanese as they ran a cement mixer, making concrete for the cribs on the reef. Trucks ran to the shore with loads of coral rock, their dimmed lights blinking faintly.

Crawling inshore to the high-water line, the secret scouts mapped the cribs for later destruction. They crept within fifty yards of their busy foes ashore.

About an hour before midnight, there were three bursts of heavy machine-gun fire aimed at the team's left flank where Ensign Martin Jacobson and two men were working from a rubber boat at the reef's edge. Bright tracer bullets flamed close to them. When the firing stopped, the men nearest on the reef tried to contact the trio. There was no answer.

Just after midnight a Very pistol flared from the transport as recall. All got back to the landing craft except the three who had been under fire. The ships withdrew, leaving one gunboat with Ensign Bert Hawks aboard which cruised off the reef looking in vain for the three missing swimmers. Finally it was decided that they and their boat must have been hit.

As dawn was breaking, the destroyer *MacDonough* spotted the three men swimming more than a mile offshore. They were safely picked up, suffering only from exposure and acute loneliness. The machine-gun fire had holed and sunk their rubber boat without touching them. They took to the water for protection, swimming most of the night, cold and miserable, hoping they'd be sighted by their own side rather than shot by Jap snipers at daylight.

With the lost sheep welcomed back, the team proceeded to the business of the day—four successive trips to the beach. The first was a fake, an early-afternoon "diversionary reconnaissance" on Dadi Beach just south of Apra. As the *Dickerson* approached, the Japanese shore batteries on Orote Point and Yona Island opened up, narrowly missing the thin-skinned transport. The destroyers, transport, and battleship fired back.

From his command ship *Appalachian*, Admiral Conolly ordered the battlewagon to close the beach within a mile. The battleship commander pointed out that at such short

range his heavy guns couldn't drop their shells on the top of
Orote Peninsula. Conolly said he wasn't figuring on the
heavy guns: "I'm sending you in because you have a lot of
40mm guns. Fire point-blank."

The curtain of fire over their heads protected the demolition men from snipers, but it didn't silence the Japanese
mortars hidden in the hills.

The team's landing craft sped toward shore into heavy but
luckily inaccurate mortar fire. The Japs never did really
learn to "lead" their targets like skeet shooters. But one
battery hidden in a protected position on a hill straddled a
gunboat and then landed a shell aboard, wounding five men.
A heavy salvo from the *Idaho* created a landslide above the
hill battery, covering guns and gunners with earth.

Half an hour later, at 1330, the flotilla moved farther south
to scout Agat Beach, the real target for the southern landing.
One loading craft drew such heavy fire from Agat Town that
it had to withdraw, but the other three boats dropped a pair
of swimmers apiece. The ships blasted the newly disclosed gun
position in Agat Town while the gunboats and the landing
craft machine guns poured fire over the swimmers' heads.
Guns and planes laid smoke on the beaches. The swimmers
were able to finish their job.

This was only a preliminary survey. Team Four was due
the next day to take over the southern beaches off Agat. The
job was obviously another tough one. A long continuous line
of coconut-palm "log cabins" were filled with rock. These
cribs were not quite as numerous as on the northern Asan
beaches, but they were bigger, and wires were strung between them. Closer inshore, a line of three-inch posts held
a barbed-wire fence.

The reef was flat and solid coral rock for 200 to 300 yards
offshore. Its seaward edge was only a foot under water at low
tide. Long narrow fingers of growing coral stretched out
irregularly for another 150 yards under water to seaward, with
occasional coral heads spotted between the clutching fingers.

That jagged reef edge immediately proved itself a hazard to landing craft.

While picking up its two swimmers, one UDT boat grounded on a submerged coral head. Enemy mortars opened fire. The trapped crew raced forward and aft, in the open cockpit, rocking the craft while the coxswain raced the motor. Finally the landing craft crunched off the coral pinnacle and, chased by inaccurate mortar bursts, limped back to its transport for repairs.

Moving a few miles farther south, the three craft made a feint reconnaissance. One UDT boat was circling close to the reef when it drove hard and fast onto a long finger of submerged coral. Another boat raced in to free the grounded boat—and it too grounded on the coral.

Unable to get the first boat off, Chief Warrant Officer Blowers started to lower a rubber boat over the side. A sniper from the offshore isle of Aluton cut loose with a machine gun. Carpenter Blowers was shot through the head, killed instantly. Several other men in the boat crew were slightly wounded.

Too late, the snagged boats backed off and escaped to make their way seaward. Admiral Conolly sent his chaplain to the *Dickerson;* taps sounded at sunset and Blowers was buried at sea by his teammates.

The weather was thickening, but Admiral Conolly ordered a night reconnaissance of the northern beaches. An hour before midnight, the landing craft set out through tropical rain squalls, hunting for the protecting gunboats as starting points for the beach. It soon became impossible to keep track of the boats and gunboats even by their "pips" in the radar screens. Gunboat 472 radioed for its location, and the *Dickerson's* harassed officer answered: "I don't know which pip is the 472. There aren't any numbers on this radar screen!"

One landing craft went hopelessly astray, but the destroyer *Dewey* spotted its wanderings on the radar and guided it back. The operation was called off an hour after midnight.

The team spent the next day shadowboxing with the

enemy, making a full-scale daytime feint at Tumon Bay, northeast of Asan, and taking part in the night bombardment of Agana's beaches.

The next day, the Japanese learned the teams were beach-combing in deadly earnest. Lieutenant William Gordon Carberry arrived with Team Four in the morning of July 17, W minus four, aboard destroyer-transport *Kane*. They promptly started a daylight beach reconnaissance under the fire cover of a newly borrowed group of LCI gunboats.

Admiral Conolly had asked the over-all Expeditionary Force Commander, Admiral Turner, whether he could spare some Saipan gunboats by the 19th. Turner jumped the dead-line by immediately detaching eight gunboats under Lieutenant Commander Blanchard to reach Guam on the morning of the 17th, just in time to back up Team Four's first re-connaissance. The gunboats shelled the shore heavily to dis-courage snipers and machine gunners.

The team's landing craft spent two hours along the reef edge, dropping sheet-metal buoys to guide night demolition. They counted almost four hundred cribs in a single mile-long line. Most of the cribs were six feet long, four feet wide and four feet high. The stout log frames were reinforced with wire netting and filled solidly with heavy coral blocks, cemented by sea water. The cribs were barely six feet apart, with half-inch trip wires strung between them. The Japanese had obviously spent thousands of man-hours of labor, constructing the reef barriers.

That night, on both northern and southern beaches, the two teams made a secret assault on the barricade. Carberry's team started for the southern Agat beach sectors at eight that evening. With muffled underwater exhausts four landing craft purred toward the reef, dropping twelve rubber-boat crews. One six-man crew stopped at the line of cribs, and placed tetrytol packs to open forty gaps, two cribs wide—passageways which could let boat waves through.

The other two boats beached on the drying reef, and their crews waded or walked to the sandy shore to load smaller charges against the posts strung with barbed wire. Gaps in the wire fence would be blown in line with the gaps in the cribs.

An occasional light ashore proved that the enemy were awake. They could be heard talking and working on their defenses. The UDT men on the reef were working, too; but silently. Things went wrong in the pitch-blackness. Parts of the barbed-wire fence were too far up on the sand to be located. Some of the crib-blowing crew landed too far north to link their fuses with the other boats', so they set their fuses for a separate explosion.

After two hours of hard work, the crews paddled back to their landing boats off the reef. The fuse pullers checked their watches, triggered five-minute delay firing assemblies, and rushed for the boats.

One fuse puller, Ensign Hoffman, made his boat all right— but the racing motor didn't budge the craft. It had drifted onto a finger of coral reef in the ebbing tide. There were only seconds of fuse left to burn, so everybody in the boat ducked flat. Along the mile of reef, the posts and cribs blew in a hundred flares of light. Wood and coral splattered into the stranded boat, but nobody was hurt.

Another landing craft hurried up and tried to tow the craft off, but its propeller fouled the towline and it too went on the reef. One boat finally pulled free. The men hastily stripped the stranded boat and abandoned it. At daylight, the ships' guns destroyed the boat with incendiary fire, leaving it a twisted marker on the reef edge.

Next morning was sunny and calm. One of Carberry's boats counted the seventy-five remaining cribs sticking up irregularly like a small boy's front teeth. A second boat crew worked to blast out landing ramps on the reef edge with their explosives. In the afternoon, the team's other two boats took over. One crew loaded sixty of the cribs, fixing the explosive packs so that most of the debris would fall toward shore on the defenders hiding there.

The next day, William minus two, continued clear and

fair, with slight surf breaking on the reef edge. In the morning, a crew finished off the fifteen cribs remaining in the mile of landing beaches. Another crew under Ensign Thomas Nixon cleared the underwater coral boulders out of the mouth of a natural boat channel into the reef south of Gaan Point.

From behind a wrecked Japanese plane lying awash, a hidden machine gun suddenly sprayed the demolition men wading and paddling over the reef. They ducked under water, their boat's radio spotted the machine gun, and the watchful gunboats and destroyers blasted the wreck and the gun.

The demolition men were so confident by now, that one of the boat crews on the reef that afternoon prepared a special stunt without the knowledge of their commander. One rubber boat kept going purposely toward shore, guided by Chief Andres F. Oddstad, Jr. "Andy" Oddstad and his boat crew, like other members of Teams Three and Four, had engaged in friendly argument with the Fourth Marines during training in Guadalcanal, as to who got to the beaches first and how far they went.

Now Oddstad and three of the other men got out of the rubber boat. Hurrying through the water to the line of posts and barbed wire at the high-water mark, the quartet were carrying something bulky.

"Those men are getting in too close." Carberry frowned. "I'll have to warn them later about that."

The four huddled at the fence for a minute. A sniper narrowly missed them. Then they splashed back to the rubber boat, and paddled to sea.

On the Agat beach fence, facing seaward, was a five-by-two-foot plywood sign, carefully lettered with black paint:

WELCOME, MARINES
AGAT USO TWO BLOCKS
COURTESY UDT 4

The sign was discovered by the Marines on W-Day morning while the Japanese were throwing all the lead and steel they could at the assault troops hitting the beach. Even the hard-fighting, hard-bragging Marines grinned when they saw the sign.

The laughter echoed throughout the fleet. Carberry reported with a straight face to Admiral Conolly that he had properly reprimanded the men who had violated landing-plan security. Admiral Turner, who took a naturally paternal pride in the Underwater Demolition Teams, repeated the story with gusto. It grew in the telling until the Marines' amtracs had practically crawled under an arch of triumph erected by the UDT.

Other teams claimed the credit. Actually Team Three had also prepared a somewhat similar "Welcome Marines" sign, but Lieutenant Crist discovered it and confiscated it at a time when the team was still making feints on other beaches to fool the Japanese. Other UDT teams tried to repeat the stunt on other invasions but it was firmly suppressed as a breach of security.

UDT was first on the northern beaches off Asan, too. Tom Crist's Team Three didn't miss a day in its full week of pre-assault beachcombing. They started their actual demolition on the same night as Carberry's team, W minus four, July 17, approaching the shore an hour after midnight. Mortar fire from Asan Point chased two landing craft off course. One of the destroyers had The Marine, Lieutenant Lahr, as the team's fire spotter; he directed five-inch fire on the Jap mortars and silenced them. The team's other two landing craft dropped their rubber-boat crews near the reef. The men paddled their explosive-laden rubber boats to the reef edge, then splashed through a foot or two of water carrying 40 pounds of tetrytol apiece. They crossed the reef to the line of cribs nearest the shore—only 50 feet from Japanese patrol routes. Working fast but silently, they loaded 120 rock-filled cribs with explosive packs, and laced the charges together with a network of primacord fuse—this wasn't a job anyone wanted to have to repeat because of a misfire.

At the extreme right flank, nearest the enemy-held point,

the UDT lieutenant in charge of the loading detail heard loud talking. He was furious at the breach of orders. Hurrying through ankle-deep water toward the offenders, the lieutenant suddenly stopped short. The men beyond him were cheerfully chattering in Japanese. The enemy workers were busily piling rocks into some half-finished wire cribs, to complete their "impassable" barrier.

Very quietly the lieutenant waded back to his own men. He warned them with gestures not to disturb the happy Nipponese workmen. Silently the UDT men tied the primacord from their packs to the fuse assemblies, and hurried to the reef edge. The fuse pullers triggered four-minute delay fuses and raced across the reef to dive for their boats. The dark reef suddenly lit up in a long line of flame, blowing coral, workmen, and water sky-high.

Now that Admiral Conolly had extra gunboats, he ordered daylight demolition on all the beaches. Battleships, destroyers, and gunboats poured their fire ashore. Spotting planes flew overhead to call fire on shore batteries or mortars, like Jove ordering the lightning. White phosphorus shells and gunboat rocket smoke screens blinded the defenders whenever they got too active.

The cribs were so numerous on the northern beaches that Crist's team worked all day following the night blast. The morning platoons blew up 110 rock-filled wire cribs. In the afternoon, the other half of the team demolished 154 cribs. The men working where the Jap night crew had labored made the disparaging comment: "Obstacles on Blue Beach were not completed, therefore only half as much tetrytol per obstacle was used."

On the final morning before the landing, Lieutenant Carberry's Team Four paid a quick last-minute visit to the beaches, clearing coral heads from the reef edge and laying buoys to mark the channels and beaches. In one boat, Chief Walter Loban looked up on the side hill above the beach he was approaching, and stared right down the barrel of what seemed to be a 6-inch gun. As he could see several Jap mock-ups (dummy guns) elsewhere in the hills, he paid no attention. But on the next run along the reef, he looked for that gun—and it was following the boat up the beach. Most mock-ups weren't movable. Loban grabbed his radio and called the fleet fire control. The ships' guns went into action, and within three minutes scored a direct hit on a very real Japanese gun. Its crew had just been waiting for the order to fire.

On that afternoon of W minus one, Lieutenant Logsdon, whose Team Six had been impatiently standing by, was called aboard the *Appalachian*. Admiral Conolly said that while no mines had been found on the reef, he had reason to believe that antitank mines might be planted in the sand behind the reef, on the northern Asan beaches. Although UDT work was supposed to stop at the high-water mark, Team Six was ordered to make a night search of that sand strip.

Logsdon arranged that gunboats, destroyers, and cruisers would not fire unless the men on the beach were discovered. In that event, an intensive "walking barrage" should start 1,000 yards inland and move toward the shore, while the UDT men escaped to the safety of the sea.

The men were liberally smeared with white grease to camouflage their bodies on the white sand, and they duly crawled ashore in the night. They found no mines on the beach, and to their great relief and surprise they got back without being fired on. They naturally assumed that they had not been detected. (A few days later, Marine Intelligence gave Logsdon a complete description of their raid, as reported by a captured Japanese officer who had been in the beach defenses that night, asking his headquarters for permission to attack, and never getting an answer!)

Meanwhile the constantly growing fleet off the island spent the remaining hours before dawn pouring barrages onto the beaches, with bombing planes adding their strikes to prove that the previous "battle against the island defenses" was only a mild foretaste.

William Day, July 21, dawned clear and bright. The dawn

bombardment and strafing covered the beaches with smoke and fire for more than an hour, then the barrage moved inland and the first waves of amtracs were guided to the buoyed beaches by UDT men. At H-Hour, 0830, the Third Marine Division hit Asan's northern beaches, while the First Provisional Marine Brigade swarmed onto Agat's southern beaches past Team Four's "Welcome" sign.

On the ragged-edged Agat beaches, Ensign Thomas Nixon stood on the reef waving the loaded craft into the channel he had cleared. A sniper on Gaan Point fixed Nixon in his sights, and killed him instantly. Shellfire shattered the point; landing craft kept pouring ashore.

One of the early amtracs running onto the northern Asan reef hit a mine and blew up. Admiral Conolly immediately ordered a search for other mines. Crist took a group of his men to the beach, and found two more scattered mines. But in general, the Japanese had trusted completely in their Maginot Line of rock cribs, neatly destroyed by courtesy of the UDT.

While the Marines fought their way inland up the slopes swept by shell and mortar and machine-gun fire by dug-in Japanese, the demolition teams had the usual postassault tasks of blasting channels for boat traffic, and chewing wide ramps through the reefs so that several tank landing ships could unload side by side. After the troops closed their pincers between the two beachheads to capture Apra Harbor, Team Three had the fun of blowing Japanese barges, sampans, and a big freighter out of the channel.

When Team Three finally completed its mission at Guam and prepared to sail away, Marine Lieutenant Lahr wanted to stay with them instead of rejoining his unit as scheduled. The Marine liked UDT work, and Lieutenant Crist liked his performance. Without further ado, his temporary duty was made permanent and the team sailed for the rest area with The Marine aboard. By the time of the team's next operation, at Leyte in the Philippines, The Marine was a regular swim-

ming platoon officer commanding Navy UDT men on reconnaissance—all somewhat irregular but highly successful.

Team Six, which had again drawn the painful role of
standing by to watch their comrades demolish the beaches,
was given a quick postassault job—blasting a reef channel
onto Dadi Beach. In two days they hand-placed and exploded
38 tons of tetrytol to clear ramps and channels through which
supplies could pour ashore.

Admiral Turner, the commander of the joint task force for
the entire Marianas "Operation Forager," reported: "Results
achieved by Underwater Demolition Teams in Forager had a
considerable if not decisive [at Guam] effect on the success
of the operations. These results fully justify the extraordinary
efforts which have been made to organize, train, and equip
the Teams."

Admiral Conolly, commanding Task Force 53 at Guam,
stated officially: "The need for and results accomplished by
the Underwater Demolition Teams exceeded that contem-
plated for the operation. The work of the Teams was an
inspiration for the entire Task Force. Positively, landings
could not have been made either at Agat or Asan beaches nor
on any other suitable beaches without these elaborate but
successfully prosecuted clearance operations."

In addition to such high commendation, all officers and
men of the teams at Guam received Silver and Bronze Stars
respectively. Six hundred and forty cribs and coral heads were
officially counted as destroyed on the northern Asan beaches,
and over three hundred bigger obstacles on and under the
reef on the southern Agat beaches by the naked warriors
working at night or in broad daylight before their enemies.

More than ten years later, in his office as President of Long
Island University, Admiral Conolly said: "A truly wonderful
piece of work. It *was* decisive at Guam. I cannot praise
Crist and Carberry and their devoted and skillful men too
highly. In my estimation both should have had Navy Crosses,
considering the importance of the job and their effective execution of it."

10. Surprise Attack

THE UNDERWATER SURVEY OF TINIAN STARTED FROM THE SKY. On July 1, Lieutenant Commander Kauffman, on board a carrier, climbed into a torpedo bomber and flew over the island, hedgehopping to as low as 25 feet. An air cover of ten F4F wildcats flew fighter escort as Kauffman scanned every yard of shore line, and sighted the reefs down through the clear water.

Earlier surveys, on which the operation plans were based, had shown three possible beaches on the twelve-mile length of the island.

Down in southwest Tinian, a concave 2,500-yard stretch of lagoon and barrier reef marked the harbor of Tinian Town, the heavily fortified capital held by the enemy's main force. The other obvious landing place was Asiga Bay to the northeast; air photos showed it was lined with pillboxes. Just as they had done at Saipan, the Japanese had particularly strengthened the beaches they could best defend, assuming the Americans would walk into their trap.

On the extreme northwest nearest Saipan, were two dangerously narrow breaks in the cliffs, disregarded by the Japanese but not by the secret Operation Plan, which named them Beach White One and Two. If they could be used, they offered hope for that rare event in warfare, even rarer on the small Pacific islands—a complete tactical surprise.

In considering these beaches, Admiral Turner had accepted them as possible landing sites, providing: that they were not fortified, that the sea was not rough at the time of landing, and that they were scouted secretly at the last minute to confirm conditions. With this knowledge, Kauffman took to the air. He returned with a fish-man's version of a bird's-eye view. By chance, he had made a real discovery, a usable beach between the cliffs, on the west side between the narrow White Beaches and the guarded Tinian Town harbor. In the earlier air photo reconnaissances, this beach had always been obscured by fog. Kauffman named his discovery "Orange" beach in his strong recommendation to the high command.

The force commander, "Kelly" Turner, and the troop commander, "Howling Mad" Smith, listened briefly before they blasted out: "You do the reporting; we'll make the tactical decisions." They reasoned that his "Orange" beach was not much better than the White Beaches for landing and for inshore exits; and it was beyond the range of shore artillery based on southern Saipan, which could cover the White Beach landing.

The Marines had not desired to make an alternate landing plan, so Admiral Turner played tough and refused to make a final decision until all conditions were satisfactory. General Smith hoped the White Beaches would prove practicable, because the other landing would involve street fighting in fortified Tinian Town the minute his Marines left the beach. The first UDT task on Tinian was shared with the crack Fifth Amphibious Corps Reconnaissance Battalion—Marine veterans of thirty-odd landings on islands in the Gilbert and Marshall groups, including many islets which the battalion had taken singlehanded.

Kauffman and the Marine commander, Captain James L. Jones, were briefed on the beach surveys. They held a boat-to-shore rehearsal (too wet to be called a "dry run") in a Saipan bay the night before the actual survey. The Marines and the UDTs were used to very different systems of operating, and everything went wrong in rehearsal. It started at midnight, but the last swimmers weren't picked up till dawn, even though the teams' best scroungers had collected aviators' dye marker and shielded pen-flashlights which they waterproofed in the usual prophylactic fashion so that each swimmer could signal his position in the dark.

The teams rested through the day of July 10 while their

officers tried to iron out the mistakes. That evening at 2030 (8:30 P.M.), UDT craft left the transports for Asiga Bay and the White Beaches. Two of the landing craft with muffled underwater exhausts, towing rubber boats filled with Company A Marines and Team Seven swimmers, approached Asiga Bay in the dark. The rubber boats cut loose and paddled within 500 yards of the beach. Marine swimmers started toward one side of Asiga Bay and the UDT men headed for the other. Captain Jones and Lieutenant Burke had been strictly warned not to alert the enemy in case Asiga should later have to be the target for the assault. They must retire immediately if the defenders became suspicious.

Burke and his exec Onderdonk waited in their rubber boat while the swimmers went in. Team Seven's swimmers were close to the beach when several explosions were heard on the dark shore ahead of them. In accordance with orders, the UDT swimmers promptly turned back to their rubber boat, which silently paddled back to sea, hunting most of the dark night for the ship. They believed that the Japanese guards ashore had been alerted, and were shooting blindly into the darkness.

The Marines, less concerned with instructions or enemies, continued on in to the beach, crept ashore, and completed the reconnaissance despite the presence of Japanese working parties on the bluffs around the beach. They reported later that the supposed shots were not an alert, but were probably light charges set off by night workers strengthening Asiga's defenses.

The Marine report was sufficient to damn Asiga Bay as a landing beach. There was no need for further underwater survey. Reefs were heavily mined. Barbed wire and pillboxes ashore were ready and waiting. Hundred-foot cliffs at each end flanking the beach were being busily strengthened with more gun positions, ready to enfilade a landing with deadly crossfire.

On the White Beaches, Team Five and the Marine Company B were having different troubles. The northern beach,

White 1, was only 60 yards wide, separated by a thousand-yard stretch of rocky coast from the southern beach, White 2. The southern beach was about twice as large, but not all of it was usable. A two-knot current was reported running southward off the beaches, so the rubber boats angled a little north against it when they cut loose from the landing craft 2,000 yards from the beaches.

Nobody knew till later that the tide had reversed, running northward with increased strength, so the boats were paddling with the tide. The group heading for the southern beach hit northern White 1 Beach instead, and surveyed its unaccountably shrunken length as best they could. The men were completely camouflaged with aluminum grease paint to blend with the night sand. The Marines got ashore fast for a "sneak-and-peek" surreptitious reconnaissance beyond the beaches, noting the size and location of exits inland through the hills and dunes. The UDT men found that the shelving reef had only a few ragged breaks in its sea edge for the amtracs to avoid. A special detail under Lieutenant (jg) George Suhrland crawled onto the beach itself, looking for a line of marks in the sand above high-water line which air photos hinted could be land mines. The UDT found no trace of mines, but their favorable report met with considerable doubt.

The other group, heading for the northern beach, was carried half a mile north of its target. Lieutenant Jack DeBold reported in his log:

Water was breaking high on the shore. . . . Suddenly I reached the cliff's edge and had the daylights scared out of me by this sudden meeting with the island. I turned north. I had only my head above water. As it was only about 1½ feet deep I could pull myself along with my hands.

I must have gone north about 300 yards without finding a beach, investigating any place which seemed to curve in like a cove. I returned . . . and headed south some 300 yards, had no luck. It was about 2300 and the moon was about to escape from the cloud hiding it, so I started back for the sea.

There was no sign of a boat, so I just swam as straight out as possible. You could not get a view unless you were on top of a wave. I soon found out the current was taking me north. After bucking it for several minutes and not getting anywhere, I decided to inflate my life belt and swim slowly seaward.

My pencil flashlight refused to work. . . . I drifted for what seemed hours. Finally a ship hove in sight bearing down on me. I flashed them by using my dive mask and the moon. It was a minesweeper and they took me aboard to join four other swimmers. Later we picked up three Marines.

A light fog increased the confusion. Often two swimmers circled each other warily, to make sure the other wasn't an infiltrating Jap swimmer. (Actually, the enemy was never alerted.) Even in these touchy circumstances, the men found time for horseplay. A Marine grabbed Kauffman from behind, and started garroting him instead of asking the password. Rumor hinted that he had been bribed by someone in the team.

Time was running out. The Tinian assault force commander, Rear Admiral Harry Hill, kept watch on his attack transport to check on night raiders. Hill's code name was "Pin-up," and the operation code was "blondes" for recovered swimmers, "brunettes" for men still missing. Every half hour that night, on the TBS (Talk Between Ships, voice radio), Hill's call would go out: "How many blondes? How many brunettes? This is Pin-up himself."

The last brunette didn't get a bleach until 0430, barely before the betraying dawn, when a minesweeper found the last exhausted swimmer far up the Tinian-Saipan channel. Admiral Hill had already scheduled a full-scale air-sea rescue search for dawn. It was fine for the men's morale that the force commander himself stayed up till morning worrying about their safety.

The commanders of the teams and the Marine companies reported at eight to the sleepless admiral, then went to Saipan to see General Smith. He ordered a repeat survey that night on the omitted southern White 2 Beach. The report from

Asiga Bay made him even more determined to use the White Beaches if he could.

Things went better that night. A dozen demolition men and six Marine swimmers were guided by radar to the middle of the beach. The UDT men found the ragged edge of the reef had too many potholes for the wheeled "ducks" but could be used by amtracs. The Marines went inland to check the beach exits, while the UDT men split up to search the sand for the reported mines. Another group even went north to repeat the survey of the northern White 1 Beach.

Chief Orr and another UDT swimmer had a narrow escape while crawling over the southern beach to locate the shore mines. A working party of Japanese came into the scrub undergrowth on the dune line overlooking the beach, carrying oil lanterns. The hooded grease-covered UDT pair on the beach lay flat, hoping the lanterns would spoil the Japs' night vision.

One Japanese sentry came down onto the sand, and began to patrol the beach. The two stranded swimmers figured discovery was certain; they felt as big as houses, despite their light trunks, silver camouflage grease, and gray concealing monks' hoods.

The swimmers clutched the handles of their sheath knives, their only weapons, as the sentry walked toward them—and right past, still half-blinded by his lantern glow. As he went back to the dunes, the two wriggled off the beach into the concealing water.

This time there was no fog or wrong-way current to slow the recovery of the swimmers. Back on the *Gilmer,* they made charts of the reef, beach, and the low coral slopes and sea wall. Kauffman and Jones reported to Admirals Turner and Hill and General Smith, getting an intensive cross-questioning on their vital information.

The net result confirmed the command decision to try a surprise landing over the narrow White Beaches, even though only a handful of amtracs could land abreast.

For the demolition teams, the result was a new assignment.

On Jig minus one Night, only a few hours before the landing, the teams must do a demolition job to smooth that ragged reef edge, and go ashore to find that still-unlocated line of land mines about which the air-photo interpreters had warned. The problem was to float tons of explosive ashore without alerting the enemy and getting blasted out of the water.

A rehearsal using overloaded, topheavy rubber boats full of tetrytol proved a fiasco. Finally an inventive enlisted man thought of using sealed-off lengths of the fat rubber hose which refueled ships at sea. Sure enough, a test showed that explosive packs could be tied onto the inflated hose.

Meantime Burke's team made a bold daylight feint at the heart of the enemy defenses. Covered by battleships, cruisers, destroyers, and air strikes, the UDT landing craft dropped swimmers who crossed the reef to the inner edge of the long, wide lagoon in front of Tinian Town's entrenched defenders. They reported that they could have gone right to the beach if this hadn't been a feint—the fleet's fire support was so successful that they counted only three sniper shots from the battered Japanese.

Tinian Town was flattened with considerable loss of life among the defenders, who may have been convinced that this was the prelude to an actual landing in this area.

That night, things didn't go so smoothly. The weather was thickening, promising rough landings in the morning if the surf got too high. The wind was offshore. The landing craft towing rubber boats and explosive-festooned rubber hoses made slow progress into the choppy waves. An hour before midnight they cast off the rubber boats, but had misjudged the distance from the beaches and were far offshore.

The men paddling their awkward rubber craft and the dragging explosive sea serpents were hit by two successive squalls, pushing the light boats back to sea. Doggedly they kept paddling. About 0130 a much heavier squall scattered the rubber boats all over the local ocean. Reluctantly Kauffman gave the order to sink the hoses and jettison the explosive, while half a dozen men swam in to make sure that the Japanese had not laid any last-minute mines or underwater traps on the reef.

The landings were scheduled some three hours later that morning of July 24. The vastly complex operation of an amphibious landing could not delay its H-Hour for any minor mishap such as inability to polish up the reef edge. Jig Day dawned, and the Japanese sun started setting on Tinian.

The landing waves hit the two pocket-sized White Beaches, the Marine-filled amtracs crawling safely across the shelving reef as the UDT swimmers had promised. Some amtracs couldn't find space on the tiny beaches, so they nosed up against the rocky cliffs which the combat troops climbed. The elusive line of inshore beach mines, which the UDT searchers had discounted, proved to be an air-photo illusion, beach flotsam or old buried pilings. The landings on these "impossible" beaches were practically unopposed.

In the meantime, during the feint landing demonstration at Tinian Town, Japanese guns opened up. The battleship *Colorado* was hit 22 times by 6-inch shells, and the destroyer *Norman Scott* suffered 6 hits.

The Marines poured inland, wave after wave crowding across the narrow beach. They never let the groggy Japanese get set again, after being so completely caught off guard at the landing beaches. The new and fearsome weapon of "napalm," jellied gasoline set afire, burned the reeling defenders out of their caves and dugouts.

On the narrow beaches, storm-whipped surf tried to upset the crowded supply shuttle of boats and tractors. The busy demolition teams searched the reef and shore for unexploded "friendly" rockets left over from the bombardment before the landing. Then, as willing slaves of the beachmaster, they cleared coral heads and helped the SeaBees set up pontoon causeways over the reef.

The balance of the Tinian operation was happy anticlimax for the teams. After Tinian Town was taken, its lagoon harbor was searched for mines. Following the troops ashore in the capital, Team Five found a Japanese haberdasher's stock hidden in a dry well. The next day, on the *Gilmer's* deck when it fueled at sea from the battleship *Texas*, every man was wearing the finest of cheap silk shirts in polka dots and gaudy colors. The battlewagon's outraged captain signaled a tart dispatch: "Remain reasonably within uniform regulations."

The UDT's were always the despair of more conventional Navy officers. The demolitioners were, almost to a man, Reserves. They sometimes made mistakes of administration or discipline or form; but their very unconventionality and originality worked amazingly well in the pinches. Most of the innovations in the new art of underwater demolition were suggested by enlisted men, chiefs, or very junior officers. The Underwater Demolition Teams found that there is no place for epaulets on a wet, sunburned shoulder, but there is plenty of room for mutual confidence and genuine discipline when officer and enlisted man alike know that the other will get every man back, or drown trying.

The high command did not complain. Admiral Turner awarded a Silver Star to every officer and a Bronze Star to every enlisted man in Teams Five and Seven. Lieutenant Commander Kauffman received a Gold Star in lieu of a Second Navy Cross (he won his first in Pearl Harbor bomb disposal).

With the battle-seasoned Marines rapidly securing Tinian, the teams split up, preparing for the westward sweep through the Carolines—Yap, Peleliu, and Ulithi—on the direct route to the Philippines.

11. Peleliu—Portal to the Philippines

A GIANT PINCER MOVEMENT WAS THRUSTING ACROSS THE PACIFIC to liberate the Philippines. South of the Equator, Rear Admiral Daniel E. Barbey's Seventh Amphibious Force prepared to seize Morotai in the Moluccas (the famed "Spice Islands") on September 15, 1944. In the Central Pacific, Vice Admiral Theodore S. Wilkinson's Third Amphibious Force would simultaneously invade Yap and Peleliu in the Western Carolines, halfway on the direct westward route from newly seized Guam and Saipan, and dangerously close to the enemy fleet and air force in the Philippines.

All nine demolition teams in the Pacific were slated for the twin landings. Teams Three through Seven were veterans of Guam, Saipan, and Tinian. A makeshift Team "Able" was thrown together, using six-man demolition units which had been in the South Pacific. Three new Fort Pierce trained teams, Eight, Nine, and part of Ten, arrived at the Maui base in June for advanced UDT combat training.

Team Ten merits special attention because it was reinforced by the OSS Maritime Unit who "sold" the swim fin to the UDT, leading to the wide postwar sport popularity of the splayed flippers.

The hush-hush OSS (Office of Strategic Services) played many roles behind enemy lines. It had trained one hardy group of swimmers in secret warfare, to be used as raiders, or as limpeteers placing mines on the hulls of warships in enemy harbors. The OSS Maritime Unit under Lieutenant Arthur O. Choate, Jr., included Navy, Marine and Coast Guard officers and men, professional lifeguards, and an Army officer. They trained in wintry water at Camp Pendleton, California, and on Catalina Island. Transferring to Nassau, Bahamas, they trained with British units in ship demolition, developing underwater skill with face mask, fins, and oxygen diving gear.

Meantime the head of OSS, Major General William Donovan, was deciding their fate in a Pearl Harbor conference with Admiral Nimitz. When the General showed the Admiral his top-secret list of specially trained units, Nimitz put his finger on the Maritime Unit, saying, "I can use your swimmers."

Some of the Maritime Unit were detailed to England or the China-Burma-India theater of war, but the majority, twenty-nine of them, landed in Pearl Harbor. Instead of employing the underwater experts in defensive, preventive limpet warfare, America, being on the offensive, would use them in UDT, as the antennae of the Amphibious Force on the assault.

Taking command of Team Ten, Lieutenant Choate trained all men with swim fins, demonstrating their superiority in speed and endurance. The training officer, Commander Koehler, and the other UDT team commanders recognized their value, and fins became standard equipment as fast as the novel gear could be procured from the States.

Meanwhile air and periscope photos of Peleliu and Yap showed that the enemy were busily building underwater obstructions. Admiral Wilkinson's chief of staff, Rear Admiral Paulus P. Powell, requested a special detail to scout the beaches from a submarine, a surreptitious technique by which much valuable intelligence had been gathered without casualties in the South Pacific's big, thinly patrolled islands.

Five men from Team Ten volunteered for the dangerous mission, together with Chief Howard "Red" Roeder of the original UDT group, who was currently a UDT training instructor at Maui. The submarine group was organized under Lieutenant Commander C. E. Kirtpatric of the Waipio Amphibious Operating Base, together with Lieutenant (jg) M. R. Massey and three more Waipio men.

Admiral Powell briefed Roeder personally about the task
and its hazards, and asked: "Do you still volunteer?"

Red just grinned, and the Admiral wished him luck with a
hearty handshake.

The volunteers boarded the submarine *Burrfish* on July
9, 1944. They were a tough-looking crew, full of bravado,
but aware that they had a good chance of not returning. In
a final thorough briefing, Commander Koehler warned the
UDT men that if captured they would be forced to talk, and
in that event they should state that UDT amphibian doctrine
had been changed. The Japs should be told that in the future
all UDT operations would be carried out from submarines.
This at the time, of course, was pure fantasy.

The submarine surfaced at night between Peleliu and
Angaur islands under a half-moon. A finned, glass-masked
UDT swimmer went over the side to repair the sub's sea
valve; the vital undersea air-conditioning had been out of
order.

Japanese radar spotted the *Burrfish,* and constant air and
sea patrols with depth bombs tried to destroy it or keep it
blindly submerged. Nevertheless the harried submarine again
surfaced one night off Peleliu. Lieutenant Massey and Chief
Roeder had picked their five-man boat parties as if they were
choosing sides for a baseball game. Roeder cut high card for
the first reconnaissance, so he paddled toward shore with
his crew, swimming in to the Peleliu reefs in the moonlight
with three men while Chief Ball of Waipio kept the boat offshore. The swimmers got back safely with their close-in
beach report.

Other nights, the enemy search was too intense. For two
weeks the submarine dodged its foes and took periscope
photos of the shore lines, before setting its course for the
small and strongly held island of Yap.

The submarine's radar located the island at night. The
Burrfish surfaced close to the south shore at midnight, and
Lieutenant Massey's crew paddled toward the reefs. One
Waipio man was sick, so John MacMahon offered to make

the extra trip, along with his three UDT teammates Warren Christensen, Leonard Barnhill, and William Moore. Mac-Mahon anchored the rubber boat while Lieutenant Massey and the three UDT men, masked and grease-camouflaged, swam onto the reef and back. They discovered that discolored patches shown in air photos were only sea grass instead of reefs which would strand a landing craft.

Two nights later, on August 18, the *Burrfish* surfaced again two miles off the strongly guarded east shore of Yap. It was Roeder's turn again. He had Chief Ball and Carpenter of Waipio, and UDT men Robert Black and John Mac-Mahon (making his third successive swim). They paddled within a quarter mile of shore and found a barrier reef just below the surface. Fearing the breakers might carry the boat ashore, they dropped the hook and left the best navigator, Chief Ball, aboard. The four started for shore. Fifteen minutes later, Black brought Carpenter back to the boat—the sea was too rough for a man without UDT swim training. Black rejoined MacMahon and Chief Roeder, swimming toward the island. There were barricades on the Tobaru islet reef, palm-log cribs full of rock linked with wire. Lights moved along the shore.

Time passed without any sign of the swimmers returning through the breakers. Ball and Carpenter became worried, and finally decided to hoist anchor and search for the swimmers. They made a sweep along the reef, but there was no sign of the three swimmers. Time had run out and they had to return to the submarine, hoping against hope that the others had swum straight out to the *Burrfish*. No such luck.

The submarine searched close inshore until dawn forced it to dive and move farther to sea. The next morning the *Burrfish* patrolled under water off the reef in another vain search. It surfaced twelve miles away, while Jap radar searched in its direction. The three surviving UDT men pleaded with the commander to let them go back to the barrier reef that night, being sure the lost men would try to make it after dark; but the sea had grown rougher, and the commander made the hard decision that having alerted the Japs and lost three men, he did not want to make it six. The *Burrfish* gave up the missing men and left for its next mission.

The three swimmers had indeed tried to come back to the reef against wind and breakers. Perhaps, carried off course, they could not find their rubber boat, and finally had to turn back to shore. Three grease-covered men in swim trunks, armed only with sheath knives, hid all day on that small island teeming with enemies. They tried the reef again the next night, but there was no boat there to make the rendezvous. Exhausted, they tried to hide again. Months later a captured Japanese document revealed the following:

ANNANSAKI   22 August 1944
Special Report   GOTTO Unit
                              Intelligence Office   (JOKOSHITSU)

On the 20th we seized 3 American prisoners at the TOBARU Battery on YAP. They belong to the FIFTH Demolition Unit. These men were transported by submarines. They jumped into the sea at points several miles distant from shore and by swimming reached the reefs off TOBARU Island, LENG and LEBINAU. When they tried to return they lost sight of their submarine and swam back to the sea coast. They were captured while hiding. In view of this situation we must keep a strict watch especially in regard to infiltration of these various patrols and spies from submarines.

In view of this case, every lookout, whether it be night or day, shall carefully watch the nearby coast line, and if he observes any examples of the above, shall report it immediately without fail. He should without hesitation emulate the above captures. We are confident there is safety in this manner.

The report and the three prisoners were sent to Peleliu, with more detailed information about the "Bakuhatai"— demolition unit. The ruthless interrogators had learned that demolition units had four "LVPs" with sixteen men per boat, dynamite and electric igniters, to open underwater passages through the reefs. It was reported that each man could swim over ten miles, and that they only operated from submarines; the exact instructions of Commander Koehler who states, "I still recall the strange feeling I had when I read that CincPac Intercept of the Jap message."

On September 2, Roeder, MacMahon, and Black were placed aboard a Japanese sub-chaser for transfer to Davao and Manila in the Philippines. Nothing more was ever heard of them. Whether the ship was sunk, or they were killed or died on board or in a prison camp, nobody knows. They were not among the liberated prisoners when the Philippines were freed. Nothing is known except that they gave their lives for their country. They were posthumously awarded the Silver Star.

Their luckier mates returned to Hawaii in December. Moore, Barnhill, and Christensen joined the Maui training staff (their Team Ten was already in Hollandia, New Guinea, preparing for its fourth beach mission). The three survivors were also awarded the Silver Star and the right to wear the submarine insignia.

The information gleaned from their night forays had gone immediately by the *Burrfish's* radio to Pearl Harbor, being added to the air and periscope pictures of the landing beaches.

Peleliu and its neighbor Angaur, and the more distant island complex of Yap, were heavily defended by underwater obstacles.

One group of UDTs joined the convoys heading for the Palau Islands, Peleliu and Angaur. The other group were already at sea heading for Yap when the radio reported a life-saving change of plans. A Philippine guerrilla report via a rescued Navy pilot had stated Japanese defenses were light, and the high command approved bypassing and isolating Yap. The four teams scheduled for Yap were rerouted at sea to the Admiralties, to prepare for the duly advanced date of the Philippine invasion.

There was no reprieve for Teams Six, Seven, and "Able"

en route to Peleliu, and Teams Eight and Ten set for
nearby Angaur. But one team was knocked out before it
got into action. Just before dawn of September 12, the
destroyer *Fullam* rammed into the stern of Team Able's
transport *Noa,* near Peleliu. Hopelessly holed and sinking,
Noa was evacuated by its crew and UDT men without a
casualty. Three of the team's boats were salvaged, but the
ship sank with all of Team Able's tons of explosives and
gear, leaving the team powerless.

Team Able was sent back to Maui to merge with other
teams. Its third of the Peleliu beaches was assigned to
Team Six. Lieutenant Logsdon's team, which had been
griping over its limited action in Saipan and Guam, would
have two teams' work.

Logsdon had already been in on the Peleliu planning.
A staff conference headed by Major General Rupertus of
the First Marine Division and Rear Admiral George H.
Fort, commanding the Western Attack Force, discussed the
plan to land the troops on three western beaches, and the
artillery in a southwestern cove. Admiral Fort called on
Logsdon for a UDT reaction to the beach plan.

Despite the natural trepidation of a two-striper with only
a year's Navy experience, Logsdon pointed out that air
photos showed a jagged reef, just awash, cutting off the
cove's seaward side; while UDT could demolish that, the
cove was ringed with three lines of pillboxes which might
stop both the UDT demolition operation and the artillery
landing. He suggested that UDT could more easily clear
paths for the artillery across a flat drying reef just south of
the main landing beaches. After some debate, this plan was
adopted. Now he must prove his claim.

By 1100, Rear Admiral Jesse B. Oldendorf's fire-support
destroyers were pouring 5-inch and 40mm fire onto the
western beaches where landing craft were dropping the
swimmers of Teams Six and Seven.

The tide was low on the long, shelving reef, which was
barely awash a hundred yards from shore. Snipers in the

coconut palms took pot shots at the swimmers, and machine guns spat from camouflaged pillboxes. The landing crafts' heavy machine guns answered them, and spotters radioed the gunfire-support ships, which knocked out pillbox after pillbox by accurate fire.

The water was too shallow over the reef to allow the men to swim all the way to the beach. They needed two feet of water to cover them. A sniper in a coconut palm was getting the range of one man in trunks spread-eagled in shallow water, unable to move fast or to go under water. A boat's radio call located the tree on a destroyer's grid map. A 40mm shell burst squarely in the treetop, and the sniper dropped from the tree. The swimmer later reported: "It was a very comforting sight."

On the northern third of the beaches, Lieutenant Burke's Team Seven swimmers found a heavy blockade of tetrahedrons on either flank, pyramids of steel that looked old and rusted by sea water. A double row of wooden posts 75 yards from shore was noted for later action. On the sand above high-water mark were rock-filled log cribs, concrete cubes, a sniper fire trench and a deep ditch to stop tanks. But those were assignments for the Marines' demolition squads protected by tank armor, rather than for naked UDT swimmers who would be fish out of water on dry land while facing sniper fire.

The previous air color and stereo-pair photos had reported the reef dangerously studded with big potholes, some an improbable 50 feet in depth—a bad hazard for amtracs. The swimmers found instead that the supposed "potholes" were just patches of dark moss or seaweed; the reef was flat and smooth, with an easy approach. Burke reported that one day's demolition should clear the posts and open the northern beach. That was lucky, because he would only be allowed one day. As soon as his swimmers were aboard and their reports delivered, his transport was dispatched to tow the *Noa's* boats to the fleet's newly mineswept sea anchorage to the northward, Kossol Passage.

Meantime Logsdon's Team Six had swum like beavers, charting the southern two-thirds of the beach and the drying reef farther south.

Both nature and the Japanese had made the task far harder than on the adjoining northern beaches. The reef was studded with coral mounds and boulders which would obstruct amtracs and DUKWs. The southern shoal, which was scheduled for an LST landing channel, was similarly rough.

Inshore, besides the inevitable posts (which might well be mined), the swimmers spotted numbers of steel tetrahedrons, and a new obstruction, chevaux-de-frise. These were massive sawhorses of coconut logs, man-high, strung with barbed wire. There was also some wire fence, strung on posts and "spiders"—three leaning posts cabled together at the middle.

Team Six reported, and was given its timetable for the two days remaining before D-Day. They would be full working days, under rather unusual conditions—the men would be stripped to trunks on a coral reef under Japanese sniper fire, which even the best fire support from the close-in destroyers could never stop entirely.

By 7:30 A.M. of September 13, the team was heading for the reef, where they would work in and out with the changing tides. On the southern beach, they loaded packs against the boulders, blowing two wide pathways for the waddling DUKWs.

Moving onto the drying reef, UDT 6 blasted a wide ramp into the coral for tank landing ships and pontoons. They worked all the way to shore, setting off a train of explosives. They had to be careful not to blast too deep, for their vehicle roadway must not have any craters.

This road construction job was hot work under the broiling sun and periodic sniper fire, the men exposed on a broad apron of reef too shallow for diving. Quitting time was 1530. A refreshing swim (under fire) to the landing craft, and back to the ship, hot chow, and rest. Nothing to do till the next shift, an hour after midnight.

That night they worked for four hours without any fire support from the destroyers or their own hovering landing craft. In the darkness, any fire from the ships behind them would silhouette the working UDT men, making them easier targets for the Japanese ashore.

Strangely enough, not a shot was fired—until the swimmers had withdrawn, and the fuse pullers did their job before hastily following to sea. The team fired one shot, a mighty blast clearing a line of posts and pyramids and chevaux-de-frise close to the startled defenders on the beach.

The team was granted sack duty aboard ship until noon, then back onto the reef and shoal in tropic sunshine for their last four-hour assignment of blasting ramps, smoothing roadways, and cleaning up boulders.

Throughout the operation, Japanese snipers kept up a spasmodic fire, but happily they were so harassed by the ships' gunfire that not one single demolition man was wounded during the entire clearance of the beaches. The only injuries were coral infection and the inevitable embedded sea-urchin spines.

The perfect score held true on the night before D-Day, when Team Seven got back from their transport's side trip. Two ten-man squads swam in and crawled ashore to load the northern beach's posts strung with barbed wire, and set tripods and range markers on the right flank.

Fearing interception by the Japanese, who must have been alerted by the previous night's explosions, the swimmers had an identification signal—waving a piece of primacord. Despite this, one eyewitness commented: "You'd be surprised at the number of drifting logs that were stabbed that night!"

Night operations have their inevitable confusions; but the result was good—the proposed landing beach was cleared.

The UDT then guided the troop waves to the beaches, and placed anchor buoys off the reef.

The next job was up to the Marines, and a bitterly tough

one it turned out to be. Peleliu had a bigger and better
garrison than intelligence could evaluate, and the mountains
were honeycombed with galleries and artillery positions.
This was one of the least-publicized invasions of the Pacific,
but it cost the First Marine Division alone over 5,000 casualties—more than bloody Tarawa. The Army's 321st Regimental Combat Team joined the bitter mountain fighting
in the north. Not until the end of September were the last
hard-fighting Japanese cornered in a small mountainous area
north of the notorious "Bloody Nose Ridge" where they
held out for two more months, costing over 2,000 more
Marine and Army casualties.

The Marine artillery landed successfully across the southern drying reef and stormed the southwestern cove. The
pillboxes were still manned and cost casualties even in a
land attack; they might indeed have given serious trouble
to the UDT and artillery, as Logsdon warned, if approached
by sea.

The UDTs were not standing idly by. Three days after
the invasion began, Lieutenant (jg) Onderdonk and a morning patrol of Team Seven, walking across the barely awash
southern shoal, discovered a newly laid minefield. Wily
Japanese had infiltrated the Marines' lines during the night
and strewn the area with 50-kilogram airplane bombs
electrically wired to shore. These were duly disconnected
and removed to a safe area to be blown up.

That same day Lieutenant Burke and two platoons gingerly cleared a southeastern cove where concrete cubes
and railroad rails and seven-foot steel tripods were thickly
backed up by a row of 39 horned mines laid under water.
These had to be carefully removed (although the Japs had
failed to arm many of them).

Following the Marines up the low-lying east shore of the
six-mile-long island, Ensign Robert Phelps took a platoon
of Team Seven toward a northwestern beach, close to the
front lines. It was early on the morning of September 21,
D plus six. As the landing craft headed into the reef, the

battle-wary Marines along the shore suddenly jumped behind palm trunks and leveled their carbines. The UDT crew hastily broke out an American flag and waved it vigorously. Luckily the Marines decided the gray craft was not one of the many Japanese barges which were sneaking onto the uncaptured north end of the island to reinforce their hard-pressed garrison. The UDT platoon was allowed to conduct its morning reconnaissance. Then they spent the afternoon blowing up 300 yards of concrete and wooden posts and steel tripods, to the accompaniment of frequent bursts of firing farther to the north. This proved to be the last underwater demolition clearance needed on embattled Peleliu.

Meantime, two other teams had paved the way for the invasion of Angaur Island, six miles to the southwest.

Angaur was less than three miles long, with 200-foot-high hills in comparison to the rugged mountains of Peleliu, and with far fewer men in its garrison. Rear Admiral Howard F. Kingman began the naval bombardment of Angaur on the same day as Peleliu, September 12.

The UDT started their tasks on the 14th, one day before Peleliu's "Dog" Day and three days before Angaur's "Fox" Day. They were assigned three beaches—one on the northeast face of the roughly diamond-shaped island, one near the eastern mid-point, and the third farther down on the southeast face.

Lieutenant Commander Donald E. Young, the senior UDT officer present, took his Team Eight on a morning feint at the southeast beaches, covered by a battleship, two cruisers, and three destroyers.

The swimmers swam two hundred yards to the beaches and back, while one landing craft's machine gunner bagged a sniper in a tree, another boat's officer took 35mm photos of the beach defenses, and a third boat investigated a suspicious oil slick. It proved to be traces of a minesweeper, sunk the day before when it hit a mine. The search located another moored mine.

Farther north, Lieutenant Choate's Team Ten was finding

good exits from the central beach, with no underwater obstacles. Scattered sniper fire and a few "shorts" from the supporting ships' guns landed in the water but nobody was hurt. A fast current running past the beach was only a minor annoyance to the strong OSS-trained swimmers.

The next morning, both teams tackled the northern beach. They found neither reef nor mines; but there were rocky caves full of Japs at both ends of the beach. The only obstacles were some fifty steel rails wedged in holes in the hard coral, blocking the left half of the waterline.

Young's team took care of those in the afternoon. Under the welcome umbrella of shells screaming overhead, one boat headed straight for the left side of the beach with the team's executive officer, Lieutenant Harold W. Culver, and the demolition platoon. The team's other three landing craft covered the working party with machine-gun fire.

The cruiser *Cleveland* suffered a disappointment at this time. A concrete pillbox had been located ashore, and the cruiser catapulted a plane to spot its fire. Then came a hasty order to hold the fire as friendly patrols were in the area. The demolition crew was already ashore. With packs of tetrytol they wrecked the pillbox, cheating the cruiser's gunners of their prey.

In a fast twenty minutes, the embedded steel rails along the shore were loaded with packs of tetrytol and strung with primacord detonators; some of the looser rails were "demolished" by brute force as the athletes, bracing themselves on the coral, hauled them out by the roots. Racing back to their boat, they watched the delayed "shot" blow a clear swath across the beach. Although the embankment behind the beach was honeycombed with Japanese caves and gun positions, not a shot was fired at the daring demolition men.

The next day Rear Admiral William H. P. "Spike" Blandy, in command of the Angaur Attack Force, ordered the teams to make a last-minute check of the currents they had reported running parallel to the north and central target beaches. On Fox Day, two regimental combat teams (321st and 322d) of the Army's 81st Division must land on those beaches.

During this afternoon reconnaissance, Ensign Robert Parmelee of Team Ten radioed from his landing craft that he saw signs of Jap activity at the point near Blue Beach. Ensign Arthur Garrett, the team's observer on the bridge of the transport *Rathburne*, duly reported the fact to a gunnery officer aboard ship.

"Tell Art I see Japs—they're dragging something out of a cave," Parmelee went on. (Exact communications procedures were not an early specialty of UDTs.)

"Japs? I don't see any Japs," the gunnery officer protested, staring through his field glasses.

"It's a howitzer!" Parmelee reported from his boat inshore. "Fire on it!"

"I still don't see any Japs," the gunnery officer repeated.

The first shell landed on one side of the *Rathburne*. The second was on the other side—a neat straddle. The *Rathburne's* captain took over, fast, and got out of there at flank speed.

"What about Parmelee?" Ensign Garrett protested.

"Let him catch up," was the answer—which the landing craft did, later, some miles at sea. Meantime a nearby destroyer took care of the howitzer.

On Fox Day, September 17, each Army Regimental Combat Team established a firm beachhead, fighting steadily inland. The demolition men guided the waves of tank landing craft and DUKWs ashore. One of Team Ten's boats spotted an anchored mine five feet under water, 300 yards off the beach in a boat approach lane. Lacking equipment to cut the mooring cable, the demolition men buoyed the mine and warned other craft away. A swift search of the area discovered eight such mines, anchored near the hundred-fathom line. The whole area was buoyed, saving the incoming craft from an unsuspected hazard.

During the next day's operations another undersea menace appeared. Team Ten swimmers were busily clearing coral obstacles from a landing ship channel when a school of sharks moved toward them, triangular fins ominously visible above the water, and huge bodies visible under water to the masked swimmers. The commanding officer temporarily called the swimmers out of the water, wasting a priceless opportunity to discover whether a UDT man bites sharks. Finally the sharks moved away, and this small sector of the war got under way again.

Angaur was secured in four days, and the attack force was ready to chew off another mouthful of Jap territory. Admiral Blandy embarked the third, uncommitted regiment of the 81st Army Division, the 323d Infantry Regiment, and set out for the atoll of Ulithi, halfway back to Guam.

Ulithi was believed to be lightly garrisoned, and only Team Ten was assigned to Rear Admiral Robert W. Hayler's Ulithi Fire Support Unit. Five little islands on the northern rim of the atoll's barrier reef were put on Lieutenant Choate's schedule, for exploration and clearance before "Jig" Day, September 23.

The job was easy. Under the usual naval bombardment cover, the team's swimmers surveyed one island's beaches in half an hour during the morning of the 21st. At noon, they charted the beach on Falalop Island, and by four o'clock they had blown two channels through the fringing reef. The next day Team Ten swam up to three more beaches, running the complete gamut of islands.

On Jig Day morning, the UDT officers reported to Admiral Blandy on the *Fremont* that the coast was clear. It actually was clearer than that. The landings were unopposed; the small Japanese garrison had been secretly evacuated a month earlier.

Underwater Demolition Teams had only one more mission in this ocean area—but it was a dangerous one.

Back at Peleliu, on the twelfth day of the fighting, the Marines had battled their way almost to the north end of the island. Across a long, narrow strait, some 600 yards wide, lay the smaller island of Ngesebus, still garrisoned by Japanese troops. The two islands were joined by a causeway at the eastern end of the strait. The causeway was too perfect an artillery target. The Marines wanted to make a shore-to-shore assault across the middle of the strait itself, if it wasn't too deep for tanks. The UDTs must find out.

In the middle of the afternoon, two chiefs and five other good swimmers from Team Six splashed off a landing craft near the southwest corner of Ngesebus, and started swimming along its southern coast in to the strait. The nearest swimmer was within fifty yards of the Jap-held shore.

Across the strait, a landing craft dropped three ensigns, a chief, and two more top swimmers from Team Seven. They swam parallel to Peleliu's northern shore, where the cornered Japanese troops were not too busy to take potshots at them.

As the thirteen swimmers spread across the strait and started eastward toward the causeway, Japanese mortars and machine gunners fired on them. The swimmers dived and porpoised in evasion.

The destroyer *Richard P. Leary* came close to the open end of the strait, but shoals and reefs kept it at a distance. Its gunners had to aim carefully to avoid hitting the swimmers instead of the Jap snipers.

From time to time, Navy planes swept low along the strait, strafing both shores to keep the snipers down.

Steadily the thirteen swimmers stroked their way eastward, taking soundings as they went. It was a long and hazardous mile-and-a-half swim. When they got near the causeway blocking their path, Japanese snipers hidden on the causeway itself started shooting at them. That was the signal to turn back. On the return trip, the swimmers kept closer to the center of the strait, sounding its middle depths—a slightly safer three hundred yards from the snipers on either bank.

At last they finished the three-mile round trip, and got out of the strait to their circling pickup boats. They were a lucky thirteen—not a man was wounded. They were able to report safe, shallow paths where tanks would not drown out.

As a result of their gallant swim, the troops were able to cross in tanks and amtracs and overrun Ngesebus, stopping the Japanese from their nightly efforts to reinforce Peleliu's last-ditch mountain fighters.

Commander Hutson recommended Team Six for a unit citation for its day and night work on the reef, and also recommended that the thirteen swimmers be cited for gallantry in action.

All four teams next proceeded to Seeadler Harbor in the Southwest Pacific, where the Third and Seventh Fleets were staging for the imminent liberation of the Philippines.

Team Seven was finally ordered to leave for Maui to give combat training to the new teams there. Their transport backed up to the *Clemson*, so that Team Six could take over their unused explosives. Both teams worked with a will all day hauling the powder on deck and passing it over to the *Clemson*. Evening chow came, and the teams knocked off temporarily, setting a watch on the fantails of the two ships. The smoking lamp was out, of course, in the neighborhood of the tetrytol packs still on deck.

A stiff breeze was blowing from the bow to the stern of the front ship, as is natural when moored in an open seaway. Somebody smoking in the bow flicked a lighted cigarette overboard. Perhaps it blew onto spilled grains of powder. Suddenly smoke and flame burst fiercely from the canvas-covered packs of explosive. The tetrytol burned viciously, but didn't explode. Nearby rubber boats and radios caught fire.

The demolition men raced onto the fantails, and started heaving packs and burning boats overboard. The lines were cut, separating the two ships. Fire-fighting ships and other craft in Seeadler Harbor hastily came to the rescue, and landing craft evacuated men who couldn't help fight the fire. At last the blaze was put out before it caught any detonators or the ships' depth charges. It was a shocking lesson to all hands.

12. The Navy Returns MacArthur

EARLY IN SEPTEMBER 1944, ADMIRAL BILL HALSEY CALLED A signal, and General MacArthur picked up the ball, on a play which speeded up the already furious tempo of amphibious warfare in the Western Pacific. Fast carrier strikes on the Philippine Islands had met with little resistance. Halsey declared that the center of the Japanese line was wide open for amphibious assault.

The Halsey-MacArthur play called for a long forward pass, an 800-mile first down into the heart of the Philippine Islands, bypassing Yap.

Vice Admiral Kinkaid acted as the quarterback of the team; and into the planning huddle came Admiral Halsey, Commander Third Fleet; Vice Admiral Wilkinson, Commander Third Amphibious Force; Rear Admiral Dan Barbey, Commander Seventh Amphibious Force; Lieutenant General George Kenney, Fifth Air Force; and Lieutenant General Walter Krueger of the Sixth Army. This All-American team wrote out a series of plays, which were later executed with precision and outstanding success despite a raging typhoon, a major attack by the Japanese main fleet, and suicidal air strikes. Under the best of conditions an amphibious operation is the most complex and difficult maneuver in the whole gamut of military activity. The planning of this operation, under pressure, was brilliant; its execution a masterpiece.

MacArthur had promised the people of the Philippines that American forces would return and liberate them. In order to make good this promise two mighty fleets rendezvoused in Hollandia, New Guinea, and Seeadler Harbor, Admiralty Islands. The Seventh Fleet, which had been called "Mac-

Arthur's Navy" due to the many naval assaults the Army leader had made in the Southwest Pacific, sortied under the command of Vice Admiral Kinkaid to lead the attack.

As Kinkaid's second in command, Admiral Wilkinson led the Southern Attack Force, which would land the 7th and 96th Infantry Divisions on the southern beaches of Leyte's eastern shore. Ten miles farther north, the 1st Cavalry Division and the 24th Infantry Division would be landed by the Northern Attack Force, under Rear Admiral Barbey. A-Day was set for October 20. General MacArthur was aboard the cruiser *Nashville* with his staff, commanding more than 190,000 Army troops. Leyte, in the southeastern Philippines, half again as large as Long Island, was chosen as a major battleground and chief steppingstone toward freeing the entire archipelago.

On October 16, a typhoon roared down squarely in the path of Rear Admiral Oldendorf's advance guard, which included the Underwater Demolition Teams. Changing course as Admiral Kinkaid's aerologists advised, to circle its outer edge, the ships still ran into winds over a hundred miles an hour. Fifty-foot waves broke over ships' bridges, breaking light equipment, twisting radar antennas and threatening to carry away landing craft lashed on deck.

The small minesweepers detailed to clear the entrance to Leyte Gulf took a terrific pounding in the typhoon. One was sunk and all were behind schedule. The fire-support ships ordered to cover UDT operations were delayed but went on despite many unswept mines.

Leyte's eastern shore lay ahead. Miles of flat beach with scattered villages and hills marked its central valley. As the nine destroyers and UDT transports cruised in single file, it was clear that the town of Dulag had not been razed by preliminary bombing and bombardment.

Despite delays, the bombardment and beach reconnaissance planned for the morning of the 18th got under way by 1400. The battleship *Pennsylvania* and three cruisers stood five miles off and fired at the southern beaches from Dulag to

San Jose. Four destroyer transports with demolition teams aboard, sandwiched between five destroyers, closed the beach to 3,000 or 4,000 yards and launched the UDT landing craft.

As soon as the landing craft got within half a mile of shore, the Japanese opened up. Perhaps they thought it was a landing. The enemy fire was heavy, especially from the untouched houses of Dulag. Rifle and machine-gun fire was punctuated with mortar bursts and shells from 75mm guns.

Zigzagging and changing speed, the UDT boats approached the beach to within two to five hundred yards, then dropped their swimmers, who stroked their way toward the beach through gunfire.

Neither the plan nor the delivery of gunfire support was good at Leyte, and the teams suffered. Distrusting the results of the belated and limited minesweeping close to shore, the battleship and cruisers stayed several miles out, and some beach areas received no heavy shelling. The destroyers similarly stayed two miles from shore, optimistically relying on their 5-inch guns to silence sniper nests and batteries.

The operation plan, though excellent in other details, blithely stated that the UDTs did not desire air support. By the time the UDT officers got a chance to change this misunderstanding, it was too late to supply planes. But the Maui training paid off; by diving and swimming zigzag courses under water, the UDT swimmers were able to evade the small-arms fire.

Commander C. C. Morgan, in charge of the Beach Demolition Group, saw what was happening and ordered his transports to close the beaches, even though they had only 3-inch guns and were loaded with UDT explosives. He brought Team Three's *Talbot* up to a fish weir 2,400 yards from the beach, shelled the enemy gun positions, and set afire the town of Dulag—a hotbed of snipers and gunners.

Although the teams' own landing craft were pitching in the swell which followed the storm, they peppered the fire trenches and gun emplacements with their heavy and light machine guns.

Lieutenant Thomas Crist's Team Three, at the southern-most beaches below Dulag, received heavy fire on its landing craft, but two boats dropped swimmers. The water was murky with mud and sand churned up by the storm, and nobody could see under water more than three or four feet, often not that far. The swimmers took soundings until they touched bottom 50 feet from shore, then they searched the muddy water for mines and obstacles before returning to safety.

The other three teams were not so lucky in escaping in-juries under the Japanese fire. Lieutenant Commander William Carberry's Team Four had the beaches to the northward, between Dulag and the hill north of town. Under the cross-fire, two boats had to turn back and circle before making another pass. In the leading craft, Carberry had just dropped his swimmers 150 yards from the beach when a shell hit the bow, and another shell hit the stern. All of the seven men still aboard were knocked down, three of them wounded. Carberry himself was stunned—as he comments:

"Not hurt, just scared to death."

As Carberry grabbed the wheel and turned the boat sea-ward, its motor conked out. The shattered wooden craft was sinking, but the wounded radioman Thomas Hannigan stayed with his radio till it drowned out, calling for the re-serve craft to come in. The coxswain and gunner inflated the life belts on the wounded men and gave them first aid. Chief Thompson manned the forward machine gun and fired on the beach over the swimmers' heads, until a third shell knocked it out. A fourth shell hit near the motor housing, and the boat sank within a minute.

Carberry and the others towed the three wounded men seaward and the nearest landing craft picked them up. Japanese machine gunners ashore fired on the rescuers.

Meantime the team's transport was closing the beach to give fire support to its harassed boats. A Japanese shell hit the ship's No. 1 stack, causing 21 casualties. B. W. Kasman of the team was killed, and five of his mates were wounded.

Despite the disaster to Carberry's landing craft, and the

heavy fire which stopped the other boats from dropping swimmers, the eight men in the water kept swimming toward shore. Ensign Guinnee signaled his men to spread out and cover the whole beach. Two swimmers reached the actual beach under fire. Bentley and Swygert crawled along the shore for a hundred yards on their stomachs in the shallow surf, searching for mines and studying the shore, until the waterproof watches showed the pickup time. The landing craft zigzagged and circled, picking up man after man.

On the beaches to the north, Lieutenant Commander Donald E. Young's Team Eight dropped its swimmers under fire. A mortar shell nearly landed on one swimmer, Ensign Donald E. Nourse, gashing his forehead with shrapnel and smashing his glass dive mask onto his face. He managed to swim out several hundred yards to meet the pickup boat, where he was hauled aboard and given first aid by Edward Tilton. While Tilton was kneeling in the boat's stern, a sniper's bullet tore through his back. He died the next morning. In addition, the team suffered four more casualties.

The right flank beaches farther north opposite San Jose were surveyed by Team Five under Lieutenant J. K. DeBold. As executive officer at Saipan, he had been griped at having to stay back in a landing craft while his commander, Kauffman, went in with the swimmers. Now DeBold was commanding officer and could name himself a swimmer.

As DeBold's boat neared the beach, its wooden sides were suddenly punctured by several bullet holes. The swimmers splashed overboard just as mortar shells began dropping close by. The exec, Lieutenant Marshall, got on the radio and called shellfire on shore positions. He commented: "We had the only plane support to be had that day, simply by getting on the radio and screaming for it without letting up until it arrived."

As the boats were picking up the swimmers, machine gunner B. B. Audibert was shot through the head and instantly killed. The last two swimmers, one of them Lieutenant DeBold, were safely picked up 150 yards from shore.

The team commanders reported to the senior UDT officer, Lieutenant Commander Young, aboard his transport. News for the fleet was good: The underwater slope of the beach was steep, which would permit the tank landing ships to drop their ramps close on shore. There were no obstacles or remaining unswept mines. Fortunately the Philippines had so many islands surrounded by usable beaches that the Japanese just didn't have enough obstacles to protect them all. It was a lucky thing for the underwater demolition teams, who had lost three men killed and fourteen wounded in the ninety-minute reconnaissance.

The far-northern beaches still had to be surveyed; up in San Pedro Bay the support ships had a narrower part of the gulf for maneuvering. Due to the typhoon-caused delay in minesweeping, Admiral Oldendorf postponed the survey until the next morning. These beaches stretched from Palo north to San Ricardo, not far from Tacloban, capital of Leyte.

The weather on the 19th was clear and calm with almost no surf, but the water was still too murky for good observation. Once more the fire-support ships stood farther out to sea than the demolition teams wished—battleships and cruisers five miles out, destroyers two miles; too far for 40mm covering fire.

As three teams went in from their transports, the Japanese opened up at long range. One shell landed short of the *Rathburne* and skipped over it amidships! Mortar and machine-gun fire chased the boats coming toward shore. One "friendly" destroyer started "walking" its fire ashore, increasing the range with each salvo, but to the dismay of Lieutenant Choate's Team Ten, it started its range short of them, and the shells "walked" past the landing craft. The OSS team continued to hold its reputation as the "Golden Horseshoe" team, however. Not a man was scratched either by enemy fire or their own destroyer's shorts. The fire was heaviest at the southern end of this beach, where the swimmers reported their inability to get closer than twenty-five yards to the Japanese gunners ashore.

Lieutenant Logsdon's Team Six had no problems to report, covering the area between the two northern beaches safely and on schedule.

The swimmers on these beaches took accurate soundings, but the turbid water played them a dirty trick. Unable to see bottom, they could not tell it was undulating, and some of their soundings were taken in the troughs. Their report of the gradient (the underwater slope) was unduly optimistic. The next day, the deep sterns of the tank landing ships grounded on sandbars, and had to wait for pontoon causeways to get their loads ashore.

A real baptism of fire awaited fledgling Team Nine, facing the enemy for the first time on the northern flank. Waiting on the seaward side of their transports two miles from shore during a half-hour preliminary bombardment, the four landing craft headed toward the beach at 1130. Shells and mortar fire soon began dropping around the boats, but they kept on.

At the south end of this beach, swimmers got within five yards of shore despite machine-gun fire from grass huts along the beach. They took soundings, but could not be sure about mines; the water was so muddy swimmers could only see six inches or a foot under water.

Lieutenant Commander James B. Eaton's boat was about four hundred yards from the north end of the beach when Japanese mortars got the range. Two shells straddled the landing craft, then a third hit the stern, knocking out the fuel tanks and rudder. Another mortar blew a hole in the boat's starboard side and it started to sink. The craft got 150 yards farther out before the motor quit. Crossfire from a house on the beach and a small nearby island was hitting the craft, and one bullet went through K. B. Lauderdale's head, killing him instantly. Wallace Bryan's arm was shot through and nearly severed. Although mortar shrapnel had wounded Lieutenant Commander Eaton in the chest and arm, he and Walter Sieminski used a sounding line as a tourniquet on Bryan's arm. The radioman's hand was smashed and bleeding, but he broke open his radio and removed the secret crystal. Nine other men were wounded by shrapnel.

The boat sank before rescue craft could reach it. Two boats came in under machine-gun fire, picked up the survivors and headed for a battleship's sickbay.

Two hours later two boat platoons were reorganized and swimmers went back to complete their mission. Jap snipers and mortarmen were not going to stop UDT 9 from its appointed task of surveying that beach.

After the teams reported their findings, Admiral Kinkaid sent them a dispatch:

"You have reason to be proud of the part you played in the Leyte operation. Well done and good luck."

During the early morning of October 20, the Navy team of over 700 fighting ships ploughed through the minefields and steamed into Leyte Gulf. After intensive bombardment, amphibious Admirals Wilkinson and Barbey landed four divisions of Army troops on schedule. The Army fought its way steadily inland. On that afternoon General MacArthur debarked from the cruiser *Nashville,* waded ashore and broadcast to the waiting Filipino guerrillas and to the world, his famous message, "I have returned."

13. Through Hell and High Water

THE PHILIPPINE ISLAND ASSAULT WAS A BITTER GAME, PLAYED in two major halves. Following the great amphibious assault on Leyte, an unopposed landing on Mindoro established airfields. The principal target was Manila. The MacArthur, Kinkaid, Wilkinson backfield again went into a huddle. MacArthur called the play; the landing would be in Lingayen Gulf, 100 miles north of Manila, a surprise end-around run. The Leyte line-up of forces would be used.

While the Gunfire Support Group under Vice Admiral Oldendorf, aided by carrier strikes, PT and submarine attacks, broke the backbone of Japanese sea power in a series of surface actions, the UDTs withdrew to French Caledonia to reorganize and train. Months of confinement on transports had broken down their physical strength. Replacements were needed for the casualties suffered at Leyte.

Rest and recreation in Noumea included liberty in the tropic city and swimming parties in the clear, cool mountain streams. Next came a long stay in Hollandia, New Guinea. The swimmers reconditioned themselves there in Humboldt Bay. An Army recreation beach was nearby, with a section reserved for Wacs. UDT men set several speed records swimming from their landing craft to the beach, although they never reported the results of these reconnaissance swims.

The local officers' club made the mistake of asking Team Nine to clear a channel through the sandbars to a proposed boat landing. The team generously used six tons of explosive-filled rubber hose left over from the canceled Yap assault. The effect was spectacular. When the debris settled from the sky-high blast, and the mud dropped off the top and side of the clubhouse, the results showed a poor channel, a missing front door, all screens destroyed, no glasses on the bar, and

157

a piano hopelessly out of tune. Demolition was a dirty word around there for weeks.

More serious work was afoot. Oldendorf detached Lieutenant Commander Eaton to serve as Commander, Underwater Demolition Group, on his planning staff for the Luzon attack. A major step toward a better "beach umbrella" was assigning a number of gunboats, whose value for close-in UDT protection Rear Admiral Conolly had already brilliantly proved at Guam.

Meantime Vice Admiral Turner had not forgotten his pet project. The teams had always suffered discomfort and even loss of physical condition because of the unbelievably crowded conditions aboard the transports reconverted from old four-stack DD destroyers. Now Turner made the newer, roomier DE destroyer escorts available for conversion as APD transports.

Two newly trained teams were dispatched from Maui aboard such new transports, *Bull* and *Blessman*, reaching the advance group's rendezvous at Kossol Roads (the anchorage north of Peleliu) just before New Year's, 1945. Team Fourteen was the first of three teams which Admiral Turner had assembled by an all-Pacific roundup of combat-experienced volunteers. UDT veterans Lieutenant Bruce Onderdonk and Lieutenant (jg) C. F. Emery became its commander and exec. Team Fifteen had trained at Fort Pierce and Maui, and Lieutenant Houston F. Brooks took command.

Admiral Turner made another important contribution to Underwater Demolition in time for the Luzon invasion. He had decided that the teams needed a separate commander who was not trying to do double duty by running his own team as well as the entire group. He wanted an officer with sufficient rank, moreover, to take tactical command during the operation of all the transports and fire-support ships assigned to cover the teams' approach to the beaches. Admiral Nimitz approved the plan, and Captain Tom Hill told Turner: "I know just the man—Red Hanlon."

They found Captain Hanlon about to take command of a

large assault (APA) transport, and used Admiral Nimitz's authority to change his orders to Commander, Underwater Demolition Teams, Amphibious Forces, Pacific. This was abbreviated ComUDTsPhibsPac, which in turn was abbreviated by all demolition men to Mudpac, as the nickname for the staff.

Captain B. Hall Hanlon, USN, a big square bulldog of a redheaded Irishman, who looked as if he "could lick any man in the house," was a good man for the job. The highly individual, rival teams had a short-lived resentment of anyone being put over the heads of their beloved commanding officers, but Hanlon quickly got the respect and loyalty of teams and commanding officers alike. One of Hanlon's line officer colleagues remarked about his new assignment: "The Navy spent $30,000 educating you at Annapolis, and $30,000 in postgraduate instruction in ordnance including modern weapons and ballistics. Now you spend your time swimming into beaches to throw rocks at the Japanese."

Admiral Turner was less conservative, instructing Captain Hanlon: "Have patience with screwball ideas and people. . . . Many of them have value."

Hanlon gave the new, scattered teams a needed central organization and coordination with the rest of the Amphibious Forces, plus holding the rank to make their recommendations heard.

The old war horse *Gilmer* was equipped as a flagship, with accommodations for staff, communications, and machines for fast reproduction of the teams' undersea charts for the assault forces. Lieutenant Commander Draper Kauffman became Mudpac Chief of Staff, to plan beyond Luzon for Iwo Jima.

Meantime Hanlon and two newly appointed staff officers with UDT combat experience flew to Kossol Roads, taking command of the four teams from Hollandia. Eaton joined Hanlon's staff and briefed the new arrivals on Admiral Oldendorf's planning. Hanlon wisely made no major changes in the actual beach operations, but he cured one major weakness in UDT methods. Very often the information for which the swimmers and boat crews risked their lives reached the force commanders so near H-Hour that it could not fully be used by the lower levels of command. Captain Hanlon set up a more elaborate pattern of information which the swimmers must obtain; he arranged to have it duplicated (by gelatin pads until *Gilmer's* white-print machines would be available at Iwo). Thus the regimental commanders could get the latest picture of their beach targets, with less danger of last-minute confusion.

Captain Hanlon accompanied Admiral Oldendorf in the battleship *California* while the six teams in their old and new transports boned up on their reconnaissance plans while passing through Leyte Gulf and up the western coast of the Philippines toward Luzon. This trip proved to be no tourist winter cruise. They were to meet a horribly different form of warfare, meteors of death hurtling down from the sky, exploding in fire on the bridges, decks, and hulls of ship after ship.

UDT transports had left Leyte prior to the serious onset of the "Kamikaze," named after the "divine wind," a typhoon that scattered a Mongol fleet trying to invade Japan in the Middle Ages. This modern man-made version of the storm consisted of bomb-and-gasoline-loaded airplanes, which were aimed at American ships. Their pilots had no chance of survival and were dedicated to the destructive principle of one man—one ship. As Admiral Oldendorf's advance group passed the Cuyo Islands south of Luzon on the morning of January 4, four suicide planes attacked, all within sight of the demolition teams. One kamikaze crashed into the escort carrier *Ommaney Bay* and set it hopelessly afire, another hit a destroyer.

The next day, the kamikaze attacks were heavier and more frequent. More and more kamikazes were set afire, due to the newly improved radar gun-direction and the new USN radar-brained proximity-fused shells which exploded when they "saw" they were close to their plane targets. Unless a pilot was killed, however, he could still direct his exploding meteor into the ships.

There was no rest from general quarters. The Combat Air Patrol overhead was busy trying to break up attacks. The teams' transports fired frequently with their 3"/50 antiaircraft guns and claimed some kills. On the *Blessman*, team gunners manned light machine guns on the fantail and fired vigorously, though futilely—still, it was better than standing around cursing the Jap planes. Several ships were hit. A hazy overcast made the enemy planes harder to spot.

In the middle of the following afternoon the group steamed into fishhook-shaped Lingayen Gulf, following the mineswept channel with great care—Filipino guerrillas had reported this obvious invasion target was sown with several hundred mines.

The *California* led the column, with the Mudpac staff aboard as observers. Two other battlewagons followed, then the cruisers, then three more battleships, with the destroyers and transports and LCI gunboats spread out along the flanks as a screen. Steaming east past the southwestern barb of the fishhook, the column moved toward the palm trees fringing the flat shore line of the southern bowl and the miles-long eastern shank, the entrance to the great central valley.

Suddenly the Navy air patrol overhead reported a headlong swarm of planes, more than they could possibly handle. The planes had come low over the hills to dodge radar warnings. The first Japanese plane left formation to sweep along the column and crash into *California's* after fire-control tower, spreading flaming gasoline and death. The American cruiser *Louisville* and the Australian cruiser *Australia* were hit for the second and third time. The cruiser *Portland* was hit by two kamikazes. Attacking planes were downed right and left but some got through, hitting smaller ships and sinking some. The scheduled shore bombardment turned into a fight for survival. Finally the Admiral had to lead his wounded fleet out of the gulf, assigning the UDT transports along with destroyers to screening duty that night—hardly a restful prelude for the morrow's daylight swim!

Oldendorf reported the bad news to Admiral Kinkaid: a

score of ships hit or sunk. Promptly Admiral Halsey sent every available carrier plane against Luzon's widely scattered airfields, trying to smother the kamikaze threat at the source. Without knowing whether the carrier strikes could slow down the attacks in Lingayen Gulf, Admiral Oldendorf returned in the morning to accomplish the shore bombardment which the kamikazes had postponed. January 7 was clear, bright, and peaceful—and miraculously it stayed that way, without a single kamikaze.

A fairly heavy swell was running to the southward along the shank of the fishhook, rolling with little surf on the eastern beaches opposite San Fabian, but crashing four or five feet high against the southern beaches opposite Lingayen Town.

After the beach bombardment between 4:30 and 5 P.M., the teams took off in their landing craft. The six teams were evenly divided. Teams Five, Nine, and Fifteen took the southern Lingayen beaches where Vice Admiral Wilkinson would land his attack forces; and Teams Ten, Fourteen, and Eight surveyed northern San Fabian where Vice Admiral Barbey had the landing responsibility.

Two swimmers of each team were given a special assignment of looking for underwater cables for firing the minefields, while all swimmers searched for mines as well as sounding the underwater gradient to determine where tank landing ships could beach. It was no easy assignment. The surf-churned water was so murky that the swimmers could only see two feet through their face masks under water.

Even the blast-happy swimmers could hardly complain about their fire support. Each team was covered by a battleship or cruiser waiting for important targets; by two destroyers and its own transport stationed a mile offshore; and by two or three of the welcome gunboats with a UDT liaison officer aboard, pouring their 40mm and 20mm fire over the swimmers' heads from point-blank range.

The boats full of swimmers headed toward the beach on a carefully prearranged, staggered time schedule, taking roundabout courses, making every effort to avoid the appearance of a landing wave which might trigger heavy Japanese fire on them.

The boats dropped their finned swimmers, weird-looking in their silver grease camouflage. Other UDT landing craft swept parallel to shore taking close-up pictures with 35mm and big K-20 airplane cameras. The bombardment was so effective that only a few swimmers or boats encountered enemy fire. The gunboats cruised in so close that more than one UDT boat officer had to ask an overenthusiastic gunboat to pull back from the 300-yard line so that it would not interfere with his pickup of swimmers. A few mortar bursts from the hills splashed near the boats, without hitting. There were no casualties.

Cartoonist Chic Young would have appreciated the compliment of the UDT radio voice code of the day. "Dagwood" said that the landing craft were en route to the beaches. "Blondie" gossiped that the swimmers were all in the water. "Baby Dumpling" told that the landing craft had picked up the swimmers, and "Daisy" signaled their return to the transport. There was no need for "Mr. Dithers" to report that demolition charges were ready to be fired, for the swimmers found no use for their hundreds of tons of explosives stowed aboard their transports.

Lieutenant DeBold delivered the Lingayen teams' reports, charts, and exposed film to Captain Hanlon on *California*. The San Fabian teams sent a dispatch, and were told to bring charts of beach gradients, hydrographic charts and exposed film aboard, pronto.

When one team commander had first reported to Captain Hanlon in greens, white swim shoes, and a baseball cap, he was told to report in uniform. He commented, only half-jokingly: "Captain, this used to be a good racket, now you are changing it into a business."

Hanlon reported to Admiral Turner later that the comment was made with no implication of impertinence, and that he himself could not understand why some of the Navy called the UDT a pampered and temperamental group: "There is a healthy, youthful freshness and boldness, though a shortage in the outward signs of military manners, due to an energetic enthusiasm. As for pampering, that is absurd. The teams train at the base with the crudest accommodations and mediocre food. They stay at sea in APDs for long periods in crowded, uncomfortable quarters, with worse food. Combatant troops do not stay in their crowded transports for such long periods."

The exposed film and charts were flown to the carriers by *California's* spotting plane, and thence to the approaching task force commanders. The reconnaissance news was unexpectedly good. The tank landing ships could drop their ramps on most parts of the beach, except where sandbars were found. Due to the swells and turbid water, one sandbar was not located and an LST grounded there on S-Day, but this was a minor mishap. The best news was negative—no mines! UDT swimmers had been unable to find the feared minefield, reported by guerrilla intelligence. The Filipino guerrillas, sweeping at night with a rope between two native boats, had cleared the area better than they thought.

The teams rested aboard their transports on screening duty, fighting the kamikazes which returned the next dawn and dusk, though in lesser numbers.

Near twilight, a kamikaze swooped through antiaircraft fire straight for the stern of *Rathburne*. As the plane dived, so did a dozen of Team Ten's men, hitting the water on either side of the ship and setting new records swimming away. Luckily the Japanese pilot overshot his mark, flying the length of the ship and crashing into the water ahead.

The swimmers got back aboard, to be chewed out by *Rathburne's* skipper—although, as they pointed out (to their teammates), they had no duty stations and their job was in the water. . . .

Meantime the main invasion fleet was approaching Lingayen Gulf. Before dawn of S-Day, Captain Hanlon and Lieutenant Commanders Eaton and Young carried the charts

THROUGH HELL AND HIGH WATER

and information to the task force commanders, Vice Admirals Kinkaid, Wilkinson, and Barbey. Other team officers delivered information and charts to the transport group commanders, tank landing ship group, and the regimental combat teams.

The landing ran off like clockwork. The Army's 37th and 40th Infantry Divisions went ashore at San Fabian, the 43rd and 6th at Lingayen. The troops swept well inland before encountering opposition in the hills. The Japanese had expected a Lingayen Bay landing all right, but they were sure it had to be at the northern end around San Fernando where they had landed three years before and where their shore defenses were stronger. They knew the southern beaches were too shallow, too choked with sandbars. But the inscrutable Occidentals fooled them again.

Except for guiding waves in to some of the beaches, the Underwater Demolition Teams stood by on S-Day. Their only assignment was to recheck the southern sandbars.

In the transport area that night, a new Japanese weapon struck at the fleet. Improvised torpedo boats from San Fernando circled the fleet and tried to sweep in from the west. Some were Japanese Navy landing craft with 440-pound ramming charges forward; the rest were fast Army motor launches carrying depth charges, which they tried to drop overboard close to a target ship.

They made their pass at four in the morning, infiltrating and then driving toward the anchored ships at full speed. Explosions punctuated the ships' gunfire at the elusive little targets, often screened from fire by the fleet's own ships.

It was a wild scramble, but four of the attackers were sunk and the others fled. All too many of them had laid their deadly eggs. Two infantry landing craft sank, four tank landing ships were damaged, the transport *Warhawk* had seventy-odd casualties aboard, and a destroyer was hit.

Team Nine's transport *Belknap* had sighted and fired at one Japanese boat which another ship caught and sank. Later that morning, as *Belknap* was moving to its screening station, two men were sighted in the water amid the flotsam from the damaged ships. The nearly naked pair of Japs, paddling tandem, seemed to be riding a two-man submarine or human torpedo.

Belknap quickly maneuvered with its bow to the threat, and lowered a landing craft from its davits. An armed crew from the ship and the team sped toward the enemy pair, carbines and machine guns ready. As the landing craft drew near, the crew could see the two Japanese were riding a piece of wreckage—obviously survivors of the night raid. Ordered to surrender, the Japanese tried to escape. A sailor from the landing craft threw a grapnel toward the wreckage. One Japanese pulled a hand grenade from his life jacket, to throw at the boat. The boat's machine gun put an end to that attempt, and to the swimmers.

The landing craft, joined by another, searched the wreckage intensively, all morning and afternoon. A total of eleven survivors of the torpedo boat raid were found, but none of them could be boated alive. The bodies were searched, and all material was turned over to intelligence for study.

The swimming Japanese gave rise to a report that they had swum out with explosives, a reverse lend-lease for UDT. After all, Team Ten's OSS men had been trained as limpet-mine swimmers. Actually the Japanese were using this tactic elsewhere. Nearly forty swimmers had entered a harbor in the Palaus just a few days before and damaged an infantry landing craft.

That night *Belknap* put out a boat with an armed crew aboard to patrol around the ship, as did many other ships in the screen. The Japanese torpedo-boat raid had clearly demonstrated the need for the "Fly-catcher Patrol" as it was named, and this became standard operating procedure for future invasions.

The other two Lingayen Beach teams surveyed the beach approaches for additional tank landing ship berths. They reversed the usual tactics by going ashore in rubber boats, then swimming out through the surf, taking soundings.

Cdr. Francis Douglas "Red Dog" Fane, USNR *(author's collection)*

A UDT recon party relaxes aboard the submarine USS *Burrfish* after returning from Peleliu on 11 August 1944. *(official U.S. Navy photo)*

A "naked warrior" affixes a twenty-pound Hagensen Pack of explosives to an underwater obstacle. *(official U.S. Navy photo)*

Hell Week: UDT trainees undergo indoctrination to explosives on "So Solly Day." *(U.S. Naval Institute collection)*

UDT swimmer inspects ship's propeller during a postwar training exercise. *(U.S. Naval Institute collection)*

Commander Fane *(right)* and Vice Adm. Daniel Barby with UDT swimmers of the first U.S. Navy attack swimmer unit. Man in center wears early model of the Lambertsen Lung. *(official U.S. Navy photo)*

Swimmers inspect icebergs off Point Barrow, Alaska, during a "Dew Line" operation. *(U.S. Naval Institute collection)*

Frogmen of UDT 13 attach the flotation collar and decontamination gear to the Apollo 12 capsule after splashdown on 24 November 1969. *(U.S. Naval Institute collection)*

Members of UDT 12 await the arrival of U.S. Marines at Da Nang, South Vietnam, on 8 March 1965—the first commitment of American ground combat troops during the Vietnam War. *(U.S. Naval Institute collection)*

UDT man prepares to blow Viet Cong bunker. *(U.S. Naval Institute collection)*

When one crew first hit the beach, they hit it flat. Light machine-gun bursts were whistling over their heads. They and an Army patrol ashore unlimbered weapons and prepared to fire back at infiltrating Japanese. Just in time, they spotted the source of the fire—an American landing craft! The adjoining team's boat officer was target-practicing on floating debris in the water. Frantic and profane radio calls soon put an end to that.

About seven that evening of January 10, two teams had a few hair-raising minutes in a kamikaze attack. A single dive bomber slipped through the Combat Air Patrol and dove straight at their transport. The 40mm and 20mm guns scored hits, as did a battery of nine heavy machine guns, manned partly by UDT men. The smoking plane swooped over one transport amidships, and crashed the water, fifty yards short of the other. A Team Ten landing craft picked up the pilot, who was badly shot up.

Team Nine was tragically less fortunate. Their transport, the *Belknap*, was on screening duty at 8 A.M. two days later. As usual, the transports and supply ships were covered with a concealing cover of smoke, when a couple of kamikazes made an unsuccessful pass.

The all clear sounded, and the ships were alerted that a Navy PBY was coming in for a landing. It landed—and two minutes later, four Japanese "Tony" type planes followed hot on its trail. The only large targets outside the smoke screen were the transport *Belknap*, a destroyer, and a few troop transports which had discharged their troops. The Japanese planes, under immediate AA fire from all ships, peeled off and dived. One Tony circled the *Belknap*, which was firing all guns.

The plane bore in, firing its machine guns. One of its underwing bombs was knocked off and fell into the water 500 yards from the ship. The ship's barrage set the plane on fire but its momentum carried it straight into the *Belknap's* Number 2 stack. The plane's second underwing bomb exploded on contact, and its gasoline spread fire furiously amidships on the boat deck. The two forward landing craft were carried away, and 3-inch ammunition in a ready locker atop the transport's galley deckhouse was set off, exploding shrapnel among the ship's crew and demolition men.

Another plane dived at the ship's bow. Despite the hell amidships, the Number One gun crew fired at the suicider until the destroyer raced to the rescue, blocking their range but downing the killer plane.

The survivors of crew and team alike fought the fire with portable pumps. The plane had smashed into the fireroom and defeated its own purpose, since escaping steam from the boilers and main steam line greatly aided the fire fighters to smother the flames. The ship was crippled but not sunk. The same was true of *Belknap's* brave crew and team.

The casualties aboard that small ship were shockingly heavy. Thirty-eight men were killed or mortally wounded, forty-nine were more or less seriously wounded. Of these, eleven dead and fifteen wounded belonged to Team Nine.

In all of the ten landings on hostile shores, only eight underwater demolition men had been killed. Now eleven were wiped out in an instant when they were supposedly safe aboard ship. Ensign Malfeo, Chiefs Gamache and McKnight, and their teammates Blettel, Castillo, Hopkins, Lewis, Rodriquez, Rossart, Scoggins, and Sugden had given their supreme gift to their country.

All hands helped the wounded. Two transports brought aid and a doctor, and the wounded were evacuated. That afternoon, taps sounded early as the canvas-wrapped bodies were buried at sea with full honors.

The survivors transferred by easy stages to the United States, for leave. After the double blow of their shelled landing craft at Leyte and their kamikaze-wrecked transport at Lingayen, the team was down to 12 officers and 47 men, and with hardly any equipment. It had suffered 39 casualties.

There was immediate work for one of the teams, however. Team Ten drew the assignment of surveying the Zambales beaches, near Manila. There another landing would be made to cut off Bataan Peninsula, while the main body of troops advanced down Luzon's central plain. Team Ten's transport joined Rear Admiral Struble's task group, screening tank landing ships until near the target. Then the fast transport sped ahead.

At 0300 on the morning of the 29th, in painfully bright moonlight, one landing craft cruised with muffled underwater exhaust toward the beach in front of La Paz. A dozen swimmers made a fast half-hour swim charting the sandbars off the moonlit, palm-fringed beach. The landing craft's machine gunners kept a watchful eye on a suspicious dark hulk offshore south of the beach, in case it should suddenly spit a hail of fire.

The team's luck held. Dawn showed the hulk was an old freighter stranded on one of the sandbars. Dawn also brought a native boat waving a white flag and bringing the news that the Japanese had retreated inland, and that the Filipino guerrillas had the area safely under control.

The 38th Division and the 134th Regimental Combat Team went ashore unopposed, while UDT swimmers found a few channels through the sandbars deep enough to let the tank landing ships beach. The UDT task in the Philippines was completed.

The Commander Cruiser Division Four had the last word to say regarding UDT in the Philippines.

"The results achieved by these Underwater Demolition Teams are far above anything that anyone, not informed, might imagine. It seems incredible that men in small boats, and men swimming should be able to close a heavily defended hostile beach in broad daylight to almost the high water mark without receiving such severe damage as to make their operations a failure. That they are able to do so is due not only to the gunfire and plane barrage, but to the skill and intrepidity of these men themselves. When one watches them perform under the gunfire of the enemy, one cannot fail to be impressed by their boundless courage. The Nation's future is safe when it is defended by such men as these."

14. Intrepidity at Iwo

PRIOR TO THE AMPHIBIOUS ASSAULT ON IWO JIMA IN FEBRUARY, 1945, Captain B. Hall Hanlon prepared a master Operation Plan for the teams, transports, and close fire-support gunboats and destroyers, which he would control during UDT operations. The men in the teams had been given thorough advance training and rehearsal.

Starting at Fort Pierce, they had been taken in hand by Lieutenant William F. Flynn. "Barrel-Chested Bill," a genial but driving Irishman, was an inspiration to class after class of demolition men whom he walloped through "Hell Week."

As commissioned teams, the men from Fort Pierce came under the iron hand of Captain A. J. "Ajax" Couble, USN, in command of the Maui base. He was an officer of the old school whose strict discipline was probably strongly needed to keep this new breed of aggressive, independent, and physically tough officers and men in line.

Commander John Koehler, as training officer, exerted a strong influence on the teams. He adapted the ingenious schemes invented in the heat of combat by UDT men, and molded the ruggedly trained Fort Pierce units, green in the ways of naval tactics, into effective fighting forces. Drawing on his own UDT combat experience, and that of teams moving ever closer to Japan, he constantly wrote and rewrote the basic operational doctrine, until sound UDT tactics were devised.

Commander Koehler had the thankless job of acting as a buffer between the Navy-wise commander of the base, and the hotheaded young team commanders who were eager to fight or demolish anyone they met. The teams that sailed out of Maui for Iwo Jima were the product of his schooling, and "did the old man proud."

Mudpac (Captain Hanlon and Staff) had sailed from Lingayen to Ulithi where an advanced base for UDT training was established. Four teams were shipped there for final training under Captain Hanlon's eyes and two further rehearsals with the fire-support gunboats and destroyers to be used at Iwo. Hanlon's "Op Plan" contained a minutely worked out time schedule for all units based on "Roger" Hour when the swimmers' landing craft were to cross the destroyer line en route to the beach. It contained detailed fire support areas, positions, and techniques, and provisions for widely distributing UDT information.

Mudpac incorporated the same deadly efficiency into UDT operations that marked the conduct of other amphibious units at this stage of the war. As the fleet closed in for the kill, each successive attack was calculated to inflict maximum destruction on the enemy with minimum loss of U.S. forces.

UDT 12 was led by big, smiling, tough Lieutenant Commander Edward S. Hochuli, who quickly gained the reputation of volunteering his team and himself for any duty. He had left home at sixteen to go into the Merchant Marine, later becoming a supervisor in its wartime training program, before volunteering for the Beach Battalions and then for UDT.

The team's first assignment was to send a detail by night to investigate gas drums buried in the black sand terraces above the enemy beach at Iwo. These looked suspiciously like a major "secret weapon" designed to pour flaming oil or gasoline on the landing troops.

Mudpac Staff Lieutenant (jg) Bert Hawks (of Roi and Guam experience) warned that the men detailed must not be briefed on any other part of the coming operation, due to the risk of capture. To everybody's considerable relief, last-minute intelligence reported that the drums had been sufficiently bombed to discourage any possible attempt at burning the beaches. It was later learned the drums were empties, used as sniper posts in Iwo's shifting volcanic sands.

Like Hochuli, Team Thirteen's Lieutenant Commander Vincent J. Moranz came into demolition via the Beach Battalions. Before joining the Naval Reserve he had been a lawyer, but there was no quibbling or legalistic hesitation about his militant leadership. His team included those survivors of ill-fated "Team Able" who hadn't soured on demolition after the *Noa's* sinking robbed them of action at Peleliu.

The other two teams slated for Iwo were veterans of the Lingayen landings—Team Fourteen under Lieutenant Bruce Onderdonk and Team Fifteen under Lieutenant Houston Brooks. When Rear Admiral William H. P. Blandy's Amphibious Support Force sailed for the small island of Iwo Jima near the south end of the Volcano Island chain 650 miles south of Japan, the four teams formed part of a sizable Underwater Demolition Group. UDT Captain Hanlon had tactical command of Task Group 52.4, numbering six destroyer transports with four teams embarked, seven fire-support destroyers, and twelve infantry landing craft gunboats gaudily painted with zigzag orange and green tropical camouflage patterns.

Before dawn, at 0500, the general alarm bell rang and the loudspeakers blared: "All hands, man your battle stations . . . this is not a drill."

In combat readiness, the men at stations stood watching the dawn light the fog that hid cone-shaped Mount Suribachi. The rest of Iwo Jima soon came into view, spreading out northward in a rough triangle from the 550-foot truncated mountain cone. Only five miles long, it was a small island to be so important a barrier on the highway to Japan. On the southwest end Mount Suribachi commanded the only possible landing beaches. These were on its eastern and western sides. Farther north as the island broadened out, cliffs and rocks blocked the sea approaches.

Battleships, cruisers and destroyers began a slow, steady bombardment, probing for the camouflaged gun emplacements dug in the coral cliffs and soft honeycombed mountain rock. Suribachi was a rat's nest of tunnels, even boasting an underground railway and road to supply the cave guns with ammunition. The brown mountain grimly earned its attackers' code name for it, "Hot Rocks." The invasion charts of the shores were red-spotted like a measles patient with known gun positions, but the Japanese cleverly refused to show their Sunday punch by firing at far-out ships.

In midafternoon, carefully following a group of minesweepers, Captain Hanlon's flagship *Gilmer* led the other transports toward the eastern beaches to familiarize the men with the next day's target.

Rain squalls obscured the beach at first, but lifted to give the men a good look at the black sand terraces and occasionally visible gun positions. A machine gun on Mount Suribachi opened up on a minesweeper, and was promptly silenced by ships' gunfire. *Gilmer* cruised on around the island to view the western beaches. Both beaches had good offshore approaches, but the high command preferred the eastern beaches because the prevailing winds would be less likely to pile up surf there which might broach landing and supply craft.

UDT 13's transport *Barr* dropped a landing craft carrying Commander Moranz, three ensigns, and fourteen men near the small rock islet of Higashi Iwa, two miles off the northeast coast. The working party paddled to the islet in two rubber boats. Carrying an acetylene navigation light and its platform, they started to scramble over the rough, unfriendly rocks, doused by mild surf breaking over them. From a wrecked Japanese landing craft ashore, a 5-inch gun fired at them. The UDT men on Higashi Iwa hastily crouched between the rocks. The Japanese shells landed in a neat diamond pattern, bracketing them as if the islet were a familiar target area.

The *Barr* and the cruiser *Pensacola* promptly silenced the lugger's gun with 5-inch shells. Under scattered sniper fire the work detail fastened the light in place to flash out to sea for fleet navigation, and got out of there with flying paddles.

Clear weather marked February 17. The sea was almost calm, with a slight swell. The eastern beaches stretched almost straight for two miles, with scattered hulks of beached Japanese landing craft spaced along them, any of which might hide machine gunners. At the shore line, the black volcanic sand rose steeply 220 feet in a series of terraces to the sharply outlined edge of Motoyama Airfield No. 1, some 600 yards inland. They were lined with dug-in, camouflaged gun nests. Two days hence, the Marines were to claw up this slope.

On the left flank rose Mount Suribachi; on the right, hundred-foot cliffs honeycombed with caves curved out to sea. This was the trap which the swimmers and their boats must enter in broad daylight.

The shore line was arbitrarily divided into seven 500-yard beaches. Team Thirteen had the beach on the extreme south, the left flank—nearest Suribachi's towering gun posts—which might well take a heavy toll of men and boats swimming in its front yard. Next to them Teams Twelve and Fourteen had two beaches apiece in the center. On the right flank, nearest the cliffs and a group of three beached luggers, Team Fifteen drew the two northernmost beach sections. The show was ready to start.

At 1030 seven destroyers moved opposite the beaches, 3,000 yards from shore; the cruisers and battleships farther out keeping up a slow, deliberate fire. Behind the destroyer line, transports launched twelve landing craft filled with men. The boat crew from ship and UDT were in kapok life jackets. Ten swimmers in each boat were covered with cocoa butter (for warmth in the cool 65° water) and silver camouflage grease; one of the developments pursued by Commander Koehler. Aboard the *Gilmer*, Captain Hanlon took tactical command of all destroyers, gunboats, and transports. His chief staff officer Commander Draper Kauffman would run the beach operation as commander of the Underwater Demolition Unit.

Up steamed the column of infantry landing craft gunboats, making a vivid spectacle with their zigzag orange and green camouflage. Under Commander M. S. Malanaphy, USN, the gunboat flotilla had just arrived at 0600 that morning from the tropics. Seven of the gunboats took stations 2,000 yards from the beach, with Lieutenant Commander W. V. Nash on the right flank near the cliffs and Commander Kauffman in the middle of the line opposite the central beach.

Planes overhead peeled off, strafing the beaches. When gunboats began shelling the enemy positions, the Japanese opened up with mortars and flat trajectory shellfire. The destroyers answered with 40mm and 5-inch guns as they spotted targets. On the gunboats, men stood by the 20's and hosed them down, and swabbed the 40's with water to keep smoking guns cool enough to fire.

Now the planes strafed the beach with rockets, and the gunboats moved abreast at 6-knot speed toward a position 1,000 yards offshore their respective beaches to fire their rockets. It was Roger Hour, and the wave of seven UDT landing craft sped through the gunboat line to drop their swimmers closer inshore. The landing craft used a stagger system, but, unfortunately for themselves, the gunboats kept to a precise naval formation which must have looked to the enemy like a genuine landing wave. The Japanese were inadvertently tricked into showing their hand. Their fire increased terrifically, from the terraces and from hitherto concealed coastal gun batteries on Suribachi and behind the right flank cliffs. The thin-skinned gunboats started taking a pounding.

The gunboat in which Kauffman had his command post was hit from a big 8-inch Japanese coast defense battery and took a heavy starboard list. After several more hits and near misses in the next four minutes, Kauffman ordered the gunboat to retire; it could only move at four knots. Kauffman's radioman was killed at his side by shrapnel. The gunboat's skipper kept all guns firing at the beach, while a working party tried to put a mattress over the hole in the ship's side.

Kauffman transferred to a reserve gunboat and moved again toward the center of the beach. Five minutes later a shell passed through one of its magazines and exploded in a troop compartment, starting a fire. The gunboat pulled back, extinguished the fire, and returned to the line so that Kauffman could resume directing the swimmers and UDT landing craft. But a hit a minute aboard the gunboat knocked out guns, killed and wounded men, and tore holes in the ship. Repeated fires blazed below decks. Commander Malanaphy ordered it to retire and get help.

By now Commander Kauffman couldn't find any gunboats operating into which he could transfer. He had outdone the general who had his horse shot out from under him, having had two gunboats shot from under him inside of fifteen minutes. As he passed alongside the destroyer *Twiggs*, its skipper, Commander George Phillips, an old friend of Kauffman's, leaned out and shouted, "Get away from here, you Jonah!"

He lowered the ladder, brought Kauffman aboard, and provided a radioman to handle Kauffman's command circuit.

In the first five minutes, all gunboats in the line had been hit, but they fought back with any guns or rockets that were still in operation. The three reserve gunboats were sent forward to relieve the worst injured, some of which had nevertheless managed to fire all their rocket salvos.

It seemed incredible that man or ship could live in that hell, but most of them did. Of the twelve gunboats in the flotilla, eleven were hit and put out of action, one was sunk. Forty-seven men were killed or fatally injured and 153 wounded, among the ships' company. In addition, Lieutenant (jg) Lee C. Yates was killed and two other UDT liaison officers were wounded aboard the brave but overmatched gunboats. Ensign Frank Jirka, wearing a pair of borrowed shoes, had both feet blown off. He only said, "I'm sorry about losing his shoes."

These unintended sacrifices nevertheless helped support the all-important swimming reconnaissance. The larger ships farther at sea concentrated on newly revealed enemy batteries and the gallant gunboats delivered substantial rocket and rapid gunfire, as well as leading the enemy batteries to concentrate on them.

The actual swimming survey proceeded on schedule despite Japanese fire. While reserve craft stayed farther back, seven landing craft zigzagged irregularly in front of the heavily shelled gunboats, halfway to the beach. The Japanese gunners did not ignore them. More than one boat was almost lifted out of the water by a close shell or mortar burst. The swimmers lined up in the low-sided craft, looking like marble statues in their white grease, and even managed an occasional wink or grin or the usual crack:

"What the hell, it all counts on twenty."

Turning parallel to the beach, the landing craft kept on at full speed, as swimmer after swimmer flopped over the side into the rubber boat and then into the water. As soon as the tenth swimmer was dropped, each landing craft zigzagged furiously at flank speed to the safety of the destroyer line.

The greased swimmers winced when they hit cold water, but it was hot enough otherwise. In order to evade the mortars, machine-gun and sniper bullets, they swam under water as much as possible. Close bursts of machine-gun fire made macabre patterns under the clear water; one swimmer said: "Bullets drifted down like falling leaves."

Nobody stopped to collect them. They had enough to do, taking their soundings with line and lead weight, and trying to get close to the enemy shore line without being killed. Each man carried on his belt ten primacord rings with delayed fuses to blow up mines, but only one mine was spotted, three fathoms down, and the swimmer was carried away by the current before he could reach it.

When the swimmers got to the shore line—and most of them did—they turned and swam fifty yards parallel to the beach, making sure there were no mines and obstacles. Some men on each beach carried tobacco bags, into which they put samples of the black sandy bottom. They could see

Japanese soldiers on the terraces above, shooting down at them.

Back on the *Gilmer*, Captain Hanlon called for heavy fire on the flanks, and ordered a smoke screen laid on the beach. But the planes were not on station, and Hanlon had to order white phosphorus shellfire on the beach, concentrating on the cliffs and on Suribachi's batteries. The cover was thin but the enemy gunfire slackened noticeably and was less accurate. At the same time, he took the calculated risk of ordering the destroyers to close the beach to 2,000 yards and give the swimmers closer fire support. The defensive fire cover improved, although one destroyer was damaged by shellfire.

The swimmers finished their job and started back to sea, somewhat startled to see that the gunboats were all gone. Their ramped landing craft picked them up, one boat coming within 150 yards of shore to get an exhausted swimmer, maneuvering erratically as mortar shells chased it. Several swimmers were carried north by the current and were picked up by the adjoining team's landing craft.

Three hundred yards off Red Beach, the partly submerged Futatsu Rocks were a hazard to the Marine landings; Team Twelve dropped two swimmers to buoy them. One, a good swimmer, got out for the pickup, but the other was washed back into the rocks. He was an eager youngster who had pleaded for the duty although he wasn't a particularly good swimmer. The landing craft returned and he tried to swim out to it. The life ring was tossed to him as the boat passed at full speed. He missed it. The boat circled under fire and tried again. Again he missed.

The boat officer knew that he should head back to sea for the sake of the other men; but he was unwilling to leave the youngster behind. On the third try, the landing craft stopped dead in the water alongside the kid. The boat crew reached over the side, hauled him aboard, and slammed him down hard onto the floor boards, as the boat got under way and out of there.

Another boat from that team searched for a missing swimmer, A. E. Anderson, who had been last seen swimming in an area where mortar shells were landing. Ten minutes after the deadline for the boats' return, the crew had to admit that he had been killed.

As Team Fifteen's landing craft was retiring out of range, a sniper's bullet hit boatman Frank W. Sumpter through the head, and he died shortly thereafter. He was the last UDT casualty, in all that barrage of shot and shell.

Aboard the landing craft, en route to their transports, they climbed into long underwear and took a warming slug of brandy. Officers from each team collected reports and met aboard the *Gilmer* to chart results: good approach depths for all beaches to the shore line; no underwater obstacles or mines; good destruction of known defenses, and the exact locations of important gun positions newly revealed.

The tobacco sacks were emptied and the sand was studied. Nobody had been able to get above the waterline, but the undersea sand had enough "fines" (small particles) among the bigger slippery grains, and was well enough packed so that the officers, after some debate, reported that the slopes could be used by all types of vehicles.

D-Day's stalled jeeps would prove this to be a mistake. The sea had ground and packed the offshore volcanic sand. Above high water, however, the dry sand was as loose as a pile of ball bearings.

The teams were right, however, about the underwater approaches. Even more important, they had lured the enemy into revealing its hidden artillery strength, particularly on the right flank bluff. As the naval gunnery officer of the Marine V Amphibious Corps reported to his commanding general:

"A hitherto undiscovered four-gun battery was disclosed on top of the bluff in a position which enfiladed the entire landing beach. This discovery of additional enemy defensive positions as well as this full realization of the heavy fire power the enemy was able to bring to bear, was of paramount importance."

Stepped-up naval and air bombardment during the afternoon and the next day knocked out many of these guns which otherwise would have fired down point-blank on the landing Marines.

The ordeal of the gallant gunboats was a successful if unintentional sacrifice play. Admiral Blandy sent a dispatch: "Greatly admire magnificent courage your valiant personnel."

Nash's gunboat group and Malanaphy's flagship were awarded the rare Presidential Unit Citation.

Radio Tokyo reported its own version of the UDT reconnaissance: "A major landing force was repulsed with heavy losses. A battleship was hit and sunk instantaneously."

The sunken gunboat had received due tribute.

Aboard *Gilmer* the Underwater Demolition Group command faced an immediate problem. Their schedule required a daylight reconnaissance of the alternate western beaches that afternoon. Only one gunboat and Commander Malanaphy's large infantry landing craft were still operative, so gunboat support had to be forgotten. Captain Hanlon decided to postpone the reconnaissance one hour to permit heavier preliminary bombardment. He would then cover the swimmers with carrier aircraft and white phosphorus smoke on the beaches, moving the destroyers to the 2,000-yard line for close-in fire support.

Fresh platoons were put into the landing craft for the afternoon reconnaissance. The swimmers were greased with silver camouflage, the boat crews wore heavy shrapnel-proof vests and aprons. All wore helmets.

The landing craft were launched. A long line of 20mm splashes promptly traced its way from shore almost to the boats—a discouraging welcome! A cruiser spotted the rocks where the firing originated, and removed the rocks with a barrage of 8-inch shells. At 1415 the landing craft moved through the destroyer line 2,000 yards from shore.

A smoker plane had laid a thin but helpful curtain between shore and the Japanese guns. The destroyers covered the swimmers with a heavy curtain of 5-inch and 40mm fire, laying white phosphorus smoke on Suribachi and the slopes. Strafing planes poured lines of rockets into the beach until the swimmers got too near.

Whenever the smoke lifted or the covering fire slackened, Japanese coastal guns fired at destroyers, and mortars and machine guns rained shells down on swimmers. The swimmers stroked doggedly toward shore, swam along the beach, and turned out to sea. Covering fire redoubled while the landing craft scurried in to the pickup line. Lieutenant Brooks, commanding Team Fifteen, had to cruise within 100 yards of the sand, nearly getting caught in the surf, to get two exhausted swimmers.

Not a man was scratched. The afternoon reconnaissance was a happy anticlimax. The western beach was clear, although its slope was less favorable than that of the eastern beaches; there were no obstructions, and the only mine discovered was neatly blown up. No further demolition would be needed before D-Day.

The officers reported aboard the Gilmer, and made the master chart and reports, running off three hundred whiteprint copies. Two Mudpac staff officers and an officer and Marine observer from each team boarded two transports for a high-speed run southward to meet the two "tractor groups" of transports in Admiral Turner's Task Force 51, on their way to assault the beaches. The commander of each assault regiment would get a UDT officer's eyewitness description of his beach area, a day before the landings, plus an accurate chart. Captain Hanlon's innovations were paying dividends.

The next day the bombardment ships worked overtime while the teams took a break, their most dangerous task completed.

Aboard the Blessman, breezing along at 20 knots to replace another ship in the outer picket screen of the anchored fleet that night, Team Fifteen was congratulating itself that the Japanese kamikazes had not attacked the advance bombardment group. Only one plane had been sighted and shot down, just before the advance group reached Iwo.

The night was dark and overcast, with occasional rain squalls. The water was highly phosphorescent; the ship's wake shone in the darkness.

It was 9:20 P.M. The mess hall was filled with men writing home to their families, carefully vague letters since everything about UDT was still top secret. At a few tables men were playing cards and risking more than they knew.

Suddenly there was a terrific detonation. The ship shook from keel to bridge and the lights went out.

Four Japanese Bettys had swept onto the fleet's fringes. One dropped a bomb on the minelayer *Gamble*. Another twin-engined bomber followed the *Blessman's* wake, circled and came in on the beam, dropping two 500-pound bombs. One exploded in the water alongside. The other crashed through the steel overhead and exploded in the starboard mess hall, killing most of the occupants instantly.

The mess hall blazed up to the sky with a flame seen twenty miles away. The whole mid section of the ship was a burning geyser. The survivors helped each other out of the mess hall, leaving the dead behind. The smell of burning flesh spread through the ship.

In the main deck troop compartments, men helped their injured crew or teammates outside in a race against the spreading flames. One group was isolated forward; most of the team were aft on the fantail.

Every bit of fire-fighting equipment that could be reached or operated was mustered. The blast had cut hoses and ruined pumps. The ship had no power or steam to work fire mains. Under the cool orders of the *Blessman's* skipper, Lieutenant LeBoutiller, the crew forward and the UDT men aft fought the fire amidships between them, with buckets and whatever hand hoses could be worked. The fire spread through the troop compartments and galley to the clipping rooms and magazine areas, exploding stored ammunition.

Everyone knew that forty tons of UDT tetrytol explosive were stored under the hot decks. The ship was a floating bomb.

Ship was not abandoned, however. A radio message had been sent and acknowledged; help was on the way. First aid was given the injured. Officers and men formed a bucket brigade, passing fire buckets and even helmets full of water from the sea below to the hottest area, wetting down the deck and the explosives to keep them from catching.

The *Gilmer* was the nearest ship that could leave a screening station. Steaming at 25 knots through the night, it raced toward the stricken ship. More than an hour after the bomb hit, the *Gilmer* halted short of the flaming, explosive-laden *Blessman* and dropped two landing craft.

Commander Kauffman led the boarding party, to report whether the *Gilmer* could come close enough for fire fighting without being blown up along with the *Blessman*. In the second landing craft Lieutenant (jg) R. M. S. Boyd of the Mudpac staff stood by to evacuate wounded.

The newcomers could see the shattered side and the flames in the troop compartment, mess hall, and through the main deck cargo hatch which was blown open. Stranded forward and aft, the survivors were fighting the fire while ammunition exploded in scattered bursts. Silhouetted against the flames, the UDT bucket brigade on the fantail were singing "Anchors Aweigh."

Kauffman got aboard and checked quickly. There was a chance that *Gilmer* could come alongside to help without being blown up. Hastily he spoke into his radio mike: "Recommend you come alongside. The fire hasn't reached the explosives yet."

Captain Hanlon dryly phoned back: "I gathered that."

While Lieutenant Boyd loaded some of the wounded into his landing craft, the *Gilmer* moved up fast through the wind and rough sea. The first approach ended with the

Gilmer fifty yards away, hosing water across onto the fire.
Then she circled and approached from the *Blessman's* stern
at full speed, reversed full, and came alongside with a slight
bump; both ships' bows matched evenly, despite swells, a
superb demonstration of seamanship. Every hose and pump
on the *Gilmer* poured streams on the fire. The *Blessman's*
40mm clipping room aft, not far from the stored tetrytol,
was on fire and the exploding 40mm ammunition didn't
aid the rescue work, but nobody faltered. Two hoses were
put on the tetrytol to wet it down—it was getting dangerously hot.

Lieutenant Commander D. K. O'Connor, Mudpac staff
operations officer, came aboard to supervise the fire fighting.
As the 40mm ammunition burned itself out, a new batch of
20mm went off like giant firecrackers. Nevertheless Ensigns
R. H. McCallum and E. F. Andrews of the team went into
the burning troop compartments to fight the fire. The boat
deck had been ruled unsafe but Ensign E. B. Rybski got
special permission to lead a volunteer party there to jettison
flammable material, and work hoses from the *Gilmer*.

Thirty-eight dead were counted that night, almost evenly
divided between the *Blessman's* crew and the team. The
wounded were transferred to the flagship in relays. Fifteen
were walking, fifteen on stretchers.

By an hour after midnight, the fires were under control,
and an hour later the *Gilmer* could stop pumping water into
the smoldering but still floating ship. The *Gilmer* delivered
the wounded to the *Estes*' sickbay and hurried on to her
scheduled dawn rendezvous with the newly arrived *Auburn*,
flagship of Attack Force Commander Rear Admiral Harry
Hill.

A fleet repair ship gave the battered *Blessman* gasoline and
pumps to keep afloat, while the team sadly hunted through
the wreckage for their buddies and prepared them for burial
that afternoon. Almost all casualties were enlisted men,
caught in the mess hall and troop quarters. Eighteen members of the team and one Marine observer were killed.

Twenty-three were wounded or burned. It was the heaviest blow underwater demolition suffered in any Pacific operation—more than 40 per cent casualties, second only to Omaha Beach's unhappy record.

The hard-hit team was given a month's recreation at Saipan. The officers relaxed hard, as the aftermath of one officers' club party suggests. Recently promoted Lieutenant Commander Houston "Tex" Brooks, the team's commanding officer, left the evening party under his own steam (a full head of it) and hit the sack. An air raid blackout sounded. Something bothered him. The lights were still on. Like a good Texan, he got his .38, leaned out of his bunk, and fired three shots. Just as he was about to finish the job, a duty officer came charging in, and put him on report, which resulted in his temporarily accepting the hospitality of the captain's brig, aboard ship. The upshot of the case can be judged by the official report: ". . . and this officer, at 50 yards, did draw his revolver and fire at three light bulbs, hitting same (good shooting!)."

Meantime, the three other teams stood by during D-Day. The reconnaissance officers who went in with the first waves to guide them into the eastern beaches thought the enemy fire was less intense than on their own swim two days before.

Ashore, the Marines met heavy machine-gun fire that slowed them on the beach and the first terrace. More waves kept coming, and the Fourth and Fifth Marines slowly fought their way up the steep, slippery slope, sinking ankle-deep into the sand with every step. Finally they reached the top terrace and the airfield, along with the few tanks which had not been knocked out by hits or land mines and had been able to climb the shifting, steep sand.

Two hours after the landing, the first amtracs with supplies started going in. Wrecked landing craft and broached amtracs began piling up along the shore line. Jeeps were landed and promptly stalled hub-deep in the treacherous sand, blocking the way. Only tracked vehicles could climb those slopes until engineers laid an artificial surface.

Studying the beach ninety minutes after H-Hour, Force Beachmaster Captain "Squeaky" Anderson, in his torn jacket and shorts, said to Commander Kauffman, who was assigned to him to handle the UDT beach clearance: "I think she look all right. Want to go in?"

Kauffman answered: "No."

"All right, I go in myself." Squeaky shrugged, and got into an amtrac. Kauffman followed, saying, "You asked if I *wanted* to go."

Captain Anderson walked the mortar-torn beach, where Marines were dug into shallow sand craters, marking spots for supply dumps. When a near miss would cover him with sand, he'd just brush it off as if spoiled kids were playing games. Kauffman, properly taking cover as he went along, remonstrated, but Squeaky said: "They can't hurt me. They've had too many chances."

Nor did they. Beachmaster Anderson was secure in his command post—a shallow crater dug in the first terrace— by afternoon when he was joined by other UDT officers and Major T. W. Wood, observer from the Fort Pierce JANET testing board.

There was no demolition left to do that day, or the next. By D plus two, however, the four-foot surf and Japanese fire had packed the shore almost solid with wrecked landing craft, amtracs, and even pontoons from a tank landing ship causeway that had been swept sideways by the current and broached along the already cluttered beach. At 0800, February 21, the three surviving teams took their landing craft full of powder in to the beach, still intermittently pounded by shells and mortars. The voices of "Squeaky" Anderson and his assistants roared out of fourteen loudspeakers ashore.

The UDT men could not demolish anything but wooden landing craft, loading them with light charges of powder. Blowing up the metal wrecks of amtracs and amphibious trucks would spread more shrapnel than a Japanese barrage;

besides, the supply men could salvage them later. After each loading of a group of wooden wrecks, it took an hour to move dug-in troops and busy supply men out of a 75-yard safety zone.

The UDT men had to tow the rest of the wrecks away later. On the southernmost section nearest Mount Suribachi, the "Hot Rocks" were still so hot that the beach was ordered abandoned temporarily till the mountain's gunfire could be neutralized. The radio reported tersely: "Green Beach abandoned temporarily. Demolition work continuing."

More beach had to be cleared; supplies must reach the Marines fighting up and down the island in both directions from Iwo's narrow throat. While all three teams were busy hauling wrecks off the eastern beaches, the beachmaster requested a survey of a beach on the western side. The Marines had crossed the throat of the island, cutting off Suribachi, and presumably held the western shore securely.

The Mudpac staff, acting almost like a combat team, made the survey in a couple of ramped landing craft. Commander Kauffman, Lieutenant Hawks, and the coxswain, all beach reconnaissance veterans, took along a staff yeoman who was begging for action. As they closed the beach, Marines on the top terrace waved at them, and they blithely waved back. They could already see that the surf was not bad, and that although the beach was shallower than the eastern ones, it could be used. The yeoman looked at a line of splashes approaching them. "See the fish jumping!" he exclaimed cheerily.

Hawks stared. "Those aren't fish, they're fifty caliber!"

They yelled at the Marines ashore, and the heavy machine-gun fire stopped. Kauffman started stripping to swim in closer. Suddenly a new group of splashes walked toward them —bigger ones. Mortars. One hit under the stern and lifted the propellers out of the water. The men got out of there, radioing furiously ashore to try to stop the mistaken "friendly" fire. Later they learned that the machine-gun and mortar fire were neither mistaken nor friendly. There were still plenty of dug-in Japs in the area. The staff reconnaissance, however, did establish that the beaches could be used for supplies, when really secured.

On the morning of the 23rd, the demolition men, who were still busily clearing wrecks from the beaches, cheered when they saw the American flag go up on top of Mount Suribachi. It promised a fast mop-up of the gun caves that had been harassing them for days, though without hitting a single demolition man.

A tired man in grimy greens hitched a ride out to Squeaky Anderson's boat. And though the UDT crew could see he carried a camera, neither they nor cameraman Joe Rosenthal were aware that one of the exposures he carried would become perhaps the most famous photograph of war, immortalizing the six Marines who raised the flag on Mount Suribachi. Few people know the true story of that flag. It was borrowed from an LST beached near Suribachi to replace one which had been raised earlier. This was the *second* flag which the Marines had planted!

Secretary of the Navy James Forrestal had been a deeply concerned observer of the entire operation aboard a command ship. When it became apparent that the landing was an assured success, he sent a dispatch to the demolition teams:

"Congratulations and the highest admiration to the underwater demolition personnel for their gallant and effective part in making the landings on D-Day possible."

For five more days the teams hauled away like beavers, clearing away over 100 craft and disarming 60 Japanese land mines and a number of booby traps. Supplies could flow ashore—and casualties could be evacuated. The battle on Iwo lasted two months, with over 20,000 casualties. UDT had cleared the beaches in nine days despite storm and enemy fire. Now the teams were ready, after a brief rest at Ulithi, to tackle the final Japanese sea bastion—Okinawa.

15. A Thousand Swimmers

A THOUSAND MEN IN SWIM TRUNKS SPEARHEADED THE INVASION of Okinawa, key to Japan itself. The Underwater Demolition Teams had come a long way in little over a year.

Captain B. Hall Hanlon aboard his flagship commanded ten hundred-man teams, embarked in a flotilla of fourteen high-speed destroyer transports, with a score of destroyers and gunboats assigned to his command for fire support.

The largest UDT operation to date triggered the greatest single naval operation in the Pacific. Admiral Turner had over 1,200 ships in the task force which he directly commanded, along with uncounted swarms of personnel landing craft, and some two hundred other large ships on temporary duty at various times around Okinawa.

The operation order which Captain Hanlon wrote for UDT at Okinawa was a masterpiece of detailed planning, giving the teams the best protection they had ever received. Many lives were saved by this plan, which is still used as a guide in UDT training.

The "fleet that came to stay" and did stay for months was hammering on the outer gates of Japan's homeland. Okinawa lay only 350 miles south of Kyushu, a major Japanese war industry area and the fleet's next target.

More than 100,000 fighters-to-the-death defended Okinawa's 58 mountainous miles. An American field army embarked in the fleet converging on the island—four Army divisions, three Marine divisions, another Army division in reserve. More than 450,000 of those troops would be committed to battle, arriving on "Love Day," April 1, 1945.

An American surprise attack knocked out a suicide weapon the Japanese had in hiding to destroy the American fleet

before the first gun was fired in the main battle. With underwater demolition teams leading the way, an American advance group hit Kerama Retto, a small group of islands
eighteen miles west of Okinawa. The wily Occidentals caught
the cunning Orientals with their anchors down. Several days
before the attack, the crews of Japanese suicide boats had
gone over to Okinawa for special training. The arrival of
the Amphibious Support Force prevented their return.
Nearly four hundred plywood suicide boats, hidden in caves
and camouflaged from air observation, were destroyed before
the Japs could creep forth in deadly night raids to blow up
their heavy explosive charges and themselves against the
American fleet.

The demolition flotilla arrived south of the Kerama Isles
just after daybreak on March 25, seven days before Okinawa's
L-Day. Four of the new-style destroyer escort transports
carried three veteran Iwo teams (Twelve, Thirteen, and Fourteen) and the new Team Nineteen. Captain Hanlon, Commander Kauffman, and the Mudpac staff were aboard the
flagship *Gilmer*; another converted four-stacker freighted
explosives.

The demolition group formed part of Rear Admiral
Blandy's Amphibious Support Force of old battleships, escort
carriers, cruisers, destroyers, gunboats, and rocket craft.

Minesweepers, always the unsung advance guard of amphibious assault, found Japanese mines so thick off western
Kerama Retto that they slowed the swimmers' schedule
twenty minutes. Three teams boldly pushed into the heart
of the islands, making up for lost time. Fire control was
perfect. As the swimmers started for one beach, a native
horse dashed onto the sand, running wildly up and down
to escape the terrifying bombardment. The gunners changed
their aim to spare the panicked horse.

The few Japanese defenders were pinned down. Only a
few shots disturbed the swimmers, except on one central islet
where the green Team Nineteen came under mortar fire.
The new men steadily swam in to the beach, while a barrage

from the gunboats and destroyers silenced the mortars. The men lived up to the training of their veteran commander, Lieutenant George Marion, one of the first Naval Combat Demolition men in the Pacific, who had been executive officer of Team Three in Guam and Leyte.

The swimmers gasped when they first hit water—not because of the Japanese, but because of the cold. The water temperature was in the sixties, and the men had been training in the warm waters of Leyte and Ulithi. They were smeared with aluminum-colored axle grease, however, which it was hoped would serve the double purpose of camouflage and warmth.

Eight beaches were explored that day, on almost as many islands. Since the over-all invasion must include so many landings, these beaches were code-named Zebra (for Z), as well as having the customary color code names. Gelett Burgess's Purple Cow was put to shame by Commander Hochuli's team which surveyed a Green Zebra, a Violet Zebra, and an Amber one. Lieutenant Commander Moranz's men examined Orange and Purple Zebras on the largest island, Tokashika. Lieutenant Marion's Zebras had the more usual beach color names of Red, Yellow, and Blue on as many different islets.

The teams reported that ramped landing craft could ride up to all beaches except the two westernmost ones, where amtracs must be used. The survey forced a change in plans. All the islands would be attacked in the morning except the western pair, which must wait another day for the arrival of the slower tank landing ships carrying the amphibian tractors.

In the morning, Rear Admiral I. N. Kiland's attack force carrying the 77th Infantry Division and the balance of the UDT flotilla (six teams and ten transports in charge of Captain R. D. Williams, USN), arrived. "Red" Williams would henceforth be the right-hand man in the top command of UDT.

Of greater concern to those teams already on the spot— in more senses than one—was the first daybreak raid by

Japanese kamikazes. Eight suicide planes swept down from
the north around dawn to attack the transports, a foretaste of
the hell to come. One destroyer was immediately hit and
seriously damaged. A single-engined Tony was knocked down
so close to Team Nineteen's transport *Knudson* that two of
the ship's crew were injured. Fifteen minutes later another
Tony skimmed across Captain Hanlon's flagship *Gilmer* amidships, one wing grazing the galley deck and wrecking an ammunition ready box, killing one crewman and injuring three
others. The wreck splashed into the water close alongside.

Two Tonys were downed but the raiders' sacrifice didn't
delay the fate of Kerama Retto. Officers from the three UDT
teams guided the landing craft of the Army division onto
five beaches at 0730 as scheduled. Only scattered snipers
opposed the landings. Hochuli's team blew up a sunken lugger
which was blocking a boat channel, and went ashore on the
heels of the troops to demolish a sea wall on one island so
that supply DUKWs could roll inland. Another team went
ashore to blow up a thick stand of trees blocking a beach exit.

When the amtracs rolled off the ships the next day, the two
western islets were duly overrun. Kerama Retto had become
an American stronghold. Heavily spiked nets were stretched
to make the roadstead between the islands safe from Jap
submarines, and most of the Orientals' suicide craft were
caught inside the area. They were studied in their hiding
places along the eastern island, Tokashiki Shima, with intense
interest; nobody could know how many more might be lurking around Okinawa itself.

The nightly "Fly-catcher Patrol" was doubly alerted to
swat suicide craft on and under the water, throughout the
fleet's long stay off Okinawa. A cruiser and a destroyer were
assigned to augment the patrolling gunboats with searchlights
and heavier guns.

A more immediate task faced the UDTs. Between Kerama
Retto and Okinawa lay a small island group named Keise
Shima. Its eastern island was needed as a base for heavy artil-
lery to pound the western Okinawa landing beaches and

southern strongholds, only eight miles farther east. Mine-sweepers found so many Japanese mines around the islands, however, that the teams got a day's rest while the busy sweepers cleared the seaway for gunboats.

The teams led by Moranz and Marion tackled Keise Shima. During the night of the 27th, Major James L. Jones and his Marine Amphibious Reconnaissance Battalion made a sneak raid on the islands, and found no sign of enemy resistance.

As a result, an overconfident boat crew from Lieutenant Marion's new Team Nineteen decided that as veterans of Kerama Retto they could rewrite the underwater manual. They paddled ashore in a rubber boat to inspect the beach of Keise Shima's eastern islet, Kamiyama, planning to swim back while making their reef and water survey. Their plan backfired.

Japanese snipers had hidden in the hills of Kamiyama while the Marines had scouted the shore. Now they opened up. Their rifle fire pinned down the men on the beach and trapped a boat crew off the reefs.

The UDT men on the beach were better armed than usual. Besides their sheath knives, one man carried a carbine, and Ensign William Cullen wore his .45 automatic. They tried to keep the snipers busy by firing their two guns. The offshore crew managed to paddle out of range, but the snipers hit Cullen twice—through his gun wrist, and through one leg. Ensign Robert Killough grabbed the falling pistol, ordered the men to carry Cullen over the reef, and ran ahead, firing at the hidden snipers. Killough fired clip after clip, as he dodged behind rocks and trees. The hidden Nipponese tried to dislodge him with hand grenades. Only after the little UDT group was safely beyond the reef did Killough follow, swimming out to sea under fire.

Meanwhile their transport *Knudson* had closed the beach to cover its men. The team called for ships' gunfire on the Jap position, but Captain Hanlon vetoed the request until his widely scattered men were out of the area. Then the snipers were duly shelled.

Ensign Killough won a Silver Star for gallantry—and all teams got a tart reminder that their responsibility was strictly under water. Their job should end at the high-water mark. Raiding behind the beach was a task for better armed and specially trained men.

Lieutenant Commander Moranz's veteran Team Thirteen came under a different sort of fire at another Keise Shima islet. It was preparing to blast a channel through a reef and sandbar off Nagannu, to help land heavy radar equipment for spotting kamikaze raiders from a distance, when three patrolling Navy Wildcats mistook the men for Jap suicide swimmers. The planes attacked the swimmers with bombs and machine-gun fire. Fortunately their aim was wild on the first pass. The pilots' ears were nearly burned off by frantic radio warnings, and they hastily veered off before making a return attack. Nobody was hurt, and the team continued on schedule.

While two teams opened Keise Shima, the other two teams of the advance group, led by Commander Hochuli and Lieutenant Onderdonk, joined the main UDT flotilla for the main push. Eight teams poised off the Okinawa beaches—a larger number than had previewed Leyte for General MacArthur's return. The Okinawa teams faced a harder task, for aerial photos had spotted lines of man-made obstructions on the reefs guarding the chosen beaches.

The Demolition Teams had to wait a full day for the minesweepers to finish their Augean task. More than three thousand square miles of ocean were eventually swept clear of anchored and floating mines, the largest single assault sweep ever attempted in the Pacific, but even so, five ships were sunk or badly damaged by mines.

On the morning of March 29, three teams explored the northern half of the selected beaches, on the west coast of Okinawa. Lieutenant Commander Richard Burke's veteran Team Seven drew the dangerous right flank, opposite the town of Hagushi, where the Bishi River flows through the reef to divide the northern and southern landing beaches.

Cliffs along the river were lined with caves and burial vaults, ideal spots for Japanese gun and sniper nests. The "vaults" were particularly suspect, and labeled as such for special attention on the gunfire plans.

The other two teams were new to combat demolition, although all the officers and men had served in combat areas throughout the Pacific. These were "fleet" teams, volunteering for demolition in response to Admiral Turner's directive authorizing such transfer for Maui training and UDT combat. Team Sixteen was commanded by Lieutenant Edward A. Mitchell, who had been on duty with the fleet. Team Seventeen had a veteran UDT commander in Lieutenant Arthur M. Downes, Jr., who had served with Team Four at Guam and Leyte.

Downes' team got an early foretaste of action against the Japanese. At dawn the previous day, two dive bombers with red meatballs on their wings had made a suicide attack on the transports off Kerama Retto. One suicider headed for Team Seventeen's transport *Crosley*, boring in through the gunfire. The *Crosley* made a tight turn and the bomber splashed only 30 yards from the explosive-filled transport.

On the morning of the 29th, the kamikazes failed to strike. A line of battleships cruised three miles off the beaches, with cruisers closer in, ready to plaster Japanese shore batteries. Six destroyers patrolled a mile from the beach, pouring 5-inch and 40mm shells ashore. A thousand yards off the reef, nine gunboats rapid-fired their 40mm and 20mm guns at the northern beaches, and two similar mortar boats added mortars to their 40mm fire on the flanks.

A dozen UDT boats sped past the destroyers and gunboats, eastward into the sun. The bombardment deafened them. Ahead lay the hidden water-covered reef. There was almost no surf except near the river channel, but lines of posts sticking partly out of water marked their target plainly. The high tide was turning.

The landing craft made their run, dropping gray-hooded and greased swimmers into cold water. The men swam vigorously to keep warm; water temperature was in the low sixties and they'd be in it for an hour or more. As they swam to the reef edge, dropping their sounding lines, they knew that every man in the water was backed up by a thousand guns on ships. Small wonder that the enemy pillboxes and caves could manage only very scattered sniper shots and a few mortar bursts from the river area!

The ghostly-gray swimmers made a "string" reconnaissance as prescribed by Commander Kauffman, who was present as chief staff officer of UDT. The swimmers took soundings every 25 yards as they swam across the three- or four-foot depth of the reef.

Half the area was blockaded by long lines of wooden posts six inches to a foot thick, higher than a man, wedged firmly into coral crevices in the reef's flat floor. The posts were six to ten feet apart in a checkerboard pattern, but there was no barbed wire. The swimmers found no mines on the posts or reefs, and went on past the obstacles, to within fifty yards of shore.

Chilled and exhausted, they got back to their pickup boats safely despite the cold water. Blankets and the standard combat UDT postswimming ration of brandy and coffee revived them.

At 3:30 that afternoon, with the sun behind them, three more teams tackled the beaches south of the Bishi River. The most dangerous beaches near the river were assigned to old hands—Lieutenant Commander Carberry's Team Four.

Next came the new Team Twenty-one, commanded by Lieutenant Edward P. Clayton, USN—one of the few Regular Navy officers in the UDT. He had earned a Navy Cross as an enlisted man before the war, diving for the sunken submarine *Squalus,* and had become a "Mustang" (commissioned from the ranks). As an officer, he led a Naval Combat Demolition Unit on the beaches of Utah and Southern France. Although many other Normandy veterans stayed in demolition, and got to the Pacific in time for the occupation of Japan, Clayton was the only one who commanded a Pacific team in World War II combat. His green team had tasted action before this afternoon reconnaissance.

At dawn, the lookouts and radar of their transport *Bunch* simultaneously reported a small boat a mile away. The ship was already at general quarters for the dawn alert, and UDT men were manning one of the heavy .50-caliber machine guns, as they usually did when they didn't have swim duty. The high-speed destroyer transport headed for the strange craft and quickly saw that it was a Japanese suicide boat! The *Bunch* immediately started firing with machine guns, 20mm and 40mm batteries, and the boat exploded, completely disintegrating 500 yards from the ship.

Twenty minutes later, a second Nipponese motorboat was spotted, heading at top speed for the *Bunch*. The UDT and ship crews laid their machine guns on the suicide craft and stopped it dead in the water. The Japanese crew heaved their explosive charges overboard, and they immediately exploded. Then they jumped over the side themselves. The *Bunch* started lowering a UDT craft to take prisoners, but an oncoming destroyer opened up with its 5-inch battery and completely obliterated the enemy boat and the swimmers. The two suicide boats had evidently come from a small Kerama Retto island which had not yet been mopped up by the infantry.

The third team swimming in to the southern beaches that afternoon was getting its first combat action. Lieutenant Louis States' Team Eleven had been cheated out of the Iwo assignment by training accidents, but they would have a real chance to distinguish themselves at Okinawa and later. The team had a UDT-experienced executive officer in Robert Wells, Chief Warrant Officer, who had swum the Charan Kanoa channel to the Jap barges at Saipan.

The afternoon reconnaissance was at low tide, the drying reef almost completely exposed, with a slight surf breaking over its sheer seaward edge. The men took soundings up to the reef edge, but did not have to crawl across it; they could see any potholes or coral heads on the three or four hundred yards of flat reef. Ships' gunfire and neatly timed carrier plane strafing kept the beach defenders quiet except for occasional rifle fire at the swimmers.

The survey was successful and almost uneventful. At the last minute, it was decided to explore an additional area between two teams' beaches, so Ensign Frank Jameson and another Team Eleven swimmer dropped off their boat to swim to the reef. Jameson had no silver grease, and wore underwater goggles instead of the standard round face mask. He also sported a drooping black mustache reminiscent of an Oriental god. As he turned back from checking the reef's edge, he saw another officer just swimming in toward him. Jameson waved in greeting. The other officer, sure the tanned swimmer from an unassigned area was an armed Jap swimmer defending the reef, hastily dove for a long-distance underwater swim, and porpoised back to the landing craft at top speed!

After the morning and afternoon reconnaissance, the men reported that portions of every beach could be used, avoiding some ragged edges and potholes. They thought that at high tide, amtracs could get past the posts or push them over, but the posts would be an easier pushover for UDT demolition—a matter of two hours' work. UDT was given the assignment for the following day.

While the six teams were exploring the intended landing beaches on the west side of Okinawa, two other teams had a similar mission on the island's southeast corner. They made a full-scale survey, although it was really a feint to trick the Japanese command into splitting its defense.

This demonstration took place in the afternoon. Hochuli's Team Twelve and Onderdonk's stand-by Team Fourteen divided the southeastern beaches between them. It was a letter-perfect, uneventful survey, with pairs of swimmers taking soundings all the way to the drying reefs, under the overhead fire of battleships, cruisers, destroyers, gunboats, and mortar boats. The Japanese fire was too weak to cause any casualties. The swimmers returned on schedule, to chart the reefs and report there were no obstructions.

Explosive packs and fuses were readied that night for the big demolition job. Team Seven made up a hundred Hagensen packs. For the most part, tetrytol blocks (stiff oblongs wrapped in waterproof brown paper) had to be used. Old inner tubes were slashed to make heavy rubber bands, which would hold the blocks tightly against the posts that were to be blown.

In the morning, all eight teams headed for the reefs. Demonstration teams Twelve and Fourteen swam to the edge of the southeastern reefs and placed their explosive packs, although no landing was planned there. As they swam back, the long line of reef blew sky-high. The feint was so convincing that Tokyo broadcast the news that the Americans were planning to land on both sides of Okinawa.

On the actual invasion beaches, six teams boarded their ramped landing craft three miles at sea. An indiscreet Japanese boat picked this moment to dash out of the river toward the line of waiting destroyers. Swift shellfire turned the suicider into a geyser of debris before it got past the reef line.

Two dozen UDT boats filled with swimmers sped through the destroyer line toward the reef. Shells roared and whooshed overhead; the thunder of guns was deafening. After passing through the inner line of gunboats the leading landing craft turned opposite the obstructed beaches and ran in a carefully irregular pattern parallel to the reef. Pairs of silver-greased swimmers dropped off the seaward side of each craft while their teammates dumped loads of explosive off the landward side. Each swimmer picked up a string of haversacks lashed together, each canvas bag filled with explosive blocks or primacord, and buoyed by an inflated jungle flotation bladder. The swimmers towed them onto the water-covered reef where the tops of the posts showed clearly above water. The men were working against time, as the tide was beginning to ebb.

Teams Seven, Eleven, Sixteen, and Seventeen tackled the heavily obstructed beaches north of the river, while Teams Four and Twenty-one covered the beaches just south. The right flank, far south of the river mouth, had no man-made obstacles, but a shallow lagoon there between reef and shore would make trouble later.

The gunboats' steady fire on the beach was screaming only a few feet over the men's heads. They worked in three to five feet of water at first, diving down to strap a block of explosive onto the base of each post. Other men strung the primacord fuse line, connecting all the posts in their team's area.

There were two casualties. One man was wounded by steel and wood when a ricocheted 40mm shell landed short and splintered a post near where he was working. Francis Lynch of Team Sixteen was missing; his body wasn't found till the day after the landings, on the beach with a bullet hole through his head.

The job was supposed to take an hour before the fuses were pulled. On some beaches it took much longer. By the time the men could swim off the reef to their boats, many of them were suffering severe cramps from long exposure in cold water. Back at the pickup boats, blankets and brandy soon cured most of them. The usual cure didn't work for Edward Higgins of Team Eleven. He had felt cramps in the water, but just assumed he had swallowed too much salt water. He finished his job, and was helped by his swim buddy back to the pickup boat. When he refused the brandy ration, they knew that he was really ill. Within an hour, he underwent an emergency operation for appendicitis.

The last men on the reef were the two fuse pullers of each team, who waited to fire until their ship signaled that the other men were clear. All along the thousands of yards of beach, successive blasts hurled columns of debris in the air. When it settled—there were the gaps.

On Team Four's beach, the men pulled their fuses as scheduled and dashed to sea. Nothing happened. The men went back, with a twenty-minute deadline, to check the fuses and fire with a new detonating assembly. This time the line of posts was shattered.

On Blue Beach, where Team Sixteen had missed its bearings and landed three hundred yards too far north, there remained a stretch of unloaded posts. When the luckless Team Sixteen did hurriedly fire its shot, the primacord fuse exploded in a lightning-fast line, with a splash like a long whip lashed across the water—but the charges didn't go off. A second attempt blew only part of the explosives.

This delayed Team Seven's fuse pullers and they failed to receive the awaited signal from their ship. They were alone on the reef, with the tide ebbing and the Japs sniping at them. They hid behind their explosive-loaded posts, and occupied the time by counting and charting enemy pillboxes and sniper posts ashore. They had started for the beach at 0930; at 1215 they got the green light, pulled the delay fuse, swam to sea—and saw their posts go sky-high.

Captain Hanlon reported a successful operation, except for Blue Beach which would have to be attacked again the next day. The landing would not wait for a second failure. Several teams aboard their high-speed transports were already speeding south to deliver the UDT beach charts and reports to the approaching assault force.

Team Eleven drew the job of going back onto the reef to finish Team Sixteen's clearance. Lieutenant States led his team back the next morning, with Lieutenant Mitchell and two other Team Sixteen officers going along as guides. As States cruised close to the reef, the swimmers towed their packs into the area which had been skipped before, and placed them over the unfired charges.

The swimmers, under sniper fire, worked fast. They swam under water from post to post seeking shelter. The trunk-line men ran out their reels of primacord.

Three quarters of an hour after they started, the ships' gunfire support slackened, and Japanese scurried from their dugouts into the shelter of the stone-arched burial vaults pockmarking the overlooking cliffs. Rifle and machine-gun fire poured onto the swimmers only fifty yards away. They were pinned down.

Mortar fire narrowly missed States' landing craft. States radioed Hanlon that the team was under severe enemy fire, giving the exact geographical coordinates of the Japanese gun position. Hanlon hurriedly checked his charts, notified the support group, and questioned: "Are they shooting from the tombs?"

Before States had a chance to answer, the *Nevada*, a heavy cruiser, and the destroyers began lobbing shells on the position, and the Navy air group came in with a dive-bomber attack. Exactly 4 minutes and 40 seconds had elapsed from the time of States' call for support to the destruction of the Jap gun emplacement! This special delivery shellfire was typical of the speed of communications, and the lightning rapidity of the attack of a Naval Support Force.

The fuse line was laid and the men swam to their boats, leaving the fuse puller and his assistant behind. Big, 220-pound Ensign Frederick G. Deiner, nicknamed "Truck" for his build, fired every fuse Team Eleven ever shot, and never had a misfire. Now he pulled the fuse and headed for sea. It was proverbial in UDT that the fastest swimming in the Pacific was done by fuse pullers, particularly when they used a less than 10-minute delay fuse. Old Reliable went off on schedule, and the last Japanese obstructions on the landing beaches were history.

April 1 bore the triple burden of Easter, Love Day, and April Fool's. The mighty landing force experienced a most welcome April Fool joke on Okinawa's beaches. Unknown to observation or intelligence, the Japanese commander had decided he could not seriously oppose the assault on his beaches. He hoarded his hundred thousand or so fighters in strong defense lines in the hills, paying involuntary tribute to the irresistible force of the Amphibious Forces assault.

The technique of ship-to-shore landing, an undeveloped art before the war, had achieved high efficiency under Admiral Turner and other American naval commanders. The massed ships lifted their gunfire inland, the last installment of over 5,000 tons of "softening up." Waves of amtracs pointed by UDT officers in guide boats crawled over the newly cleared western reef and poured their troops inland. The enemy only harassed them with sniper and mortar fire. The regimental combat teams of Army and Marines walked ashore upright, swinging a punch that met no real resistance until they hit the hills well inland.

The first tank wave following the troops onto the farthest southern beaches met resistance from its own commander. The tanks crawled onto the drying reef, but stopped short at the suspicious stretch of lagoon between reef and shore in this area. The commander would not risk drowning out his tank engines, despite the UDT assurance that the lagoon was flat and shallow. Enemy snipers and mortars from the hills farther south took the sitting targets on the reef under fire.

Gunner's Mate 1/c Samuel Conrad of Team Eleven was guiding the tanks with Lieutenant (jg) Williams. Conrad jumped out of his vehicle and stepped out on the reef, stripped for UDT action in trunks and coral shoes, his blond head covered by a helmet. He strode ahead of the tanks into the water—and waded under fire across the three-foot depth of lagoon all the way to the beach, a visible measurement of the water. Conrad led the tank wave, alone and unarmed, to the Okinawa shore, and his prompt, brave action won him an admiral's spot promotion to Chief Petty Officer.

The Love Day landing was so easily successful that there was a brief moment of horseplay. Some demolition men strayed ashore after the infantry on Love plus one, discovering a saki distillery whose product was promptly confiscated for unofficial Army-Navy relaxation.

One of Team Eleven's men, Gilbert Soto, of Mexican descent, looked convincingly Japanese when he donned a captured uniform and walked into the transport's wardroom. The team, remembering their briefings on suicide boats,

Japanese infiltration, and sly Oriental tactics, overturned many a coffee cup and wardroom chair before the hoax was discovered.

But there was little time for fun. The troops quickly ran into the strong Japanese defense lines in the northern and southern hills, and there were constant calls for the demolition teams to clear supply beaches as the troops advanced. It would be June 22 and almost 50,000 American battle casualties before the honeycombed hills and their more than 100,000 defenders would be finally crushed.

The Japanese strategy made sense—to hold on as long as possible, while their fleet and suicide planes and boats harassed the American fleet standing by the troops. A small Japanese task force did sortie from the home islands on April 6 in a vain attempt to relieve Okinawa; it was virtually wiped out by the fast carrier force. Our gunboats destroyed 71 suicide boats, and others were destroyed by bombardment. But the kamikazes overhead cost the besieging fleet dearly.

All of the available craft in the American Fleet were pressed into service on the screen and the picket lines, stationed in a wide circle around Okinawa and the surrounding islands, to give early warning of air raids and to knock down all the approaching suiciders they could. The kamikazes tried every possible trick, with feints, mass attack, and "window" —clouds of metal foil sprayed from planes to confuse the radar screens. Infantry gunboats and UDT transports added their guns to the radar picket line. Riding a boatload of high explosive into a kamikaze attack was hardly a comfortable experience.

Closer to Okinawa, the "Fly-catcher Detail" was a regular nightly assignment in the fleet, coping with the occasional suicide boats that showed up. By day and night, the surviving suicide boats were knocked off, but they damaged five large ships and three small craft. Some of their attacks were nipped off by UDT transports.

The radar picket line and its supporting ships took a

terrible pounding; 560 raids by 2,228 planes during the month and a half before Admiral Turner turned over the naval command of Okinawa to Vice Admiral Hill.

One night after the landing, Team Twenty-one had a narrow escape followed by a vital rescue mission. Their transport *Bunch* was en route to the outer screen at dusk with two other ships when a pair of Japanese bombers dove at them. One Betty bomber crashed into the nearby transport *Henrico*, causing fire, heavy damage, and 170 casualties. The other Betty, missing the transport *Dickerson* with a bomb, turned and crashed into the ship, setting it afire.

The *Bunch* came alongside the *Dickerson*, trying to get the flames under control. Swimmers from the team dove into the water while others paddled rubber boats, saving injured men who had been thrown off the blazing destroyer.

The fire and the pounding swells forced the *Bunch* to pull loose, but a UDT fire and rescue party crossed in a landing craft to board the blazing ship. Another boatload of fire fighters from Team Seventeen also boarded the *Dickerson*, as their transport *Crosley* came to the rescue.

The fire fighters managed to start the destroyer's gasoline-driven pumps, playing hoses on the fire. The *Bunch* got a towline aboard, and ran its own hoses onto the stricken ship. The tow and hoses parted in the heavy sea, and the fire started up again. The teams and crewmen from the ships worked for five hours before a salvage tug arrived to put out the fire and tow away the fatally wounded ship which finally had to be sunk. Six officers and 55 men, many of them injured, were taken aboard the *Bunch*.

Every team had its own narrow escapes from kamikazes, or helped fight fires and rescue men aboard less fortunate ships.

By day the teams surveyed beaches behind the lines, which were not always clear-cut. Lieutenant Jack Wood and Chief Walter Loban of Team Four were told to chart a channel to an Army-held beach south of the original landing beaches, on the way to Naha. Since all seemed quiet ashore, the pair climbed over the sea wall into a small village which was completely deserted. They suddenly learned why. They were exactly halfway between the Army's front line and the Japanese positions. Both sides opened fire on the village at the same time, and the two UDT men tried for a world's record covering the two hundred yards to their boat.

Beach after beach was explored as the Marines and Army moved up the island. Many offshore islands had to be scouted before the troops overran them. Team Seven drew the beach assignment at Tsugen Shima, a small island guarding Okinawa's eastern Buckner Bay (as it was renamed after the 10th Army's general, killed only three days before the island was secured). They swam to the shore, charting the reefs, without drawing a single shot. Later, the day before the landing when their transport *Hopping* was cruising off the Tsugen Shima shore, a Japanese battery of 3- and 4-inch guns, hidden on the rocky island, sent six shells crashing into the ship, one of which exploded in the troop compartments. The casualties were almost equally divided between ship and team. One of the ship's crew was killed and eleven were wounded. Team Seven had nine wounded men, one of whom died and was buried at sea the next day.

Those were the last serious injuries the enemy inflicted on underwater demolitioners around Okinawa, although the teams went on to explore half a dozen other Japanese-held islands including the major enemy stronghold of Ie Shima off Okinawa's northwest coast.

Captain Hanlon was directed to make a flying survey of possible UDT training bases for the cold-water invasion of Japan. On April 4 he turned over command of the Okinawa teams to Captain Williams as Acting ComUDTsPac. The Mudpac staff, including Kauffman, moved over to Williams' flagship, the *Bunch*, already crowded with Team Twenty-one.

The last big UDT operation in the Okinawa area was the invasion of Ie Shima, which was managed by Red Williams. Teams Four and Twenty-one surveyed the beaches on the

13th and 14th of April. The latter team also swam to the smaller nearby isle of Minna Shima. The teams found no obstacles except the reefs themselves, which again required the use of amtracs.

The swimmers charting Ie Shima's beaches were of course under orders not to go beyond the high-water mark, as the island had a strong Japanese garrison. As a pair of swimmers reached the shore, one of the men stayed in the surf while his buddy crawled inland between the enemy's sand dunes. On the nearest gunboat, Chief Loban, who had to keep track of the swimmers, marked the man's name down as lost, never expecting to see him alive again. But the man got back from the Jap-held shore, and reported back aboard with his beach information. Chief Loban bawled him out for exceeding orders (something Loban himself had done a little earlier near Naha!). The swimmer replied in a hurt tone: "I was perfectly safe, Chief. My buddy was covering me with his knife."

One can judge how safe he really was, from the fact that it took the 77th Army Division five days to capture that bitterly held three-by-five-mile island. It was there that war correspondent Ernie Pyle was killed by a sniper and buried.

The reefs around Ie Shima kept the two teams busy for days, blasting channels and reef ramps so that ships could supply the troops fighting their way to the top of the island's 1,200-foot peak. There was never any shortage of fish for chow, as the demolitioners dynamited the reef waters.

Meantime the other teams had been happily leaving the kamikaze country, two and three at a time, for Guam, Ulithi, and Pearl Harbor. Commander Hochuli's Team Twelve was honored with UDT's first Presidential Unit Citation for its heroism in front of Iwo's Mount Suribachi and its later Okinawa work. Finally only Team Sixteen remained at Okinawa, ably atoning for its misfire by successful clearance of landing beaches all along Okinawa's shores. By April 25, this last team left Okinawa. But the battle ashore still continued, and a month later Team Twenty-one was recalled from its rest in Guam, to assist landings and clear beaches on other outlying islands near Okinawa which were needed for radar sites—Iheya Shima, Aguni Shima; more clearance on Okinawa and Ie Shima. Finally on June 26 newly promoted Lieutenant Commander Clayton's team accompanied Major Jones and his Marine Reconnaissance Battalion to seize Kume Shima, fifty miles west of Okinawa, as a last stop on the route to Japan. Clayton's Team Twenty-one left Okinawa on July 1, after blowing up more than seventy tons of explosives, and experiencing two hundred air raids.

Okinawa was the last UDT operation for Captain Hanlon, who had been hoping to get back into more conventional Navy duty. He was invited to dinner on June 6 aboard Vice Admiral Turner's flagship at Guam. In his cabin, the Admiral said sharply: "Hanlon, stand up!"

The surprised captain snapped to attention, and Turner solemnly awarded him the Legion of Merit, for Iwo and Okinawa. Red Hanlon modestly started to sit down, but was arrested by Turner's stern: "Dammit, stand up!"

Hanlon braced, and Turner gave him the Navy Cross for the Iwo operation. Hanlon started to relax again, and Turner roared: "When I say stand up, I mean stand up!"

Hanlon stiffened once more, and the dead-pan Admiral handed him his orders as captain of the battleship *North Carolina*, perhaps the most desired award of all.

"Now sit down, Red," the Admiral concluded with a grin. It was about time, for the former commander of UDT couldn't take much more. Although this was the end of Hanlon's official connection with UDT, his rapid rise to the rank of admiral, and his very distinguished career, is a matter of great pride to his old gang of demolitioners.

Commander Kauffman took over as commander of UDT, until Hanlon's successor was appointed—Captain R. H. Rodgers, who had commanded Turner's flagship in the South Pacific and had more recently been Director of Training for the Pacific Amphibious Forces in Coronado. The new UDT commander had a big task ahead—planning beach surveys and demolition for the successive invasions of Japan's main islands; first Kyushu in November, then in March, Honshu where Tokyo is located. Surveying the beaches alone would require thirty teams on thirty transports.

Meanwhile, Teams Eleven and Eighteen spearheaded one of the war's least recorded actions—the invasion of Borneo.

16. The Blasting of Balikpapan

RETURNING FROM OKINAWA, TEAM ELEVEN'S TRANSPORT *Kline* tried to pass through the submarine net at Saipan after dark. In the narrow entrance, the *Kline* was accidentally rammed by a tank landing ship—a "Suicide LST," as the kamikaze-weary team promptly named it. There were no casualties, and the damaged ship could be repaired in a month's time. But war is so complex that this small accident in Saipan gave Australian engineers a terrible day and endangered a landing operation, half an ocean away, in Borneo.

A small Japanese fleet still survived in Singapore. Veteran Australian troops had to seize the huge oil-and-rubber-rich island of Borneo before the enemy could destroy its vital war resources or smuggle them through the blockade to reinforce besieged Japan.

At Tarakan and Balikpapan aerial surveys had shown heavy log barricades blocking two of the three chosen Borneo landing areas. Team Eleven was assigned to destroy those underwater blockades. The *Kline's* accident caused the team to be canceled out of the first landing at Tarakan Island. Australian combat engineers were assigned to remove thousands of heavy coconut log pilings and iron rails, solidly sunk in the deep offshore mud. The company of Australian sappers had never faced such a task. They did many things contrary to UDT experience, going up to the obstacles in landing craft, working without a prior reconnaissance. They tried it in daylight without enough fire support, and when they called for a smoke screen it cut down their own efficiency. They struggled waist-deep through mud all morning, and came back bravely to work all afternoon. They blew eight narrow gaps, thirty feet wide, through the barricade. Utterly exhausted, they returned without casualties, simply because the Japanese made no real effort to stop them.

There was luckily no opposition later on, when the assault boats got through the dangerously narrow channels, easy targets for enemy fire. Many of the troops waded through shoulder-deep water and climbed over the barricades. The Japanese, waiting far inshore, missed their chance.

A handful of trained American naval demolition men were available at Tarakan. Four units of six men each, trained at Fort Pierce, stood by in two special infantry landing craft converted for demolition. Lieutenants Frank Kaine, Lloyd Anderson, Bill Culver, and Carpenter George Shinners had been leading their units to clear channels through reefs and sandbars *after* the troop landings, clear across the Southwest Pacific, up the New Guinea coast at Tanahmerah Bay and Biak and Noemfoor, all the way to Leyte and then mopping up the southern Philippines. At Tarakan the beachmaster called them in on P-Day after the troops had landed, ordering them to clear up the three lines of pilings, log floats, steel railroad rails, and hardwood logs which had been left between the Australian sappers' narrow gaps. They cleaned the beach completely before P-Day was over.

Too late for Tarakan, veteran Team Eleven sailed for Leyte to report to the task force, and practice demolition on a hastily erected log barricade modeled after air photos of the Balikpapan barriers.

The team picked up a recruit in the tropics, a small monkey who promptly earned the name of Stud. The mascot's favorite sport was jumping on the back of the ship's cat and riding around the deck like a mad jockey. Stud took easily to life aboard ship, as the team joined the task force of Vice Admiral Daniel Barbey, staging in Morotai for the second assault on Borneo. This would be the capture of Labuan Island and Brunei Bay, on the northwest coast next to Sarawak where the legendary Rajah Brooke had held sway.

Team Eleven's swimmers practiced with unusual enthusiasm at a small island near Morotai, on which they discovered

native women who wore skirts, but above the waist lived up
to the best South Seas travel posters.

Team Eleven's commander, Lou States, was briefed on the
Balikpapan obstacles. When he found that they were heavier
and more numerous than those which occupied six teams at
Okinawa, he urgently requested four additional teams to help.
The high command was already planning for the fall invasion
of Japan, and allotted him only one team, the untried but
thoroughly trained Team Eighteen which would arrive in
time for Balikpapan. States' Team Eleven must handle the
interim Labuan and Brunei Bay operations by itself.

Testing obstacles similar to the Tarakan barriers, States
sent out a hurry call for Hagensen packs. Although these
were now standard items of Navy issue, a year after they had
been improvised for Normandy, the packs were in short
supply in the Pacific. A shipment of more than 5,000 was
finally dispatched by air to meet the teams at Balikpapan.

States' last problem was personal and embarrassing. His
second in command, the team's veteran Executive Officer
Robert Wells, a chief warrant officer, was junior to the team's
commissioned officers, and was still awaiting a deserved and
often recommended promotion to Lieutenant (jg). States
himself had been promoted after Okinawa to Lieutenant
Commander, so that he could have rank enough to command
the demolition task unit of underwater teams, transports,
and assigned gunboats. Now, in the last mail before the fleet
set out, he received official word that through some technical
mistake in Maui, his earlier promotion to Lieutenant was
invalid, and he was actually only a Lieutenant (jg). With that
grade, he would have no right to command the operation,
since almost every officer in his task unit would be senior to
him! Yet he was the only commanding officer in the unit
with demolition experience.

He put the problem up to Rear Admiral A. G. Noble,
commanding the Balikpapan Attack Group, and Rear
Admiral R. S. Riggs, commanding the Support and Covering
Group. While the two admirals gave tacit consent, Admiral

Noble's chief staff officer Captain Solomon solved the difficulty with a judgment worthy of his name: "Don't tell anybody till the job's done."

The acting Lieutenant Commander obeyed the order to the hilt. In the first mail that arrived after Balikpapan was captured, States received a letter authorizing him to assume rank as Lieutenant Commander as soon as an enclosed form was executed. Chief Carpenter Wells received his belated promotion to Lieutenant (jg). All this made everything legal.

The only obstacles facing States' underwater demolition unit at Labuan and Brunei Bay were mines. Borneo had originally been mined by the British and Dutch against the oncoming Japanese. More mines were laid later by British submarines. Then to bottle up the Japanese oil supplies, magnetic mines were sowed wholesale by American planes. When Allied invasion seemed imminent, the Japanese themselves laid new mines.

The minesweepers worked desperately to clear a channel into Brunei Bay but the task was too vast for their timetable. When Team Eleven and its supporting gunboats started work on June 8, two days before the "Zebra" Day for landing, they had to run a 20-mile gauntlet of death through unswept, uncharted minefields.

The "acting" Lieutenant Commander faced a grim problem. He received permission from the task group commander, Rear Admiral R. S. Berkey, to take the supporting gunboats into the minefield within six miles of the target beaches on the south shore of Labuan Island, covering the swimmers with their guns as best they could.

A cruiser and a destroyer took stations in an area cleared the previous day, at extreme range from Labuan Island. In single file, five gunboats set out behind two minesweepers at 0630 on the morning of June 8. Team Eleven was aboard the gunboats—three large support craft and two infantry landing craft, which towed the team's ramped landing craft behind them. As the column approached the entrance to Brunei Bay, the minesweepers and gunboats were surrounded by bobbing mines that had been cut adrift. They had to retrace their path and start again on a different course. The lost time could not be made up, so the schedule was postponed an hour. The change of time was radioed to the support ships, and to the 13th Air Force, bombers already en route from Morotai hundreds of miles away. Such a tight schedule could easily go wrong.

Since the gunboats reached the six-mile point without disaster, States took the responsibility for ordering them another five miles into unswept waters, to within a mile of Labuan's Victoria Harbour. The team embarked in landing craft and followed the gunboats. As the column passed an island south of Labuan, a shore battery fired on them and was promptly silenced.

The gunboats finally stood half a mile off Labuan and shelled the beaches from Victoria Town to Ramsey Point. The cruiser and destroyer contributed their fire from the sea. The first wave of high-altitude Air Force bombers arrived on schedule and dropped strings of 100-pound bombs on the shore line.

The team's craft darted through the gunboat line at 11 A.M., dropping pairs of swimmers 400 yards from shore, more closely bunched and more numerous than usual in order to search the undersea bottom thoroughly. Air photos had showed suspicious spots that appeared to be a field of mines in front of the shore. All the swimmers wore yellow, banana-shaped mine crimpers in their belts, with delayed fuses to be attached to mine horns.

As the swimmers neared shore, Jap snipers in the brush behind the beach began firing. Both flanks took heavy mortar and machine-gun fire from back of Ramsey Point and from the ruins of Victoria Town. The supporting gunboats plastered the beach with 40mm shells, silencing the snipers but not knocking out the hidden guns on both ends of the swimming line. The men swam doggedly ahead, porpoising, keeping under water more than above. They reached the high-water mark within half an hour, and turned parallel to the beach to search the offshore line.

A flight of Royal Australian Air Force Beaufighters swept the beach at treetop level, accurately strafing the sniper area. The swimmers hunted vainly for the supposed mines. Some men even dove onto suspiciously dark patches of bottom, probing the weed and mud with their knives—a fatal test for anyone hitting a mine horn. They found no mines, only small scattered rock, rotted piling stumps, and sea bottom growth.

At 1135, when the swimmers were just about to turn back from the shore line, another flight of 13th Air Force bombers roared overhead at 10,000 feet. The first four planes dropped their 100- and 250-pound bombs on the beach, as did the second quartet. The next four planes were a few yards off course, and dropped more than sixty bombs into the water, along the line of swimmers. Some bombs even fell to seaward of the UDT men.

Lieutenant Commander States urgently radioed to stop the next air strike, though he doubted if the message could get through in time, and pointed his own ramped landing craft in to the beach while the bombing smoke still hid the swimmers. He could soon see that men were in trouble. Some wounded men were towing more seriously injured buddies. Close to shore, several men were waving for help, evidently unable to swim out.

A second landing craft followed States' boat, while the other craft patrolled the pickup line for swimmers who were already well out from the beach. Some men waved the two rescue boats away—they could swim to the pickup line all right, and their teammates nearer shore needed immediate help.

Both rescue boats picked up dazed, exhausted men within fifty yards of shore, while Japanese gunners from the flanks splashed shots near the boats. One man had bomb-shrapnel wounds, others had suffered internal injuries and shock from water-blast concussion. A pair of swimmers waved for help, hardly able to keep afloat, neither buddy able to help

the other. The other rescue boat picked them up while States'
craft headed straight for the enemy beach. A swimmer, too
dazed to stay in the surf, was crawling onto the Japanese
shore.

States ran his craft aground. The man was hastily helped
aboard. The motors reversed. For a horrible moment it
seemed that the landing craft was stuck on the Jap-held beach,
hopelessly aground. Then water boiled under the hull from
the reversed propellers, and the boat surged backward into
deeper water, swirled around and continued on its rescue
mission.

A hasty check-up showed that one man was missing—
Coxswain Charles Masden. His buddy had been dazed by
concussion as several bombs fell near them, and had not seen
Masden since.

One landing craft was stripped to a skeleton crew and vainly
cruised the area under fire for nearly an hour, before States
had to call it back, and head his column of gunboats and
landing craft out to sea. Masden's body was found on the day
of the landings, and he was buried with full military honors
on the beach he had helped win.

Meanwhile the other injured men were getting medical
treatment from the transport *Kline's* doctor, who went with
the team through the minefields. Besides the man wounded
by shrapnel, five others were so badly injured by underwater
concussion that they would have to be hospitalized on the
transport; but their prompt treatment helped them all to
quick recovery.

While the column gingerly retraced its path through the
minefield, States detached one gunboat and two landing craft
full of swimmers and buoys, to make another scheduled
reconnaissance under the team's executive officer, Bob Wells.
Old British charts had shown a deep-water passage through
the mud past Daat Island into the Borneo mainland, near
Klias Point. If this channel was still navigable, troops could

make landings simultaneously on Labuan and the nearby mainland.

The landing craft and their rubber-boat crews of underwater swimmers found a good channel, within a stone's throw of Daat Island. As the men dropped anchored buoys to mark the channel, they spotted uniformed enemies on the island, watching them. The gunboat captain radioed States for permission to bombard the island. States repeated his previous instructions: "Don't start a gun fight unless they shoot first." The UDT mission was to explore and clear the way, not to kill a few unimportant defenders.

The Japs just watched warily, and so did the UDT men with one glance at the shore and the next on the water depths. They charted the channel to Borneo's mainland and got back without damage, rejoining the transport outside the minefield by 6:30 that evening.

One highly unmilitary incident occurred shortly after this reconnaissance. The team's transport *Kline* was moving in a column of ships through a mineswept channel. The team's mascot Stud had become excited during the ships' bombardment of the island. The monkey was still worked up, dashing around the deck. He liked to leap off the stern of the ship, catching the aft rail with his prehensile tail at the last moment. This time he leaped aft, the ship pitched—and his tail missed the rail.

"Monkey overboard!" somebody yelled.

Sure enough, there was Stud, swimming pathetically in the ship's rough wake. Somebody on the signal bridge broke out the "Five Flag"—man overboard.

Contrary to all rules, the ship was stopped. A UDT boat was hastily lowered, to speed back to the frantic monkey. The wet ball of fur was fished out and brought aboard in a dry blanket, as the ship got under way again. Stud got a quick medical check-up and was happily consoled with his favorite meal of mashed potatoes.

When a convoy officer signaled inquiring about the delay, he got the reasonably ethical answer, "Swimmer overboard"

—Stud was certainly swimming. At Admiral Berkey's flag conference that night, States was asked directly what happened.
He said he could think of a dozen reasonable explanations
but had better tell the truth. . . .

Incidentally, the minefield was not always so successfully
cheated. The minesweeper *Salute* hit a mine that day, losing
nine dead and thirty-seven wounded, and sinking.

Team Eleven had no further duty until Z-Day, June 10.
Wave guides steered the landing troops. The veteran Aus-
tralians swept ashore against weak opposition onto Labuan,
onto the Borneo mainland at Klias Point, and onto another
island far across Brunei Bay near Brooketon. The mission
was a complete success.

The team sailed back to Morotai to refit for the final
operation, the capture of Balikpapan near the southeast
corner of Borneo. This rich oil-producing area was guarded
with a most extensive minefield and underwater blockade.
Team Eleven arrived off its shores June 24, joining the newly
arrived Team Eighteen embarked in the destroyer transport *Schmitt*. Under the command of Lieutenant Charles E.
Coombs, Jr., Team Eighteen was facing its first combat
operation. The team had been thoroughly trained for nine
months, and its executive officer, Lieutenant (jg) Lewis F.
Luehrs, was a UDT veteran with Kwajalein, Eniwetok,
Guam, and Leyte battle stars.

Although minesweepers had been working for a week,
they still had more than they could handle during the final
week remaining before "Fox" (F) Day, the July 1 landing
date. Between the minefields and the beaches stood a continuous barrier of coconut and hardwood pilings, staggered
three or four rows deep, braced with slanting logs, bolted
together by heavy log crosspieces to make a solid, boat-
tight fence. In many places the fence was interlaced and
tied together with wire cable, and mined.

In addition, air photos showed regular straight lines of
round black marks along the surf edge—thousands of omi-
nous spots that could be mines. Lieutenant Commander

States believed they were broken-off stumps of old pilings; there couldn't be that many mines in the world—he hoped. Luckily he was right. But in each of the two mile-long areas which the two teams must clear, the busy Japanese had driven more than three thousand posts solidly into the hard sand. Using improvised bamboo-frame piledrivers and unlimited enslaved native labor, they had completed a continuous barricade some thirty to fifty yards from the high-water mark. They were well along with constructing a second line of fence in deeper water off several beaches when the fleet arrived.

The two teams first hit the beach a dozen miles north of Balikpapan itself. They made a full-scale demonstration on the beaches of Manggar and Manggar-Ketjil, reconnoitering the underwater obstacles on June 25 and returning the next day to demolish the fences.

Even this far from Balikpapan's oil refineries, the smoke from burning, bombarded oil dumps drifted so thickly over the shore that Team Eighteen had difficulty finding its beaches for the first day's reconnaissance. The unswept minefields held both teams' gunboats too far from the shore, and there was less covering fire than usual.

As the swimmers approached one beach, they could hear birds singing. The men commented bitterly that they preferred the zing of 40mm fire over their heads, protecting them. Luckily the Japanese hidden ashore did very little shooting, either suspecting this was only a feint, or waiting for the actual landing assault.

Two of the Team Eleven swimmers had a close call, however. Ensign "Truck" Deiner, the team's veteran fuse puller, and his regular swim buddy George Bender, swam toward the beach and its dark curtain of drifting oil smoke behind the palm trees, exploring the half-submerged lines of log fence. When they were almost to the breaking surf line, they split up to swim in opposite directions parallel to the beach, looking for the suspected line of mines.

Deiner marked his starting point by a lone stump in the middle of the sandy beach. He swam a few moments looking under water through his face mask, then quickly checked the beach. He was still opposite the stump. He figured there must be an unexpectedly strong rip tide along shore. He swam strongly, as every fuse puller can, and kept glancing at the marker ashore.

The stump raised up on two legs and started following him.

Deiner went under like a sounding whale, and turned to sea. He swam under water as long as his breath lasted, surfaced for a quick backward look, then dove again. He kept porpoising, to offer as poor a target as possible to the sniper ashore. When he last looked back, on his way to the boat pickup line, the stump was still hopefully waiting on the beach.

All the men got back with their underwater information. That night, four Japanese Bettys tried to attack the minesweepers. The planes dove so close to the ships that they passed between them. Team Eleven's taffrail machine guns jammed. Team Eighteen's gunners, however, were sure they scored hits on one plane, which splashed. A destroyer's gunners got the credit, however. The Japanese pilots were not kamikaze-minded, and the survivors fled.

By morning the sea, which had been calm during the reconnaissance, was choppy with whitecaps. The teams set out in their landing craft, dropping swimmers on one side and their strings of explosive packs on the other. Each man swam his floating charges, buoyed with life belts, to the beach barrier line several hundred yards away. One or two double-sized charges had to be put on every post, and primacord was strung despite the waves rolling through the fence.

Air strikes by bombers and fighters were perfectly timed, making up for the mishap at Labuan. The resulting light enemy fire caused no casualties. The team's control craft spotted a coast defense gun emplacement, which the ships duly clobbered on request. The green smoke signals flared; the fuse pullers fired their charges. Two towering columns of water and debris climbed into the sky and fell back, disclosing two 800-yard gaps through the barricade.

Back aboard ship, Team Eighteen had to launch one landing craft again at five that afternoon, to rescue seven survivors from a minesweeper which had struck a mine.

The brave little sweeps, too few at the start and constantly dwindling in number as they hit mines, were a long way from finishing their preliminary task in front of the main beaches farther south. The next day was F minus four, June 27. The minesweepers reported a circuitous route by which the gunboats and landing craft might approach the intended landing beaches.

Wind and seas were high. Heavy rain and the overhanging pall of oil smoke obscured the beach. Guided by radar, the blind column of seven gunboats followed by the teams' landing craft wove through the minefield until they were a mile and a half from the Klandasan beaches, where two thousand yards of landing beach had to be explored and cleared by the two teams. Klandasan was a settled area facing west onto the ocean, in front of Balikpapan which faced a bay to the south.

States radioed that he assumed the air support was weathered out, and got the unexpected answer that the first waves were approaching the target. The same 13th Air Force Squadron which had accidentally bombed UDT swimmers at Labuan now made up for it by blasting the beaches. Waves of B-24 bombers and B-25 strafers hit on schedule. To the teams' relief and delight, the bombers risked flying close to the treetops to drop their sticks of bombs accurately inshore.

As the landing craft approached closer to shore, they began to pick out landmarks through the haze—houses, pillboxes, a radar on a hill. Lieutenant Coombs' on-the-spot comment was: "The beach looked like the San Francisco Embarcadero —Borneo style. It was not without some qualms that we began that operation. The Aussies were fearful that it couldn't be done, and we didn't discourage them too much."

The sky was dark with smoke and shellbursts ashore. Pipelines had been observed running onto the beach, and it was mistakenly feared that the Japs would use oil to flood the sea and burn the demolition men alive. The men were briefed on methods of swimming in burning oil, such as using a splashing breast stroke to clear a path ahead.

The fire the swimmers did face was bad enough, however. Heavy gunfire from the hill ridges behind the beach started landing near the boats and the swimmers, proving that the Japanese were determined to hold the oil fields.

At first the swimmers thought the splashes in the water were "shorts" from their own heavy covering fire. It had happened before. Urgent orders were radioed to lift the support fire farther onto the shore. The splashes only got thicker. The Japanese weren't cooperating.

The swimmers kept on. The water seemed warmer than the rain-swept air. The "splashes" got one man. Ensign Frank Jameson, who had been bitten by a moray eel while spear-fishing during Hawaii training, took a worse bite from a Japanese mortar which burst underneath him, lifting him out of the water. Although suffering from concussion, he re-fused to be evacuated, directing his men while they finished the reconnaissance. Only then did he let himself be carried out to the sickbay to be treated for blast concussion.

Despite the murky water due to the storm, the swimmers measured the depths and bottom carefully, using paddle boards and measured line. They found there were no mines, only broken stumps of old pilings. But the barrier fence was new and heavy, most of the posts being a foot thick, and much more numerous than expected.

The Hagensen packs had arrived by air in the nick of time. Thousands of tetrytol blocks were also prepared with special ties. Bladder and life-belt floats were tied to the haversacks filled with charges. The loads to be placed on posts and cross-pieces were increased to insure destruction.

Even the weather cooperated the next day. Just before dawn of June 28, it was bright moonlight when the ex-plosive-laden teams set out with their column of gunboats. They wove through the minefield channels. The gunboats ventured as close as half a mile from shore, anchoring to keep from drifting into the unswept minefields on either side, and opened heavy fire on the beaches. Immediately Japanese shore batteries blazed away at them—only to be answered by the cruisers and destroyers from three and four miles out to sea.

Seven landing craft sped toward the beach, deep-laden with explosive packs, inflated rubber boats, and motored flying mattresses for pickup work. From the ridges, enemy guns and mortars opened intense fire on the incoming craft. The enemy's 3-inch shellbursts came dangerously close, but it was the smaller 37mm fire that scored hits.

Three of the teams' ramped craft were hit in quick succession. One shell went through a boat above the waterline. Two other shells hit boats and exploded aboard. Luckily both shells penetrated rubber flying mattresses before they exploded, and these cushioned the shrapnel. Although one of the supporting gunboats was so badly hit that it had to retire temporarily, the ramped landing craft ran very close to the barricades before dropping swimmers and packs.

The now-beloved B-24s made a low-level bombing run along the beaches. Fighter strafing plus steadily increased ship gunfire reduced the enemy fire still further. Still the Japanese managed to keep up a harassing fire on the gunboats and landing craft.

Near the barricades, the swimmers ran into enemy mortar fire. The splashes came close; one man was seriously injured by concussion. Busily the powdermen fastened their packs to the posts. At this stage of the tide, the pilings stood half out of water, so that the men alternately had to duck under water to tie a pack at the foot of a post, then shinny or be boosted up to load a crosspiece.

While the men were working under fire against time, they spotted a dog running up and down the beach, obviously terrified at the two-way bombardment. Several men eagerly whistled at the dog, hoping to lure him through the few yards of surf to "safety" with them. But he ran away.

It was 1025 before both teams were ready to fire their delay fuses. The swimmers streaked out to sea while the two teams' fuse pullers fired their detonators. Deiner and his buddy had barely pulled their ten-minute fuse assembly and started swimming away, when an enemy mortar shell landed squarely on a pack atop a post. Team Eleven's eight hundred yards of beach instantly erupted. The underwater concussion was brutal. Luckily Deiner and his buddy Bender were both swimming on their backs, and their vital organs took less of a shock. Both men were able to keep swimming, ducking under, after the blast, to avoid the resulting rain of debris. The pickup boat sped in to get them. The tough pair refused hospitalization.

Team Eighteen's "shot" went off on schedule without an assist from the enemy. When the smoke cleared, another 800-yard gap could be seen. Enemy fire increased against the pickup craft and gunboats, so a white phosphorus smoke screen was fired onto the beach, along with heavy fire on the enemy battery. Thereafter the blinded Japanese fired wide of their targets.

Between the areas cleared by the two overburdened teams, a 300-yard stretch of untouched fence still blocked the middle of the beach. Although landing waves could surely squeeze through the two cleared 800-yard gaps on either side, Lieutenant Commander States wrestled with his duty while he granted the exhausted teams a day's rest on Fox minus two. Both short-handed teams had been fully committed on four successive days under fire. The tension building up to any combat swim was terrific; the men had been told that one demolition mission at Balikpapan would be all. They had let down, relaxed. States' exec, Wells, was sure the men couldn't take any more.

States knew that Admiral Noble's approaching assault fleet was observing radio silence, so he concluded his demolition report to the Admiral with the tricky poser:

"Swimmers are exhausted and unless specifically directed otherwise I will consider preassault demolition on Klandasan completed. In any event cannot meet schedule tomorrow. Will dispatch you early 29 June as to physical ability this unit to operate."

He knew the Admiral would be unlikely to break radio silence in submarine-infested waters to radio any direct order sending the UDT men back to the barriers.

All day States kept studying the obstacles, his men's condition, and his duty to the Australian assault troops. Finally he decided to try to lead the men back the next day, Fox minus one. Lieutenant Coombs offered to take his own team instead, but States pulled his supposed rank and scheduled his more experienced Team Eleven, borrowing a couple of tons of explosives from Coombs' supply. Late that afternoon he ordered his team to prepare packs for another day's demolition to complete the job. He and Wells watched for signs of morale weakening or combat fatigue.

"They had as much p——s and vinegar that last day as any time," States reports. "Whenever the men had a job to do, they went at it like stomping snakes!"

Once more, on the morning of June 30, Team Eleven started back through the minefield toward the central barricade. Many of the men, including Conrad and Higgins who had distinguished themselves at Okinawa, were swimming toward the enemy's Borneo beaches for the fifth time in six days. They did not hesitate as they towed their strings of explosive packs. They even noted with satisfaction how the fleet's continuing bombardment had cut down the previous days' volume of fire from the shore, although mortars and snipers kept trying to hit them and their boats.

The skilled demolition men loaded the 300 yards of crisscrossed posts, and retired safely within an hour, without a single casualty. The green smoke signal flared, Deiner swam back to sea—and a few minutes later, the last enemy underwater barrier blew skyward, towering above the ever-present dark pall of burning oil ashore.

On Fox Day, July 1, the UDT guides in guide boats, a hundred yards in advance of the first landing craft waves, led the veteran Australian "Rats of Tobruk" toward shore, until the troops were safely pointed into their exact beach areas a thousand yards ahead.

The left flank started moving too far left. Instead of trying to correct them with signals, the UDT guide boat sped up alongside and forced the whole line to the right where they belonged. The guide boat stayed with the wave almost to the beach, under all the fire the enemy could throw.

The tough Australian troops drove through the enemy fire, running into stronger opposition inshore but driving ahead. At 1130, General MacArthur, Vice Admiral Barbey, Rear Admiral Noble, General Morshead of the 1st Australian Corps, and Air Marshal Bostock of the RAAF landed on the firmly established beachhead, in token that "Operation Oboe" was a success.

The battle continued inland. Team Eleven had some more work during the next three days, including an unscheduled boat survey inside enemy-held Balikpapan Harbor itself. The newly captured Sepinggan Beach, halfway between the beaches the teams had already cleared, had to be stripped of its log barrier so that heavy equipment could land to repair the airfield. In the last UDT demolition operation of the war, appropriately enough on July 4, five hundred yards of hard-built log fence was blown up in an hour.

For "extraordinary heroism" at Okinawa, Brunei Bay, and Balikpapan, Team Eleven was awarded UDT's second Presidential Unit Citation (Team Twelve received the same citation for Iwo and Okinawa). It was the third awarded to Naval Combat Demolition Units (the Omaha Beach units had earlier received the same award for their Normandy ordeal).

17. Samurai Surrender to Naked Warrior!

FROM FORT PIERCE TO THE PHILIPPINES, THIRTY UNDERWATER Demolition Teams were on the move, preparing for the November assault on eighty miles of code-named beaches in Japan's home islands. Casualty estimates for the invasion ranged up to a million from kamikaze and suicide submarine attack, from massive coast defenses, from the bulk of the surviving Japanese armies and the last-ditch stand of a dedicated citizenry. Ships and troops would face a hot reception; but the waters would be bitterly cold for UDT swimmers. Their mild foretaste at Okinawa led to elaborate plans for cold-water training to start August 15, 1945, at Oceanside and Morro Bay, California. Swimmers would be clad in long wool underwear, underneath watertight rubber suits.

The underwater clan gathered from amphibious training bases in Maui, Fort Pierce, and the Philippines; from advance bases in Okinawa and Guam and Ulithi; and from their recent impressive demonstration of peak wartime efficiency in the Borneo mop-up.

Captain Rodgers was now Commander of Underwater Demolition Teams and Underwater Demolition Flotilla, Amphibious Forces, U.S. Pacific Fleet, and of a Task Group for the Kyushu operation. He completed a Top Secret operation plan even longer than his titles—151 mimeographed pages with 36 charts and diagrams covering flotilla operations and movements, reconnaissance and demolition procedure, intelligence, fire support, communications, minesweeping, air support, logistics; the amazingly detailed and complex schedule needed to operate this single task group, in dovetailed and perfectly timed coordination with every other Navy, Army, and Marine phase of the assault. Amphibious warfare had become a real science under the Pacific Amphibious Force Commander, Admiral Turner. Under him, Vice Admirals Barbey, Wilkinson, and Hill would carry the troops of General of the Army MacArthur to the shores of Japan. Admiral Halsey and the Third Fleet was to operate north of Tokyo. Admiral Spruance with the Fifth Fleet commanded all naval operations south to the Philippines. Fleet Admiral Nimitz exercised over-all command of the mightiest force ever assembled.

Three thousand trained demolition men braced for a "Sunday punch" they never had to deliver. Japan was nearer defeat than America could know. Its war industry and resources were crippled by naval blockade, USN submarine attacks, and by the continuous fire raids of long-range Air Force bombers, using bases which the UDT had in their small but vital way helped to open in the Marianas, Iwo, the Philippines, and now Okinawa.

On August 10, after suffering the first and second atomic bombs, Japan openly sued for peace. As one small, immediate aftereffect, Captain Rodgers in two days rewrote his elaborate operation plan to schedule his teams for occupation instead of invasion. Peace became official on August 14. The UDT cold-water training didn't start on August 15 as scheduled. Instead, on that day, Lieutenant Commanders Coombs and Clayton took Teams Eighteen and Twenty-one aboard C-54 transport planes to Guam, thence by fast transports to Tokyo where the Third Fleet was gathering.

Clayton's team had the rare privilege of being the first Navy personnel to land on the Japanese homeland on August 29, just one day after troops had landed by plane to seize Tokyo's airport. Team Twenty-one made a quick reconnaissance of mines at the harbor approach, and unloaded from their landing craft at Futtsu Saki in Tokyo Bay. As Commander Clayton approached Fort Number One, its commander ceremoniously surrendered his Samurai sword.

With equal ceremony the surprised UDT officer accepted it, both as a token of surrender and as a priceless souvenir.

Word leaked out, and Clayton was later required to give up the sword. Nothing must mar the historic "first" of the surrender ceremony to General MacArthur aboard the battleship *Missouri*. But history's erasers often leave marks on the blackboard. UDT was there first—Samurai surrender to naked warrior!

That first day the team surveyed beaches and wharves for the Marine occupation troops landing to follow. On shipboard, the men had painted a large "demolition banner" which faced the incoming troops. Naturally it read: WELCOME, MARINES!

The Marines landed on UDT's "red carpet" the next day to occupy Yokosuka, while Team Eighteen scouted the Naval Base and erected their own banner of triumph. Sixteen Army divisions and six Marine divisions were en route from all over the Pacific for occupation duty. So were the demolition teams, all gathering for the "kill."

Peace came as a welcome anticlimax to the UDT men bracing for their biggest assault. Immediately everybody started playing the "point game," counting up their medals and months of overseas service to see how soon they could be released from service. A most unwelcome anticlimax was the arrival of a fleet of the too-familiar destroyer transports off the California coast, along with orders to embark for the Orient.

Ten teams remained at Fort Pierce, Oceanside, and Maui, along with five new teams finishing their training. The Maui base began to close down. Pioneer UDT officer Commander John Koehler, who had been supervising Maui training and doctrine through the war, returned to the States, where he later became Assistant Secretary of the Navy.

Eighteen teams sailed west, looking regretfully back at the V-J Day fireworks still filling the California sky behind them. The ships were divided into two squadrons. One squadron under Captain Williams would prepare docks and

beaches and dismantle coast defenses, for the occupation of
Japan. The other, under Captain J. B. Cleland, USNR,
would do the same for harbors in Korea and China. Captain
Rodgers hoisted his broad command pennant in Guam and
sailed directly to Tokyo.

The most famous figure in naval demolition wasn't there.
Commander Kauffman, who would have operated a group
in an actual invasion, had gone to Washington, originally
to expedite cold-water equipment, then on a long-delayed
month's leave. He was traveling on carte-blanche "temporary
duty" orders he had written himself for Admiral Turner's
signature. Unwilling to be left out of the final operation in
Japan, Kauffman caught priority flights all the way across
the Pacific, keeping just one jump ahead of Captain Rodgers'
orders canceling his vague "temporary duty." He reached
Japan just in time to join Team Eighteen in the combat-
style reconnaissance and demolition of the suicide boat
flotilla at Katsuyama, ahead of the troops. Ten days later
Kauffman returned to San Diego aboard "Scotty" Cooper's
transport to set up a permanent postwar UDT base on the
Coronado beach of the U.S. Naval Amphibious Base. (He
later realized his life's ambition to become a regular Navy
officer and is currently Captain, USN, serving as Naval
Advisor and Aide to the Undersecretary of the Navy.)

Two of the new team commanders were veterans of naval
combat but new to demolition. They command the Atlantic
and Pacific units at the date of this writing, Commander
David Saunders and Commander Francis Douglas Fane.

"Red" Fane completed UDT training at Fort Pierce, becoming Commanding Officer of UDT 13 for the planned
invasion of Japan. In a rounded Navy career commencing
in 1940, Fane had seen combat in the "Med," the Aleutians,
and the Pacific, on cruiser, destroyer, oiler, carrier, assault
transport, and finally as navigator of an ammunition ship
appropriately named after a Hawaiian volcano, the *Mauna
Loa*. When he determined to use the explosives himself
instead of ferrying them to others, there was one drawback to

his volunteering for Underwater Demolition—he couldn't swim. "That's why I volunteered for UDT," he says. "It seemed to be a last chance to fulfill a lifelong desire." He learned to swim across a pool in a Chicago YMCA, in order to honestly report at Fort Pierce as a "qualified swimmer."

The teams spent a busy September and part of October clearing beaches and harbors, demolishing wrecks, and preparing landing ramps. They inspected coast defense guns, and ripped out their breech blocks or blew them up wherever the Japanese garrison had not already dismantled them. They found hundreds of midget submarines, one-man torpedoes, and plywood suicide craft, which they destroyed with fire, blowtorch, or by towing strings of them to sea to be sunk in the "deep six" demolition treatment. It was a long time before they could round out their reconnaissance by an unofficial survey of geisha girls.

Right after the first landings in Japan, teams moved on to Korea and China to scout landing places for the waiting Army and Marines. One such reconnaissance had far more significance than was guessed at the time. Orders came after August 25 to cancel proposed Otomari (Karafuto) landings north of the main islands, as that area and Korea north of the 38th parallel had been assigned to the Russians for occupation. Just south of the not-yet-famous 38° line, two teams entered a Korean harbor on September 8 for the landing of the 24th Army Corps. Thousands of Koreans, in their then unfamiliar white garb, watched from hills and housetops. Teams Nine and Twelve tried to reach a small island named Wolmi Do but were stopped by mud, having to wait four hours till the 30-foot tide rose enough to cover the mud flats and let them get ashore to raise the "Demolition Flag" of welcome. They officially commented: "Difficulty of assault landings over beaches experiencing extreme tidal changes. . . . The mud bottom would not support vehicles. . . . Craft could be landed only at high tide except at established piers, making such an operation, if carried out against opposition, extremely difficult."

This harbor was then called by the Japanese name, Jinsen. Almost exactly five years later, another Underwater Demolition Team would be outside that harbor with a Navy fleet and Army-filled transports facing that muddy, tide-swept harbor. On that day General MacArthur made it world-famous under its Korean spelling—Inchon.

Nobody had any thought then of any future challenge to the world's mightiest air-sea-land military machine. No opposition or treachery marred the work of the small advance units. Typical of their operations was their reception on China's Shantung Peninsula, paving the way for Marine occupation of territory last visited in force during the Boxer Rebellion. A reception committee met the ramped landing craft at Tsingtao. The Chinese commander, who had taken over a big Japanese suicide-boat base, bowed, exchanged engraved calling cards with Captain Cleland, and officially conducted him about the base. This made sufficient impression to be noted in the official report by the UDT squadron commander. No official report was made of the additional Tsingtao reception committee made up of two beautiful White Russian girls who watched until the captain was on his way, then approached the other visiting UDT men with an equally hospitable offer to take them on a conducted tour of the city.

Despite such novelties, the demolition men were homesick. Team after team completed its duties and boarded ship. But it was no easy job to get back across the Pacific. Typhoon after typhoon struck Japan and China. Captain Rodgers' flagship had barely reached Okinawa when he had to escort part of the fleet westward to sea, away from the United States, to ride out one particularly close typhoon.

At long last, the final teams managed to get back to the States, late in October. Medals and citations, which had been chasing the fast-moving officers and men for two years, were officially awarded by Captain Rodgers. The teams were decommissioned, the great majority of the men being released to "inactive duty"—back to civilian life. A handful of demolition men stayed in the underwater service because they loved it, forming the nucleus of the postwar teams.

First Lieutenant Frank Lahr, USMCR, The Marine, who had stayed with Team Three throughout the war and was now its executive officer, second in command during the occupation of Japan, wanted to stay with UDT. Back in Coronado, he asked Commander Kauffman to help straighten out his dubious status. Kauffman interceded with the commanding Marine general, who ordered Lieutenant Lahr back to regular Marine duties—no transfer would be permitted!

One of the UDT officers (who may prefer to be nameless) had saved up some $4,000 in back pay. He invited all the UDT men in Coronado to a farewell party. The manager of the swank Del Coronado Hotel was briefed about the work the UDTs had done—their achievements were still a secret from most of the public. The manager turned over three suites in a corner of the hotel, with special advance warning to the obliging guests above and below. Nine admirals were living in the hotel at the time. One admiral launched the party with a magnum of champagne; three gallons of milk and six gallons of brandy were combined in a punch to get the celebration strongly under way. Kauffman kept a duty section at the UDT base, letting half the personnel off duty at any given time. A sober officer was especially stationed outside the suites' one unlocked door—this duty was regularly rotated, of course.

Giving his $4,000 to the hotel manager, the UDT host said only: "Tell us when the party's over."

The victory party lasted twelve riotous days—an unforgettable celebration of the end of America's greatest war, months after most of the country had celebrated V-J Day.

Following World War II, the reduction of funds available forced the Navy to draw in its belt. Demobilization proceeded at a near-frenzied pace in the armed forces. In the Navy Department, however, cool judgment prevailed. Outstanding officers gathered together to recount their experiences and from this well of knowledge to write up plans for the conduct of future naval warfare. Many high naval officers who merited retirement and rest spent months in the Navy Department preparing tactical publications embodying the lessons that had been learned during World War II.

In the fall of 1945 at the Amphibious Base in Coronado, Captain (now Admiral) R. H. Rodgers gathered his UDT skippers together for the last time before releasing them. He outlined the plans for an operation and training manual for the guidance of future Underwater Demolition Teams. Several groups of officers sat down and thrashed out chapter after chapter of plans and instructions; the details of preparing time fuses and firing devices, how to swim through heavy surf, how to swim into an enemy beach at night, how to place a demolition charge on a horned scully in order to blow it flat, how to call for naval gunfire support and air strikes; each minute detail of the manner of conducting UDT combat operations was explained by the veterans of combat, by those who had the real know-how. Finally in the spring of 1946 Captain Rodgers completed the *Underwater Demolition Team Training Manual*, the encyclopedia for the new breed of underwater swimmers.

As has been true following every war, there was a cry from the politicians to return the mother's son to the mother's breast, to slash to the bone the appropriations of the armed forces; politically the watchword was "peace," expected to last for decades. Funds for the Navy were ruthlessly cut, the belt was drawn in tighter and tighter. Hundreds of Navy ships were decommissioned, but the Navy ordered them moth-balled ready for immediate service on some future Dog-Day.

The ax fell on UDT as it did on many of the smaller "specialized units" bred by World War II. The flotilla of 30 transports and Underwater Demolition Teams which had been assembled for the assault invasion of Japan was cut to four. Two teams commanded by Lieutenant Commander Cooper were assigned to Commander Amphibious Force,

Pacific Fleet; two teams commanded by Lieutenant Commander Fane to the Commander Amphibious Force, Atlantic Fleet. By 1948 the four UDT teams had a skeleton complement of 7 officers and 45 men each. With this small force they had to prepare for possible future wars, and try to maintain a combat readiness.

18. Korean Mines and Guerrillas

> *But above all, it is men—men of the fleet—who will win our future battles by working together with skill and enthusiasm toward a common goal.*
>
> ADMIRAL ARLEIGH A. BURKE, USN

TWO MEN MADE THE FIRST UDT RECONNAISSANCE IN THE Korean War. Lieutenant (jg) George Atcheson III, USN, and McCormick, QM3/c of postwar Team Three had to find out whether 10,000 desperately needed reinforcements could land on a shallow beach beside the fishing village of Pohang. The excellent port of Pusan, at the tip end of Korea, was hopelessly overloaded with troops and supplies of the 24th and 25th Infantry Divisions rushing to aid the overwhelmed South Korean troops.

Less than three weeks earlier, on June 25, 1950, five years of uneasy peace had ended with a bang. During those five years, a great debate had raged in military and civilian circles throughout America concerning the conduct of future warfare. Again and again the advocates of push-button warfare claimed, "The battleship and aircraft carrier are obsolete! The days of fleet action are over." Self-styled strategists said, "Foot soldiers have no place in modern warfare." Just before Korea burst into flame, one high military official declared, "We do not need an amphibious force because there never will be another amphibious landing!"

Our responsible Navy officers, many of whom at Okinawa had faced and defeated the most concentrated aerial attack ever launched against a fleet, consisting of guided missiles piloted by fanatical humans, were not now to be panicked by the fear of Buck Rogers weapons. They trained their men for war as they knew it, and soon after the Korean attack launched a mighty counteroffensive which swept to military victory.

It is probably not generally realized that the U.S. Naval Amphibious Force is our only weapons system designed *solely for the offensive.* An amphibious assault is our fleet's combat "Sunday punch." Because of the tremendous concentration of power in ships, guns, aircraft, and men which can be brought to bear at a point of our naval commander's choosing, the amphibious assault has never been defeated.

Soon after the invasion of Korea, General MacArthur in Tokyo, as Commander in Chief, Allied Occupation Forces, Far East (CINCFE), held council of war. Troops and supplies in huge quantities must be landed to hold the line against the Communists and their Russian armament. Only two large seaports were available, Pusan and Inchon. Pusan was hopelessly overloaded. On July 4, just nine days after the initial aggression by the Reds, MacArthur was planning an amphibious assault on Inchon. The fast-moving attack of the North Koreans ruled this plan out—for the time being.

Since no seaports were available, it was decided to land over the beach of Pohang, seventy miles north of Pusan, if UDT reconnaissance showed it could be used. South Korean ROK (Republic of Korea) troops had just beaten off a Red advance guard not many miles north of Pohang, when Lieutenant Atcheson flew into the village on July 10 with a Marine amphibious landing expert and the future Navy beachmaster of Pohang.

Atcheson, born and raised in China where his father was ambassador, had been in Japan when war broke out, routinely training a ten-man UDT detachment with the Army in amphibious landing techniques. Now he must put his training into practice. Atcheson was a powerful swimmer, good at demolition, aggressive but cool under fire. Other UDT men described him with their highest praise: "a good operations man."

After sounding the depths of a narrow channel into Pohang village, Atcheson and his colleagues moved on to a sandy beach half a mile long. Through an interpreter, the friendly fishermen warned that the offshore water was shallow. Atcheson stripped to trunks, fins, and mask, and plunged into the water with a sounding line. He found that the sea-bottom slope in front of the beach was barely usable —small landing craft must drop troops in waist-deep water, while the larger tank landing ships would ground so far offshore that pontoon causeways would be required. But providing good weather and smooth surf prevailed, a landing would be possible.

Then too, "We owned the real estate"—the natives were friendly, there would be no fighting on the beach. Under such conditions the operation was termed "an administrative landing." If the North Koreans broke through to Pohang before the troops arrived, it would be an "assault landing"— a tough proposition on this beach for troops new to amphibious landings.

The UDT reconnaissance report was favorably received. The amphibious force commander, Rear Admiral James H. Doyle, a veteran of Tulagi and Guadalcanal, gave the Army's famous 1st Cavalry Division a hurried "dress rehearsal" in amphibious landing, and ferried the troops and their thousands of tons of vehicles and supplies from Sasebo to Pohang. The ROK troops held firm north of Pohang, against increasing Red pressure. On July 18, the amphibious force landed the dismounted cavalry, fully equipped for combat, across that half mile of beach in one day. Ten thousand fresh troops boarded trains at Pohang, and two days later met and repelled the Communist advance. This outstanding example of Army-Navy teamwork, employing the so-called "obsolete" weapons of troops and ships, saved the day in Korea.

But the war raged on. Korea is a mountainous land, great rugged ranges spread out from the interior to the sea. The main highways and railroads, on which the North Koreans were dependent for transport of military supplies, followed the shore line and in some places clung to the cliffs at the water's edge. U.S. Navy ships and aircraft cruised up and down the coast bombarding and bombing the bridges and tunnels, strafing the long lines of military vehicles and trains, and even blasting cliffs to pour landslides across the vital highways.

Vice Admiral C. Turner Joy, Commander of Naval Forces, Far East (COMNAVFE), conceived the idea of organizing small amphibious raiding parties to harass the enemy by dynamiting their supply routes.

To his great surprise, the junior-ranking Lieutenant (jg) Atcheson, as the earliest UDT officer on the scene, was summoned to a conference with Admiral Joy and Admiral Doyle in General MacArthur's headquarters. They decided to raid Yosu on the south coast—an important seaport with a railroad, now forty-five miles behind the enemy's front lines which were squeezing the Pusan beachhead. It would be the first of a series of such assignments for the demolition teams, usually prefaced by the words: "The admiral wants a ten-hand working party."

Yosu looked vulnerable with three bridges and a tunnel only 300 yards from the water. The high-speed destroyer transport *Diachenko*, which had carried a UDT team in the occupation of "Jinsen" (Inchon) five years before, now dropped a ramped landing craft off Yosu just after midnight of August 5. Guided by the ship's radio, boat officer Lieutenant W. L. Thede approached the enemy shore with muffled exhaust, then dropped a rubber-boatload of men and explosives.

Atcheson and Boatswain's Mate Warren Foley swam ahead of the boat for the last 200 yards, going ashore to make sure that the coast was clear. Atcheson carried a waterproofed pistol and four hand grenades. The pair climbed the steep 35-foot sea wall from the rocky beach, and approached the bridge at the north end of the tunnel. All was quiet, but the moon was rising. Only too clearly they could see the rubber boat and landing craft and the *Diachenko*. Atcheson sent Foley back in a hurry to guide the men and explosives ashore.

As if on cue, a patrol of North Koreans, armed with rifles, rolled out of the tunnel on a handcar. They stopped, and stared out to sea. Atcheson crouched under the trestle, ten feet below them, watching to see what the "gooks" would do. The patrol flashed lights onto the beach. As Atcheson reported later, "All hands were 'shook.' "

Foley waded out to meet the incoming rubber boat, grabbed a Thompson sub-machine gun and hurried back to help the trapped officer, followed by Austin and McCormick from the boat. Atcheson was meanwhile climbing silently up the slope behind the patrol. He lobbed a hand grenade at the patrol and another into the tunnel. The enemy started firing. Foley scrambled onto the sea wall and started running toward the bridge. Atcheson took him for another Red, and, as he tells it:

"I fired on Foley and so did the 'gooks.' I missed, they hit him. He fell off the wall. The gooks were behind the tracks. I poked my head over the rails and Austin shot my hat off."

Foley was wounded in the hand and leg, and bruised by his 35-foot fall onto the rocks below the wall. McCormick carried Foley to the boat. Atcheson and the others somehow made it by paddling furiously to the landing craft, which swept in to within 75 yards of shore while under fire. The raid resulted in the Navy's first battle casualty of the Korean War.

The admirals were not discouraged. A stronger raiding party was organized. Team One's commanding officer, Lieutenant Commander D. F. "Kelly" Welch, arriving with the 1st Provisional Marine Brigade, joined forces with Marine Major Edward Dupras. Atcheson was one of the attached UDT officers, along with junior grade Lieutenants P. A. Wilson and Edwin P. Smith. Altogether, the impromptu group of "commandos" numbered 25 UDTs and 16 Marines.

The Marines would establish a defense perimeter on the beach around the target, and the UDT explosives experts would do the job they loved, blowing things up.

Embarked in the destroyer transport *Horace A. Bass*, the raiders cruised up the east coast 160 miles, well above the North Korean border. Just below Tanchon, a railroad bridge and two tunnel mouths close to the sea offered a tempting target for demolition.

With Lieutenant Commander Welch in charge of the landing craft, seven rubber boats loaded with Marines, UDT men, and explosives approached the beach midnight of August 12. Although they chose a moonless night, lights and activity around the tunnels made it impossible to place their explosives without discovery, and they had to return to the ship.

The next day the ship moved north to another tunnel and track section which looked promising from the aerial photos. At night the crew started out again, their faces camouflaged black and green. They were loaded down with packs, fuses, and weapons. This time the tunnel area was quiet as the rubber boats beached; sentries could not be seen.

Suddenly one lean North Korean guard, startled by coming upon Lieutenant Smith, turned tail and ran, dropping his "weapon": a wooden rifle with a bayonet lashed to the muzzle. As the men moved up to the target, they were forced to take cover due to a passing freight train—a "tabu" target, as nothing must distract them from their main demolition mission. When the tunnel entrance and about a hundred feet of the track had been loaded with a ton of TNT, the defense and demolition personnel were withdrawn to the beach, except for Major Dupras, the UDT lieutenants, and two others. Wilson and Atcheson pulled the long-delayed fuse, then all ran for the beach. The boats got away safely, to watch a brilliant explosion wreck the tunnel mouth.

The raiders returned the next night to the scene of their first attempt. There was no enemy patrol. But in one of the concrete pillboxes guarding the tunnel, the raiders discovered four North Koreans, seemingly a family who were taking shelter for the night. They had picked a poor hotel. The raiders, unable to turn them loose for fear they'd sound the alarm, took the luckless quartet a safe distance from the coming explosion, and tied them loosely enough so that they could escape later. The demolition crew finished loading the tunnel. All hands got away in their rubber boats before 2 A.M., when a towering explosion shook the night, completely destroying the main tunnel and the bridge.

After taking other bridges in their stride, the *Bass* and its lethal crew cruised far north within thirty miles of Chongjin to tackle a rail bridge and a highway bridge side by side some two hundred yards inland. Understandably cocky from their recent successes, all hands relaxed their usual strict habit of silence. Major Dupras, after repeated warnings to the men to remain silent, decided that drastic measures must be taken. He clambered upon the railway trestle and shouted "QUIET!" at the top of his voice. The men were so startled that the entire operation was completed in shocked silence.

During this raid the party received an unusual assist from the *Bass*. The ship spotted headlights moving north along the coast highway. Knowing that the vehicles must pass over the highway bridge, the ship reported the interloper to Major Dupras ashore. As the ship's position was fixed by radar, it was a simple matter to plot the progress of the truck; its succeeding positions were radioed to the beach. When it was about a quarter mile away Dupras ordered all hands to take cover under their bridges, where they waited for the truck, loaded with unsuspecting North Korean troops, to pass. Then they completed their mission. A visual check from the *Bass* next day revealed that one span of the railway bridge had been dropped into the river below, and the highway bridge was damaged beyond repair.

The troops in the Pusan perimeter had weathered the storm, and General MacArthur was getting ready for a daring counterstroke. First would come deceptive raids around

Kunsan, halfway up the west coast, on the way to the real target of Inchon.

In bright moonlight on August 20, two landing craft and seven large and small rubber boats boldly cruised into little Piin Bay north of Kunsan, brightly visible from the ship and presumably from the shore, but not a shot was fired at them.

After another night's equally uneventful reconnaissance a few miles away, the same flotilla landed squarely on the beach of Kunsan itself, measuring the depths as they approached. The Marines set up a sixteen-man perimeter of sentries, preparing to reconnoiter the nearby airfield.

Unknown to the raiders, North Korean eyes were watching their every move. Suddenly from the surrounding hills, enemy rifles and machine guns started firing on the camouflaged figures scurrying around the beach in the moonlight. The boat's radio ordered all hands back aboard. The shooting had already wounded two men, who were helped onto the rubber boats. One boat was riddled and sunk and two others abandoned because they were drawing enemy fire. When it became possible to count noses, nine Marines of the perimeter were missing.

One landing craft immediately sped back to the beach, dropping a small rubber rescue boat skippered by Lieutenant (jg) Fielding and crewed by Smith, Atcheson, Second Lieutenant Dana Cashion, USMC, and Fred Morrison who paddled to shore while under heavy rifle and machine-gun fire. Standing patiently in the water up to their necks, the nine Marines hailed them. Not one of them could swim. Boarding the rubber boat or clinging to its side, the stranded Marines were ferried to deeper water and safety aboard the landing craft. The two wounded men were flown to Japan; the team reported that they had found the beach depths unsuitable for landing.

General MacArthur actually did not want to land so far south—he was afraid the still-triumphant North Korean armies might escape. The target was Inchon, seaport of the capital city Seoul. "Operation Chromite" was a tremendous gamble for the high stakes of immediate and complete victory. The enemy garrison was confident that no landing could be attempted because of the monstrous tides at Inchon —tides averaging almost thirty feet high, ebbing to leave a hopelessly impassable stretch of mud. Commanding the narrow channel was the heavily fortified island of Wolmi-do. Five years before, the occupying UDTs had reported that a landing there against opposition would be extremely difficult.

There would be bitter opposition now. No preliminary UDT survey was planned, however, since the approaches had been well plotted during the brief American occupation. American navigators had been using the channel until the Red invasion. Then a daring Navy officer, Lieutenant Eugene Clark, camped on an offshore island, testing the mud and checking the tide, quizzing prisoners and friendly fishermen. The difficult Wolmi-do defenses and high Inchon sea wall were all too well known.

During the night before the assault, radar-guided destroyers anchored and slugged it out with the Wolmi-do batteries, planes plastered the dome-shaped island with bombs and napalm, and the new 200-foot rocket ships (LSMRs), with ten continuously fed rocket launchers apiece, proved their power in their first combat use. The Marines came in on the morning tide and took Wolmi-do by seven. The main assault over the Inchon city sea wall must wait for the rising afternoon tide.

While the fleet bombarded Inchon the Underwater Demolition Teams scouted the low-tide mud flats in front of the sea walls, buoyed the fast-flowing channel, dove to clear ships' propellers fouled on anchor lines, and generally greased the ways for invasion.

There actually were "teams" in Korea by that September 15th, for the first time. Both of the existing Pacific coast teams, One and Three, had arrived overseas in their peacetime half "strength" of some fifty men apiece. Lieutenant

Commander Welch had gone to Japan aboard the *Bass* at the beginning of the month to pick up the balance of his Team One on arrival from the United States, where they had been alerted for war duty early in August. Team Three had assembled from all directions. Lieutenants Mack Boynton and Daniel Chandler brought half the team from Coronado. Lieutenant Commander Harry Nowack arrived in Japan with eight men from prewar swimming tests in the Arctic ice-water off Point Barrow, Alaska. Lieutenant Commander William R. McKinney flew to Japan to resume command of Team Three.

When the teams arrived off Inchon, they were happy to board their own familiar ramped landing craft. As the tide rose that afternoon, Lieutenants (jg) Fielding, Smith, Bess, and QM3/c Boswell were wave guides while the Marine landing craft under enemy mortar and machine-gun fire hit the "beaches" of Inchon—actually nosing their ramps against the high sea walls which had been only breached in a few places by ship and plane bombardment. Elsewhere the troops used scaling ladders or boosted each other up and over, to capture the Reds' fire trenches and push into the city just before sundown.

The Marine and Army divisions drove on to recapture Seoul and cut off much of the North Korean army, already reeling from American counterattack in the Pusan area. The UDT men spent the next week buoying channels, and blasting sunken Korean junks to keep the fast-flowing channel clear for incoming tanks, ammunition, and food. The demolition men found and exploded a few stranded mines, as a bare foretaste of a major task ahead. Luckily the North Koreans had only begun to mine the "impossible" Inchon approaches.

A week after the landing, Team Three sailed halfway down the west coast. The *Bass* anchored two miles off the beach of Katsupaoi-po from which the inland rail and highway center of Taejon might be attacked, further splitting the North Koreans who were already being chased from north and south. The swimming raiders had to find out whether the beach and its exits could be used for a troop landing.

It was a bright moonlight night. Nevertheless, Lieutenant Commander McKinney's landing craft went within a quarter of a mile of the enemy shore to drop a line of five inflated rubber boats. The rubber boats paddled in within fifty or a hundred yards of the beach, with Number One boat paddling close to a cliff on the right flank.

Chief Wetenkamp, coxswain of Number Two boat, reports:

"We got 25 to 30 yards from the beach and dropped one man into the water. He swam alone into the beach with the end of the flutter-board line. He lay in the water's edge while we paddled out, to take soundings every 25 yards. We no sooner got into position than we heard the crack of a rifle. As we looked over in that direction, we could see tracer hit the radio they had in Number One boat. Then all hell cut loose. I remember somebody in my boat saying, 'Those poor guys in Number One boat!'

"I figured that the men in the water were a lot safer than the men in the boats, so I gave the order to paddle out. Nobody got shook up, and they sat there real quiet as in a training exercise. We paddled out of visual range and then we turned around to pick up our swimmer, who had a pencil flashlight which he kept flashing on and off.

"By this time two landing craft were on their way in to cover us with their .30-caliber machine guns. We were the first to be picked up. We could see through binoculars that Number One boat was still afloat. We picked up three men of its original crew and the other boat picked up two, but that left two men missing. We searched up and down, though believing the two men were lost. Finally we got a radio call from the ship that they were located. One of the men told us later that a bullet shot a fin right off his web belt. Those gooks up there were shooting directly down into the boat."

Lieutenant Mack Boynton, who was in charge of Number One boat, describes the scene:

"The beach was concave with a cliff along the right flank. This was my lane to obtain soundings after scouting the beach. All hands were in combat greens with fins strapped around the waist. The weather was cold, the moon was full, visibility too damned good! I approached the beach within 100 yards and dispatched two swimmer scouts. They had just reached the beach when I heard a command from the hill directly on my right, and immediately received a heavy volley of fire from automatic weapons.

"The crew rolled off the boat and hit the water. The swimming scouts received no fire. I had glasses around my neck and a radio between my legs. The first thing I knew, a shot hit my radio, knocking it away, and I can remember the air coming out of the boat from numerous hits.

"After hitting the water, the crew scattered. At this time I had no way of knowing how many had been hit. I dove for the bottom and headed seaward. Every time I came up for air I received heavy bursts of fire. Finally I got out of range and headed seaward, fighting the terrific current prevalent on the west coast of Korea. Two UDT landing craft were patrolling about 600 yards to seaward but not in my vicinity. I swam the two miles to the *Bass* lying offshore and was picked up."

Once the swimmers were picked up, the *Bass* and its supporting destroyer lit the cliff with star shells and bombarded the snipers.

The North Korean army was collapsing fast; an additional landing after Inchon was not required. Meantime one member of the United Nations, the USSR, disputing the legality of the UN sanctions, shipped new mines and mine assemblies by truck and flatcar, to be sown thickly in the major North Korean harbors of Wonsan and Chinnampo.

On the east coast, the ROK troops were pushing north toward Wonsan against the disorganized North Koreans. Whether or not they captured Wonsan in time, the high

command determined to make another major amphibious
landing similar in plan to Inchon. Major General Edward
M. Almond embarked his X Corps, planning to land the
1st Marine Division at Wonsan and the 7th Infantry Division farther north at Iwon, around October 20, to drive to
the Manchurian border, while his 3d Infantry Division
would link up with General Walton H. Walker's 8th Army
driving north from Seoul. This would make short shrift of
the North Koreans, and reunite the artificially divided country.

The uncharted Wonsan minefields threw a road block.
The waters and minefields were too shallow for the big,
awkward destroyer-minesweepers. The job was assigned to
three 1,200-ton steel minesweepers, the *Pirate*, *Pledge*, and
Incredible, plus the wooden-hulled auxiliary motor minesweepers under Lieutenant Commander Shouldice.

Two new tools were applied to minesweeping for the first
time—a cruiser's helicopter, and an Underwater Demolition
Team. On the morning of October 11, Lieutenant Commander McKinney's Team Three aboard the *Diachenko* approached the outer channel leading to Wonsan harbor.

The crescent-shaped bay is stoppered by two outer islands,
Ko-to on the north and Rei-to on the south. Other islands
stud its inner area farther west. The ROK troops had already
overrun Wonsan on the mainland, but nobody knew who
held the offshore islands. As for the harbor, the mines owned
it—unknown numbers of unknown types in unknown patterns, laid by local sampan skippers who were then killed
or kidnaped by their Communist masters to prevent their
revealing the harbor's secrets.

Two landing craft full of UDT men set out from the
Diachenko, which had anchored in the last-swept area. They
promptly spotted a pair of wickedly horned mines under
the surface, within half a mile of the ship's "swept" anchorage. All the team, boatload after boatload, were brought
out to the newly buoyed mines in recognition drill.

By the end of the afternoon's search, the team had located

and buoyed fifty mines, the nearest within a hundred yards of the anchored ship. They went back aboard, and the *Diachenko* cautiously backed out of the area, to the loud disgust of the team assembled on the ship's vulnerable fantail getting briefed for the next day's work. It was to be a memorable day.

October 12 started with air bombardment of Rei-to Island by carrier planes, then by cruiser and destroyer batteries. Lieutenant Commanders McKinney and Nowack then approached the southern island in landing craft. They splashed eighteen swimmers into the icy water.

By now, the swimmers were all equipped with two-piece rubber exposure suits, hooded, covering them from top to toe with only the mouth sticking out below the mask. The suits were zippered together at the back, in what was optimistically intended to be a waterproof joint. The wearers claimed differently, as the men's exertions let icy water seep in; but at least the suits retained the vital body warmth.

The swimmers dove under water and searched for mine cables running from the island for electrical firing, but found none. The island's pillboxes seemed deserted. If the rumored North Korean marines were on Rei-to, they were lying low.

Nowack's landing craft intercepted a Korean fishing sampan from the northern island of Ko-to. The natives claimed to be friendly, and said that only a handful of enemy troops were on southern Rei-to. Nowack started towing the sampan toward the *Diachenko* for further questioning, while McKinney picked up his swimmers and started for Rei-to.

Meanwhile, carrier planes had staged a pattern-bombing air strike the length of the inshore islands, along the so-called "Russian Channel" close to the northern tier of islands. Air intelligence had previously seen Russian or North Korean craft entering and leaving Wonsan along this supposedly swept channel. The bombing was a new stunt, intended to countermine (explode by concussion) any mines laid in the area. Its success can be judged by what happened a few minutes later.

After the air strike, the three steel minesweepers, electrically "degaussed" against magnetic mines, approached in a staggered line, with two of the wooden minesweepers spotted strategically between them. The *Pirate* led the way, with the mine division commander, Lieutenant Commander Bruce Hyatt, aboard. The cruiser's helicopter whirled overhead, scouting in front of the sweeper line as they approached the islands.

Everything happened at once. The helicopter radioed it had just spotted three long lines of mines ahead in the area bounded by the various islands. The minesweepers' sonar pinged steadily, getting undersea echoes from mines close ahead in all directions. The *Pirate's* bow lookout shouted that there was a shallow mine close aboard the starboard bow. The *Pirate's* rudder was put over hard left, then hard right. But the mine hit amidships, spouting a 250-foot column of water and debris. The ship sank stern first, all in a matter of moments. Six men went down with the ship. More than forty others were floating injured.

The *Pledge* was next in line. Its kapok-life-jacketed men at battle stations saw the *Pirate's* stern lifted from the water by the explosion, exposing its propellers, then settle fast, turning over and narrowly missing survivors in the water. The *Pledge* stopped engines and lowered a whaleboat to go to the rescue.

At this crucial moment, hidden North Korean shore batteries finally decided they had a target they could handle. From the honeycombed fortress island of Sin-do farther west in the harbor ahead, camouflaged batteries shelled the sinking ship and the rescue party. Even the "surrendered" Rei-to Red marines showed their fangs and fired on the trapped targets.

The *Pledge* fired its 3-inch gun against the shore battery. Trying to turn inside the area swept by the lead ship, the *Pledge* then struck a mine; there was a terrific explosion.

The skipper's leg was broken. All the men on the open bridge were severely injured; one was dead, one unconscious, pinned down by wreckage. The silence throughout the stricken ship proved how heavy the casualties were. The injured men tried to help each other as the captain ordered everybody to evacuate the hopelessly damaged ship.

Planes and the supporting ships farther out to sea opened up on the Sin-do batteries. Shouldice's wooden minesweepers headed into the fight with their guns blazing.

The scattered UDT landing craft swept in to the rescue. The minesweepers' boats also picked up wounded men and towed life rafts and nets.

Lieutenant Commander McKinney's craft sped over from Rei-to Island. They pulled wounded men out of the water, dazed from concussion, bleeding from mouth and ears. McKinney took his boat alongside the sinking *Pledge* and UDT men went aboard to help stranded crewmen. The UDT landing craft pulled away from the sinking ship, loaded beyond capacity, towing its rubber boat filled with men and dragging others who hung onto its side ropes in the frigid water.

Nowack's landing craft dropped off all but a skeleton crew at the *Incredible*, to leave more room in his craft for survivors. Nowack then tied up to the fast-sinking *Pledge*, picking up five survivors from the water. McKinney's crew reported they had evacuated every survivor aboard, except one man pinned in the radio shack.

Chief Wetenkamp and three other members of Nowack's crew now went aboard to search the *Pledge*, which was almost awash. They found the man in the radio shack, mortally wounded or dead. He looked as if he were in three parts. They strained to lift the wreckage, and yelled for a blanket to carry the body. The ship gave a mighty shudder and started on its final plunge to the bottom. The four UDT men leaped off into their boat, which departed for fear the sinking ship's depth charges would go off.

The two landing craft delivered twenty-five rescued men to the destroyer-minesweeper *Endicott* for hospitalization. All but one of the rescued men survived their injuries. Twelve men went down with their ship. Seventy-five men and eleven officers were injured. In the confusion, one UDT man salvaged a camera with which a crew member had snapped pictures of the sinking *Pirate*.

Returning to the main task the next day, the *Diachenko* bombarded Rei-to Island to pin down any remaining North Koreans. Two UDT boats proceeded to the area where the *Pirate* and *Pledge* had sunk. They had to buoy the wrecks and the mine line. In the few desperate moments before the ships went down, it had been impossible to take off certain secret code materials, which could not be permitted to fall into enemy hands. The landing craft found oil and wreckage on the surface, but could not locate the sunken hulls.

The next day, after blowing up a North Korean channel marker to confuse enemy gunners, the demolition boats cruised around the area of the wrecks, and found two streams of air bubbles. They also sighted two more moored mines.

Dropping the ramp, UDT diver William Giannotti, clad in rubber suit and mask, plus heavy steel compressed-air tanks on his back with twin air hoses running from the tanks' control valve to his mouth, plunged into the water. This was the first U.S. combat operation with the "aqualung."

This self-contained compressed-air breathing apparatus for free underwater swimming was developed in France during the German occupation by Commandant Jacques-Yves Cousteau and Engineer Émile Gagnan. Its first American naval use was pioneered by Fane in the demolition of a wreck in the Norfolk ship channel, two years before the Korean War, although the lung was still considered "experimental."

Giannotti swam down trailing a line—not for his protection, but to mark the wreck if he could locate it. His teammates on the surface peered through their masks, watching him exhaling a stream of bubbles which grew larger and larger as he descended into deeper water. Giannotti could see better than he had expected to in the early-morning light. He spotted the sunken *Pledge* below him, lying on its side in the mud. Reaching its nearly vertical deck, he carefully secured the line. A Dan buoy was fastened to the line on the surface, to mark the wreck of the *Pledge*.

A large oil slick discouraged search for the *Pirate*, and the team turned to locating and buoying moored mines, of which there was no scarcity. While carrier aircraft again vainly tried to countermine the inner harbor with bombing runs, the team's landing craft were joined by five sampans of friendly fishermen from Ko-to, who gestured their willingness to help buoy the dense minefield.

From morning until night the landing craft and the small wooden minesweepers pushed deeper into the successive mine lines barring the transports' approach westward to Wonsan. UDT searchers dropped anchored Dan buoys as close to the mines as they could without rupturing the sensitive chemical horns—one mistake would destroy boat and crew. Overhead, the helicopter flew, radioing the location of new mine lines it spotted under water. The wooden minesweepers cut mine moorings, then sank the floating mines with automatic fire. The UDT marksmen hit a few of them with rifles.

Rubber-suited divers from the team swam down to pack explosives and primacord on the first mines in one line, planning to detonate the mines themselves, but the operation was overruled by the minesweep command before they could fire the charges. The mines were cut and fired according to standard practice.

Day after day the strange team of whirlybird, swimmer, and wooden fleet pushed closer to the inner harbor. Their progress through the islands was punctuated with a regular series of explosions and high, watery geysers as mine after mine was exploded. Wherever the minesweepers went, UDT ramped landing craft and rubber boats were usually in the lead, spotting and buoying the mines. The team revised the old election slogan to: "As UDT goes, so goes the Mine Force."

The work was dangerous. Lieutenant Commander McKinney made a helicopter survey of the proposed landing beaches on Kalma Pando peninsula close to Wonsan, searching for mines. Meantime the UDT men were skin-diving and using aqualungs over the sunken minesweepers, in order to locate and salvage their valuable sweep gear. Carefully the divers planted demolition charges to free the "pigs," the depth-regulated floats at the ends of the sweep cables. Then they salvaged pigs and cables.

The team was given the hazardous honor of taking over Sin-do Island, which had bombarded the crippled *Pirate* and *Pledge* survivors before the ships and planes silenced its batteries. The one-time Japanese harbor fort was a rabbit warren of galleries and gun emplacements.

Lieutenant Daniel Chandler and twenty volunteers paddled up to the island in rubber boats, loaded down with tommy guns and other weapons. They observed how thoroughly the bombardment had smashed the guns and bunkers. Two native families came running down to the shore, begging food and first aid. They told the team's Korean interpreter that 200 North Korean troops had fled from the island the night before.

The landing party were happy to find that this was true. After searching Sin-do, they paddled to a small nearby island where a white flag flew from a small-boat landing. Hundreds of haggard, deformed natives crowded down to the shore, begging for food. The island was a leper colony. No landing was made, but the boat quickly returned with a load of rice from the transport.

By now the team felt quite expert at locating the moored contact mines without getting blown up. The minesweepers were not so lucky. A contract Japanese minesweeper, rechecking supposedly safe waters outside the harbor entrance, hit a mine and went down instantly. The nearest UDT boat sped to the spot and picked up seventeen survivors, giving them first aid while rushing them to sickbay. The other hired Japanese craft promptly went on strike, rather understandably.

The undaunted little American motor minesweepers pushed into the landing area the next day, polishing off the last known mines in the channel so the Marines could land. Although the shore was held by North Korean troops, the rubber-suited UDT swimmers mapped 4,600 yards of offshore approaches, making careful soundings in the chilly waters. UDT divers swam under water close to the Wonsan docks, mapping the numerous sunken wrecks for early demolition. Everything was clear sailing.

A small string of ROK Navy patrol craft and minesweepers now cruised cautiously through the swept waters to help the mine craft near the beaches.

Suddenly a terrific explosion rocked the harbor. A second followed. The third blast erupted in the middle of the South Korean column, and the ROK Navy's minesweeper YMS-516 disintegrated in a towering geyser of water and debris.

Swiftly the UDT boats raced to the wreckage, heedless of other possible mines. Once more the UDT crews rescued seventeen survivors from a sunken minesweeper, taking them to the team's own sickbay aboard the *Diachenko*.

That explosion was really bad news. Some unknown type of influence mines, secretly sown deep in the inner Wonsan harbor itself, had been triggered by those metal ships. The divisions of troops and their big supply ships could not risk the landing as scheduled.

By a brilliant intelligence coup, Lieutenant Commander DeForest found the key to the harbor the next day. Going behind the enemy lines, he discovered some abandoned mine parts which showed that the unknown mines were magnetic monsters big enough to damage any ship. A Korean skipper who had escaped from the Communists volunteered to show where he and his fellow skippers had sowed the mine lines. From there on, it was a matter of careful navigation.

While the minesweepers used their own special methods

for coping with the magnetic mines in the inner harbor, the team of frogmen and whirlybird kept busy spotting and buoying the complex, undulating mine lines to widen the swept channel. The search was "without incident"—meaning that no more ships were blown up, nobody was killed, only the constant strain of anchoring buoys alongside triggered TNT in a choppy, cold sea. Lieutenant Commander Nowack remembers the last long line he located:

"That was the roughest of all, with a high wind and four-foot waves. The mines were moored at different depths. As we eased the small boat around, every man's eyeballs were on the lookout for mines. Some men would point and could not talk as the mines suddenly appeared directly ahead of the boat. It chilled the hearts of the toughest men."

Special working parties went ashore on the landing beaches to double-check against land mines or underwater antiboat mines at the shore. UDT spotters flew north along the coast in helicopters, Navy PBMs, and British RAF Sunderland planes, to get a bird's-eye view of any mine lines in other harbors farther north, such as Hungnam and Iwon, which would soon be amphibious targets. Along the Wonsan docks, UDT divers carefully placed explosive packs in sixty- and eighty-foot wrecks, blowing them up without wrecking the docks.

"It was a dirty, stinking job," Nowack reports, "with dead Korean bodies floating all around."

On October 26, a week behind schedule because of the mines, the X Corps started unloading the 1st Marine Division and their supplies onto the beaches of Wonsan, with UDT craft acting as wave guides through the swept channels to the beaches. The Marines immediately split up, one force moving south to mop up Red guerrillas clinging to the hills, while the main force moved north to take Hungnam and inland Hamhung, and start their perilous drive toward Chongjin reservoir and the border.

The next day, the usual "ten-hand working party" under Lieutenant Mack Boynton embarked with Rear Admiral

Lyman A. Thackrey's task force sailing north to prepare for the 7th Infantry Division landing. There the UDT detachment went into Iwon in a rubber boat, swimming a string reconnaissance to chart the approaches to the ROK-held landing beaches. During a house-to-house search ashore for enemy agents, Lieutenant Boynton was handed a present by a native—a large painting of Stalin. Boynton gave it to Admiral Thackrey, who had it inscribed: *Liberated by UDT 3.*

That night the little detachment set up a defense perimeter and signaled their tank landing ship to come ashore.

The Army's 7th Division landed on the morning of the 29th, under General Barr, met by the usual UDT welcoming committee.

Another detachment of the team had a quick and easy mine search at Hungnam harbor, where supplies would be landed for the Marines driving northwest to the Chongjin reservoir.

On the west coast, mines were delaying General Walker's offensive more than the main North Korean army. He badly needed the port of Chinnampo to supply his 8th Army with gas, ammunition, food, and winter equipment for the fast-approaching bitter weather.

Commander Stephen M. Archer, observer and technical commander of the Wonsan underwater reconnaissance, drew the Chinnampo assignment. Lieutenant Commander Kelly Welch's Team One arrived in the *Bass* to help Archer's minesweepers. For the first few stormy November days the team stood by in their chilly landing craft for rescue missions. Then they went into action.

With Lieutenant Commander Welch flying in a helicopter to guide them, three UDT boats searched the shallow channel south of Soku-to Island. They spotted and buoyed a mine line across the channel the first day. The next day they found another line, and discovered a whole mass of mines on the beach of another island, evidently jettisoned by mine-laying junks wrecked nearby. UDT mine disposal expert, Lieutenant (jg) J. O. Lyon, gingerly and deftly removed the exploders from more than a dozen mines, and made sure the others were safe for removal and destruction.

In the twin channels north and south of Soku-to, more mine lines were found and buoyed for the sweepers. Steadily, day after day, the minesweepers and the team cleared the way deeper into the tide-swept channels leading to Chinnampo's docks. Winter was closing in. The men in the open boats logged November 15 as the first sub-freezing operation. As the mines were cut loose, PBMs flying overhead blew up some of them, UDT marksmen and ship gunfire disposed of others. Sixty of the eighty mines swept were divided almost evenly between the planes and the UDT crews. By November 17 the 200 miles of channels were cleared, permitting Welch's team to make its final reconnaissance in to the Chinnampo docks.

Chinnampo was opened to supply a victorious army's advance to the Manchurian border. During the month it took to clear the channel minefields, the tide of battle changed so that the port was opened barely in time to evacuate the army's casualties.

The Army 3d Infantry Division had been recalled to Wonsan and evacuated. In abandoning Wonsan, one special security task had to be accomplished. The Reds must not get the codes that went down with the *Pirate* and the *Pledge*. The Navy salvage vessel *Conserver* borrowed five helmet divers to reinforce its own man, and anchored over the *Pirate's* grave.

Because the ships were in a depth of 100 feet of water, the order was to demolish the ships rather than salvage them. Lieutenant Thede of UDT 1 came aboard as demolition officer.

The bottom was soft, sticky mud into which the weighted divers sank from knee to hip. They could only see an arm's length in the December light. It took four dives before a helmet diver identified a 40mm gun tub of the *Pirate*.

Explosives were borrowed from the Army at Wonsan. After

five days' diving, Lieutenant Thede directed the placing of explosives, and fired the fuse igniter. After the column of mud and water settled, the *Conserver* moored over the still-buoyed *Pledge*. Two more days of diving and blasting destroyed the *Pledge*. Three more days were spent scouring the bottom for signs of the sunken ships. Dragging the ship's stern anchor finally located fragments of the *Pirate*. After another demolition charge was exploded in her wreckage, a final search on December 12 could find no trace of the brave little minesweepers in their Wonsan harbor grave. The codes were obliterated. The salvage ship pulled away, leaving the hard-won harbor to the enemy—for what comfort they could get out of it, under a continuous gunfire siege by Navy ships cruising offshore.

Fifteen miles farther north at Hungnam, the Marines and Army had formed such a strong perimeter under cover of artillery and naval guns that the Communist hordes could not have broken through. But the X Corps would be more useful in the 38th parallel line, so they were "redeployed" to fight under more favorable conditions. All the techniques of amphibious landing worked like clockwork in reverse, aided by the shipping supplied by Military Sea Transport Service. By Christmas Eve, 100,000 Army, Marine, and ROK troops were loaded and shipped out, as well as nearly 100,000 Korean refugees from Communism.

Just as UDT had a role in the overture in opening the port of Hungnam, it had the curtain line. The inevitable ten-hand working party headed by Lieutenant Commander McKinney and Lieutenant Boynton flew to Hungnam. Based on the transport *Begor*, they spent several days checking the harbor and dock area, making a few preliminary demolition blasts.

When the last troops were finally being sea-lifted, the demolition men put in a seventeen-hour working day placing more than 20 tons of explosives along the docks and harbor installations, laying literally miles of primacord fuse. It was bitterly cold.

The big ships were firing steadily over the men's heads, blasting the circle of surrounding hills to keep the Red jackals from hurrying prematurely to the corpse of Hungnam. While the UDT men packed explosives against the towering harbor cranes, the massive steel structures shook like leaves in the wind of the battleships' gunfire. At last the harbor-wide "charge" was ready.

The UDT officers pulled the delay fuse, and hurried by landing craft to the waiting *Begor*. Suddenly the entire shore line of Hungnam blew skyward.

From that point, the entire character of the war changed. In General MacArthur's analysis, the North Koreans had been completely defeated; the entry of the Chinese Communist armies started a new war. From the limited viewpoint of this account, the change was equally abrupt. After Hungnam, the Underwater Demolition Teams were fighting a guerrilla war. For months they alternated between "administrative reconnaissances" behind their own lines, and guerrilla drops behind the enemy's front.

The team surveying beaches near Pusan got a special dividend from the Army. The team's supply officer persuaded an Army depot to supply the men with winter outfits of salvaged winter Army clothing shipped back from the front lines. The clothing was warm, but all too often grimly needed a bullet hole sewed up or a blood spot washed out. The UDT men needed extra-warm clothing—one reconnaissance was made in North Korea when the transport was covered with a solid sheet of ice, and the rubber-suited swimmers had icicles hanging from their noses and eyelids. The thermometer read 12° above zero!

Even in South Korea the weather was bitterly cold. The welcome was much hotter than the weather on one beach survey, however, 150 miles south of the front lines. The UDT landing party from the *Bass* was met by the usual crowd of women and children waving ROK flags. The interpreter was told there was no guerrilla activity, due to a strong ROK police force in the west coast town of Popsongni only five miles away. The detachment mapped the beach exits, took its photographs, and returned to the transport for lunch.

A second boat crew went ashore at a deserted beach three miles north, four men landing to hold range markers so the boats could keep in line as they paddled out to sea making soundings. The survey was completed and one rubber boat paddled ashore to pick up the four men. Suddenly several white-clad men appeared over the dune line behind the beach, dropped to the military prone firing position, and started shooting at the UDT party with carbines and rifles.

Immediately the shore party dashed into the water, cold though it was. Bullets punctured the rubber boat as its crew, junior grade Lieutenants Edward Frey and R. G. Pope, emptied their automatics at the snipers on the dunes before they jumped into the water and started swimming, towing the boat. The landing craft sped to the rescue, with Lieutenant (jg) Edwin Smith emptying his carbine's two clips and the only other weapon aboard, a .45 pistol.

The landing craft tried to tow the waterlogged rubber boats, but the line broke twice, with the six men still in the water. One of the sniper bullets hit the landing craft coxswain, and a UDT man took his place.

In the water, Lieutenant Frey, a World War II veteran of UDT 18's Balikpapan operation, grabbed another line and started swimming to the rubber boat, drifting away on the strong tidal current. Two sniper shots hit him in the head. Lieutenant Pope and another swimmer tried to keep his body afloat, but the current dragged them under the landing craft and they had to let go. Frey's body was never seen again.

The men in the landing craft tried to pull the chilled swimmers over the high gunwale. Last out was Paul Satterfield. The ship's radioman and a UDT man were hoisting his waterlogged, exhausted body up the side of the boat when sniper bullets wounded the radioman and killed Satterfield.

The *Bass*, as soon as the beach was clear of UDT men,

opened up on the dunes with its shells while the landing craft spotted the fire by radio. But the guerrillas had fled.

Team One's official "action report" contains the bitter afterthought: "In Korea there is apparently no such thing as friendly territory or truthful natives."

Early in April, Lieutenant Commander J. F. Chace took over Team Three. "Spike" Chace, of Harvard rowing fame, had been a World War II UDT training officer and team commander. His UDT teamed up with the British commandos, the 41st Royal Marines, for a raid far up the east coast of North Korea. Half of the team disembarked from the *Begor* at the usual midnight hour, and started for the dark beach. Fog closed in as the rubber boats were about to drop their frog-suited swimmers. The transport's radar spotted a strange "pip" on its screen, and radioed the team that an unidentified craft was approaching them. Even if it was an innocent fishing vessel, they must locate it and avoid discovery.

As Lieutenant T. R. "Rog" Johnson and the other swimmers silently swam toward the beach, keeping close enough to see each other in the fog, their landing craft cocked its machine gun for instant action. The swimmers heard voices on the beach. They even smelled campfire smoke. It was too foggy to make out the number of people. Quietly they started swimming back to their landing craft. It wasn't there.

Their suits were leaking and they were getting colder by the minute. Hopefully they flashed their pencil flashlights out to sea in narrow arcs. One hour later a muffled exhaust was music to their ears. The landing craft located them and helped the near-frozen men aboard.

Commander Chace headed for the dock landing ship *Fort Marion* where the British commandos and their amtracs were embarked. The gunner forgot to uncock his machine gun. As the boat nosed against the big ship, the gun fouled and went off. Bullets ricocheted inside the landing craft. One man was seriously wounded, two others were hit, and Chace was momentarily knocked out with a scalp wound. He quickly regained command, taking care of first aid for his wounded men before he took them aboard ship, then reporting to the commandos that the beach was occupied.

The raid was staged in the morning nevertheless. UDT boats guided the British amtracs, steering through the fog by compass until they could see the beach. A North Korean beach patrol of a dozen men fired at the incoming craft, until they learned the strength of the raiding party. A hundred fifty commandos chased the Reds into the hills, then set up a defense perimeter. Lieutenant Johnson and his radioman served as the communication section on the beach all day, spotting for ship gunfire, while the commandos demolished bridges and tunnels, using the techniques taught them by UDT. The raiders re-embarked that night without a casualty from enemy action.

Meanwhile in Europe, Lieutenant Commander Francis D. Fane was completing a special research assignment. He had contacted assault swimmers of the British, French, and Italian Navies. On his return to the United States, he requested combat duty, which was quickly granted. His honeymoon was interrupted by orders to take charge of UDT Unit One.

In June, he arrived in Korea as senior UDT officer, and made plans for improving UDT techniques and coordinating the teams in the laboratory of war. Fane's first project was a series of guerrilla landings conducted in July. Major R. V. Kramer, USMC, was in charge of the guerrillas aboard the *Begor*.

The first mission was just below the far-north seaport of Chongjin, to "exfiltrate" (pick up) an agent. The *Begor* had to lie more than three miles offshore because of a known enemy minefield.

Lieutenant Commander Chace, now skipper of the team under Fane, brought his landing craft a half mile off the beach about midnight, vectored in by the ship's radar. Then a ten-man rubber boat left the landing craft, with Kramer, Fane, an interpreter, and two rubber-suited swimmers

aboard. They strained through the darkness but could not
see the expected flashing light of the agent's signal. Major
Kramer and the swimmers went in to the beach just as a
thick fog set in. The rubber boat's radio conked out at this
critical moment.

Nothing was heard or seen for an hour. Then the men in
the rubber boat heard a low whistle to seaward. They paddled for an hour's fruitless search—a swimmer's head could
only be visible within ten yards. Finally they heard low hails
from the water far to one side of the beach. They located the
swimmers, exhausted and cold after swimming for an hour.
Major Kramer was nowhere to be found.

A bright white light started flashing on the beach, moving
northward. This was not the code signal, but the rubber
boat paddled as close as it could. No sign of the agent, or
Major Kramer. The boat searched back and forth. Finally,
at 4 A.M., Lieutenant Chandler's boat went close to shore
and swimmers landed. They found the stranded major and
brought him back. Meanwhile Fane's rubber-boat crew paddled back to sea, lost in the fog. The men, exhausted, huddled together and slept, though cold waves washed over
them. Dawn would bring either enemy to destroy them, or
rescue.

Lieutenant Chandler's boat, radio functioning, was skill-
fully guided to them by the ship's radar. The grim game of
hide-and-seek was over, with no casualties, unless something
had previously happened to the agent. If he missed the
rendezvous, he was not supposed to try again at that point.

Fearing that the area had been "compromised" and the
enemy alerted, a beach three miles north was used for the
guerrilla landing the next night. Fane insisted on the preparation of an operation plan with emergency procedures for
locating lost swimmers. This time, three landing craft
launched six rubber-boatloads of South Korean guerrillas
safely ashore under UDT guidance.

The July 2 landing suggested a mysterious tragedy. An
agent was to be picked up at Kotan Wan, some fifty miles

northeast of Hungnam. Two landing craft were loaded down with .30-caliber machine guns, BARs (Browning Automatic Rifles), carbines, burp-guns, and rifles. As the muffled craft neared the beach at midnight, the lookouts saw a flashing amber light, the agent's signal. Just then a small, darkened, strange craft was spotted near shore. One landing craft sped over and seized a Korean sampan, a seemingly innocent fishing craft.

Kramer, Fane, and swimmers set out in a rubber boat toward the still-flashing amber light. A dog began barking. Suddenly there were two shots on the beach, and loud, angry shouts. The amber signal light vanished and was never seen again. The rubber boat paddled anxiously along the shore, fifty yards out. Somebody moved along the beach with a dim blue light—not the agent's signal. The boat came closer to shore and Kramer hailed the beach again and again with a code challenge. There was no answer. Nearly two hours later, Major Kramer decided to give up the search and return to the ship.

After landing fifty guerrillas safely at another beach farther north, the Begor picked up a new load of a hundred South Korean troops and returned to a beach only three miles from where the agent had vanished. Toward the usual midnight hour, three landing craft full of guerrillas, rubber boats, and UDT swimmers closed the beach while Chace "rode shotgun" in an armored high-ramped boat. Fane and two swimmers splashed off a rubber boat and swam to the beach. They found it deserted, although blacked-out trucks were rumbling continuously along a road just out of sight behind the cliffs. The beach was rocky with offshore ledges. There was no surf.

The men on the beach flashed their carefully shielded signal to sea. The rubber boats full of guerrillas did not see the signal. Fane swam out to the nearest boat, leading the group to shore through the reefs and rocks. The rubber boats then paddled back for more customers, while Major Kramer set up perimeter outposts. The last group landed safely, and then the whole guerrilla band melted into the hills behind the beach. Fane, Kramer, and the UDT men headed back to sea. Another "routine" mission accomplished!

Lieutenant Commander Fane's primary mission in Korea was to improve operational techniques. As a result of his critical combat report, the Commander Amphibious Force Pacific and the Chief of Naval Operations conducted a greatly accentuated UDT equipment development program.

Besides guerrilla warfare, the teams had two more tasks in the dragged-out Korean War. The fleet was bombarding Wonsan in an offshore siege which lasted during the entire two years of "truce talks." Despite Russian-made radar which improved the Communists' gunnery to score hits on a number of the besieging ships, the fleet stood firmly off Wonsan, pounding the shore batteries.

To assist in this siege, UDT crews and minesweepers moved boldly into the mined harbor approaches. Late in July 1951, the other half of Team Three aboard the destroyer transport *Weiss* started a boat-and-helicopter clearance of mines newly sown in the island area. It was a war-long race between the Red mine sowers and UN minesweepers.

Lieutenant Johnson spotted the mine lines from the helicopter while Lieutenant Commander Chace's landing craft and a group of rubber boats buoyed them. This time, masked rubber-suited swimmers led by Lieutenant Schmidt, the team's mine and bomb disposal officer, dove boldly down onto the wickedly horned contact mines. In spite of choppy waves, the divers safely packed their explosives and fuses onto the touchy mines. Two destroyers fired over their heads to keep the Communist gunners quiet. Despite rain squalls and poor visibility, part of the mine line was successfully loaded and blown clear. The minesweepers moved into the opened line and completed the job.

The war dragged on, and the Wonsan Reds industriously replaced their mines despite the toll of naval gunfire. A year later, UDT paid another visit to the Wonsan minefields. Lieutenant Commander Louis States, USNR, the World War II commander of Team Eleven at Okinawa and Borneo, had come back to active duty as head of a beach training school, then was ordered to organize a team newly commissioned for Korean war duty. Team Five included "Truck" Deiner and other World War II and Korean veterans. The team entered Wonsan waters aboard the *Diachenko* in February, 1952. Armed enemy sampans and junks were lurking in the inner harbor, and heavy field artillery in the hills overlooking Wonsan tried to control the harbor. The blockading fleet managed to keep the Reds under cover while the minesweepers and UDT repeated their task.

One morning the helicopter signaled States' landing craft that it had located a new, shallow laid line of mines off the beach. One mine was a "watcher," moored at the surface. The helicopter dropped a smoke marker. Since the mines were shallow enough to be triggered by the landing craft, Lieutenant Richard Lyon, former captain of a great Yale swimming team, and Lieutenant Edwards of Mine Disposal Squadron Three, paddled ahead in a bright yellow rubber boat. Lyon swam to the mine and held it while Edwards plugged the mine switch. Then they pulled up the mine cable, and States' crew lifted the entire deadly contraption into their landing craft. It was a brand-new type with a Russian warehouse receipt still inside. The next mine was similarly plugged, cut loose, then towed behind the craft.

The bow lookout leaning over the landing craft's ramp, a big rangy Texan, suddenly shouted: "Oh, for God's sake, stop her!"

Everybody knew he meant there was a mine dead ahead. The coxswain tried to reverse the motor. It stalled!

Leaning farther over the ramp, Tex groaned: "Don't make no difference now, it's under us."

In the breathless silence, they could hear it scraping under the hull. Slowly the boat drifted off, and the mine appeared at one side. It was a dud. Quietly they pulled away. When he got his breath, Lou States said: "I didn't think you Texas boys ever got scared."

Tex had an answer. "Commander, ain't no mines in Texas!"

The team finished its minesweeping mission safely, returning to Japan for a brief rest period. Then intensive training with the aqualung commenced. By this time, the Cousteau-Gagnan diving apparatus was standard equipment in UDT operations. In April, States' crew came back to use the new underwater tool in buoying wrecks in Wonsan harbor. The *Pirate* and the *Pledge* had been completely destroyed, but other minesweepers had been sunk there.

Guided by a helicopter, Team Five explored the harbor depths for three wrecks. Heavy weather kept the water murky. One morning, the minesweepers' drag hit a sunken object. The snagged sweep gear was cut and buoyed as a marker. That afternoon, aqualung divers from the team went down to locate the wreck. The water was too turbid for good observation, but they salvaged the valuable sweep gear. High seas forced the boat to call off operations.

The next day, the six best-qualified aqualung divers in the team went down to survey the wreck and demolish it if necessary. They found the obstruction, more than fifty feet down. Close-up inspection by masked, free-swimming, aqualung-breathing divers discovered what the official hydrographers and the minesweepers' blind draglines could not. The "wreck" was a negligible rock outcrop, too deep to disturb ships or minesweepers. Wonsan's muddy graveyard had by now buried all the wrecks.

The next major UDT operation was guerrilla work. "Operation Seanet" was planned to disrupt North Korea's military economy, based on fish as much as rice. During the summer and fall of 1952, Team Three under Lieutenant Commander A. W. Sullivan, Jr., raided far up the east coast, cutting and destroying the ocean fish nets floated by buoys and big glass balls. Sullivan was a "hot to go" redhead, like

Hanlon, Cooper, Fane, and others before them. All were of Scotch or Irish descent (Fane a native Scot) adapted by nature to war on the sea.

Sometimes the demolition crews would have to paddle close to shore, while North Koreans stood grimly watching from the beach. Once under cover of darkness, near the Siberian border, a rubber-boat crew was trying to cut the heavy anchor cable of a big net near shore. They signaled the landing craft to bring in bolt cutters. This failing, they finally signaled for explosive packs. As the landing craft came in again, a machine gun in the cliffs back of the beach commenced firing. The swimmers shuddered, but the landing craft, armed now with twin .50-caliber machine guns, answered sharply. The transport, farther out, responded to the radio call by laying shellfire accurately on the luckless machine-gun crew. The rubber-boat crew speeded the task of fastening their explosive charges and pulling the time fuse. They boarded the landing craft and raced away, while the blast tore the net loose, to be towed to sea and sunk.

This was the last extensive UDT operation in the Korean War, a combat which had proved the readiness and outstanding capabilities of the naked warriors. Though only two UDT were available for the greater part of the war, they conducted a most extensive series of combat missions. One team fought for a year in the Korean theater without relief.

Underwater Demolition Teams learned many new lessons during this campaign. With Lieutenant "Rog" Johnson, Lieutenant Commander Fane sat down and rewrote the "book" of advanced operational doctrine for the employment of UDT, a work which will guide the tactics of UDT for years to come.

19. Over the Horizon

When the art of war is so perfected that war ceases to be the umpire of disputes by its bringing certain annihilation to all parties resorting to it, then will peaceable arbitration become the resort in all cases of military controversy.

LIEUTENANT COMMANDER J. S. BARNES, USN.
U.S. NAVAL ACADEMY, JUNE, 1868

BETWEEN WARS UNDERWATER DEMOLITION TEAMS HAVE crossed other horizons. They have ranged far and wide over all the seas of the world, from Arctic and Antarctic to atomic Bikini. The world's first atomic bomb tests at sea found a team under Lieutenant Commander Scotty Cooper on the job. UDT 3 was part of Vice Admiral Blandy's Joint Task Force at Bikini during July, 1946, in the symbolically named Operation Crossroads.

The team's mission was to secure samples of radioactive water, as soon after the explosion and as near its center as possible. For once, they did not dive into the ocean; the sea was too "hot." Instead, they operated their familiar ramped landing craft as drone boats.

Unlike the earlier drone boats at Kwajalein Atoll and off Southern France, these remote-control craft worked well. UDT experts flew in control planes, radio-navigating the surface craft shortly after the awesome mushroom cloud had risen. There were difficulties, of course, and hazards. Planes had to turn back from danger zones when the "R-count" (roentgen units of radioactivity) in the surrounding air rose too high. One boat balkily circled around and around, unable to raise its anchor, until it eventually was rescued by the team's destroyer-transport *Begor*. But all the other craft obeyed radio orders, cruising in where no man could venture and live. They collected samples of water, reported the radiological activity from automatic Geiger counters, and finally returned to safer waters, to be hosed down and relieved of their "hot" cargo.

Thanks to the elaborate and ingenious safety precautions used throughout the test, the team and all the task force personnel came through the overwater and underwater A-bomb blasts with a perfect safety record.

Instead of man's startling science, primitive Nature provided the background for the chief UDT project of the next year, 1947. Commander Fane proposed that an Underwater Demolition Team could be useful on the Antarctic polar expedition in which the Amphibious Force would play a major role. Lieutenant Herman Garren, a five-winter-sports man from Lake Placid, wrote the plan for UDT 4.

The leader of the expedition, Captain Cruzen, welcomed the services of seventy men in rugged physical condition, able to operate in any climate. Embarked in the World War II command ship *Mount Olympus*, the team sailed south, an integral part of "Operation Highjump." They blasted paths through ice pressure ridges, conducted reconnaissance patrols on skis, and helped to build an airstrip.

Wearing special heavy underwear and rubber exposure suits, they pushed aside ice floes and swam in the briny Antarctic Ocean in water temperature of 28°F.—below the freezing point of fresh water! Their ability to dive in icy waters proved invaluable in inspecting ice-damaged ships' hulls, replacing bent propellers, blasting holes in the solid ice for ships' moorings, and doing other unfamiliar tasks. They confounded the skeptics who had questioned the use of swimmers in ice fields. On succeeding Arctic and Antarctic expeditions, demolition teams or detachments have played valuable roles, starting with a return visit to the Bay of Whales in the spring of 1948.

From such peacetime projects, the half-strength Underwater Demolition Teams were abruptly plunged into a shooting war in the Far East, in Korea from 1950 to 1953.

The uneasy armistice freed some UDT detachments for duty in another trouble zone, between Red China and the Free Chinese forces in Formosa. UDT experts trained teams of Chiang Kai-Shek's Nationalist China's Navy in underwater demolition and reconnaissance. Rubber boats manned by Nationalist Chinese crews paddled up to both friendly and doubtful islands.

The strategic decision to evacuate the Taichen Islands close to the China coast gave the American UDT a familiar task, charting safe passage for the Amphibious Transport Group guarded by the U.S. Seventh Fleet, and then demolishing fortifications and munitions to prevent them from falling into the hands of the Communist Chinese. Lieutenant Mack Boynton and UDT 11 gingerly trod through heavily mined terrain executing this mission. While blowing up bunkers, pillboxes and 200 tons of ammunition, mostly Japanese from World War II, UDT 11 was mistakenly fired on by a Nationalist destroyer.

Once again, evacuation in the Far East required UDT reconnaissance. "Operation Freedom," the Amphibious Force rescue of fugitives from the Communist occupation of Hanoi in Indo-China, was a humanitarian deed of the highest order. The Amphibious Force saved untold thousands of helpless, loyal people from the Communists. Such defensive operations were new duties for the men who were accustomed to swimming into enemy-held beaches a few days before an assault landing.

On a more constructive note is the most recent operation which called Underwater Demolition Teams into action. The northern rim of this continent has been a challenge since the days when the stout little sailing ships of Parry and Franklin sought a legendary "Northwest Passage." The only charts of the area consisted of a single line of "position doubtful" soundings taken by a Royal Canadian Northwest Mounted Police boat which had forced the passage many years before. No large steel vessel had ever dared the "Passage." Now, as a vital defense mission, the Amphibious Force was ordered to penetrate the passage in full force during the summer of 1955.

The Northland has meant mystery and danger from the early days of the Hudson's Bay Company to the modern, radar secrecy of the DEW (Distant Early Warning) Line. Into the muskeg and floe ice of this land of Eskimo and fur traders, came the Amphibious Force, Pacific Fleet, plowing a way through polar ice fields extending from Icy Cape, Alaska, through Simpson Strait, Canada, to a place called Shepherd Bay in the approximate longitude of the North Magnetic Pole.

Eskimos who had seldom seen a ship gazed in awe as a vast convoy of 60 vessels smashed through heavy ice to unload 116,000 tons of cargo on desolate Arctic beaches, many of which had never seen man before, populated only by the white fox and polar bear.

No less a man than Admiral George C. Towner, USN, Commander Amphibious Group Three, could have driven ships through ice fields seven feet thick, pushing down from the North Polar regions. The pressure of these tremendous floes piled ice up to heights of 60 feet where the ridges formed. Huge bergs of blue polar ice were frequently encountered.

UDT played a small part in this tremendous maritime undertaking, one of the greatest feats of seamanship in modern times. Ten detachments of U.S. Navy Hydrographic Office and UDT men surveyed the route for 1,200 miles through polar seas, entirely above the Arctic Circle. Lonely outposts of the Hudson's Bay Company and the Royal Canadian Mounted Police gave them warm welcome.

In charge of one of those detachments was Ensign Jon Lindbergh. Twenty-odd years before, Jon's parents, Charles A. Lindbergh (now General, U.S. Air Force) and Anne Lindbergh, flew their pioneer plane *Sirius* to chart hitherto unknown landmarks over frozen waters where their son would later swim. Mrs. Lindbergh was co-pilot and navigator, mapping new areas a year before Jon's birth on a turbulent flight over the ice fields. For a typical picture of that terrain, take Ensign Lindbergh's August 3, 1955, report of midnight near Terror Bay:

022400Z ICE REPORT X CONCENTRATION 80 PERCENT OF THE SEA COVERED X ICE THICKNESS 56 INCHES X WATER TEMPERATURE 27° AIR TEMPERATURE 33° X WIND VELOCITY 36 KNOTS X OVERCAST X LITTLE CHANGE SINCE LAST REPORT

These ten teams of UDT men and hydrographic specialists, under command of Commander Fane and his hydrographic assistant Lieutenant Commander Marshall Cook, traveling in small open boats, charted an area of 100 miles per team. To take soundings they cut holes through sea ice six feet thick. In exposure suits they swam and dove for hours in icy waters to check the sea bottom. Detailed charts were drawn so that ships could pass safely through to the temporarily ice-free harbors.

It was during a "recreational swim" in Cambridge Bay, Canadian Northwest Territories, that UDT men again faced guns, this time in friendly hands. The ice had started to break up in the bay in July, when Lieutenants Aquadro and Jones, apparently struck with spring fever, started to swim across the bay towards an Eskimo camp. They were clad in black exposure swim suits, rubber gloves, and large swim fins. Alternately crawling over ice floes and swimming through the water, they neared the shore. The sled dogs started howling. Eskimo hunters, who had never seen a man swim, came out of their tents, and on seeing the figures, rushed for their high-powered rifles. The UDT men had been mistaken for seals, the favorite food of Eskimos and husky. Only wild cries and frantic gestures prevented a fusillade.

Anywhere in the world, from Alaska to Hawaii, from Malta to Formosa, in seas too numerous or too sensitive to mention, the Underwater Demolition Team swimmer may thrust his way through ice, sharks, gunfire, or raging surf in the accomplishment of his amphibious mission.

Too little credit has been given to the toughness, courage and enterprise of the American fighting man. His spirit stems from a hardy heritage.

Our nation was born of men who in the early 1600's crossed uncharted oceans and made hazardous landings on a hostile, savagely defended, surf-pounded coast line; despite the burden of women, children, and livestock. Since that beginning our forefathers have always faced the sea with confidence. Our Colonial Navy was noted for audacious nautical enterprise, for Yankee ingenuity, for unique departures in naval warfare. In 1777 the Commander-in-Chief, General George Washington, sponsored the first naval underwater attack in United States history, an assault on the men-o'-war of the blockading British Navy at New York. The operation was planned by David Bushnell, a Connecticut inventor and schoolteacher, the first American to envision the possibility of submersible warfare.

General Washington in a letter to Thomas Jefferson dated 26 September, 1785, said:

Bushnell is a man of great mechanical powers, fertile in inventions and master of execution. . . . I furnished him with money and other aids. . . . He had a machine so contrived as to carry him underwater at any depth he chose . . . with an appendage charged with powder, which he could fasten to a ship and give fire to it, and by means thereof to destroy it. But, it was no easy matter to get a person hardy enough to encounter the variety of dangers to which he would be exposed—first from the novelty; secondly from the difficulty of governing the machine underwater, and thirdly, from the uncertainty of hitting the object devoted to destruction without rising frequently above water for fresh observations, which when near the vessel would expose the adventurer to discovery, and to almost certain death.

A stouthearted man was selected by David Bushnell:

After various attempts to find an operator of my wish, I sent one who appeared more expert than the rest from New York to a fifty-gun ship, the H.M.S. *Eagle*, Lord Howe's flagship, lying near Governor's Island.

Our first underwater demolitioneer was Sargent Ezra Lee. No ships were sunk by this warrior, stripped naked to the waist, sweating in the confines of his minute submersible; but the haughty officers of mighty English ships blockading our infant Navy were whipped out of their wigs by the violence of the detonation of Lee's explosive magazine. Underwater warfare had commenced, the course of naval tactics was changed by the onslaught of a single, naked warrior.

Inspired by the cause of freedom, other great patriotic Americans continued the development of submersible weapons by which to arm the underwater man. Robert Fulton constructed a submersible before the steamboat; Samuel Colt an underwater mine before the revolver; both weapons, however, became favorite tools of Hitler, Mussolini, and Stalin. But the wheel has turned, and the techniques and equipment devised by Yankee inventors have in recent warfare assisted the United States Navy in its task of maintaining the freedom of the seas. In our Navy, men have been found who can fulfill the requirement considered by George Washington to be no easy matter, that of being "hardy enough to encounter the variety of dangers to which he would be exposed." The naked warriors of the Underwater Demolition Teams now operate submersibles not unlike that of Bushnell, under conditions which would win the approval of our first great military commander.

20. UDT Submerges

Technical advances and the possibilities of the nuclear age notwithstanding, it is men who will eternally remain as the one essential ingredient to successful maritime operations.

ADMIRAL ARLEIGH A. BURKE, USN

IN THE FALL OF 1946, ONE HIGH STAFF OFFICER WARNED Lieutenant Commander Fane: "We are thinking of changing the name of Underwater Demolition Teams. It is not truly descriptive. You fellows swim on the surface, your primary mission is reconnaissance, you seldom will have to use explosives again. Your methods are known, you should henceforth be called 'Reconnaissance Units.'"

Fane admitted that some revision of tactical doctrine was necessary because of enemy knowledge of World War II UDT methods. However, a change in the name Underwater Demolition Teams, which had won such distinction in combat, would be a blow to the morale of all demolitioners. The fear of such a happening provoked action to forestall it. To retain the underwater part of the name, UDT would submerge to the deepest depths if need be.

One fact had been established which brooked no denying: The development of radar and electronic detecting devices had virtually nullified the possibility of a secret approach by UDT surface craft or surface swimmers to an enemy beach. Another way must be found. To go under water was an obvious solution, but how?

World War II research projects had been restricted to such devices as the "Stingray," "Reddy Fox," and other remote-controlled weapons designed for use on the surface

277

of the sea. Only one type of underwater apparatus existed which could be applied to submersible operations, the "lung."

"Lungs" were self-contained underwater breathing apparatus, now universally dubbed SCUBA from the initials. There were two models, the Jack Brown named for a famous diver; and the Lambertson Amphibious Respiratory Unit developed by a Philadelphia doctor of that name.

The lung permitted a man to breathe under water for periods of up to one and one-half hours, and to dive to depths of 30 feet. There was no hose to the surface. Oxygen was fed to the diver from high-pressure cylinders strapped to his body by a harness. The diver's exhalation circulated through a breathing bag and a soda-lime purifier, returning through the face mask to be breathed again. This equipment had been designed for the clearance of obstacles.

The World War II diving indoctrination course conducted by UDT was brief. Little was known about the lungs. The diving candidates were placed in a rubber boat, anchored in a depth of about 15 feet. Each man in turn had a lung draped around his neck, lashed at his sides and under his jock strap. The mask was placed on, a rope was tied beneath his armpits, lead weights were belted on; for all appearances and feeling, he was about to be hung. Then the oxygen valve was turned on, the man was asked if he was all right, at which time he was immediately dumped over the side into the water, and generally sank to the bottom. If within five minutes the line to the man was not being spasmodically jerked (which was assumed to signify distress), or if there was no movement thereof (which was interpreted to mean that the man was enjoying himself or had found a lobster bed), the trainee was hauled to the surface, the mask given another, and a diver listed as qualified. Such crude training would never do for the operations Fane envisioned.

The use of lungs, it was officially noted, was "for brave men." Neither the Experimental Diving Unit nor the Navy Diving Schools encouraged the development of these devices.

However there was no question but that lungs gave men the means of long-distance underwater swimming, if properly used.

The next problem to be solved was that of finding a way to propel swimmers at a greater speed than by their own muscles and swim fins. War records revealed that a small UDT detachment led by Lieutenant Floyd Gammill had reported to England for training in the operation of the British "Sleeping Beauty." This small, one-place submersible boat, about the size of a canoe, did not have as good a performance record as that of the "Nautilus" built by Robert Fulton (the steamboat engineer) in 1805, from whose plans the British had apparently taken the design. Two "Sleeping Beauties" lay in the UDT warehouse in California, still crated—no one knew how to use them. Fane ordered one shipped east, on the theory that all available material should be tried during the initial stages of the underwater development.

The next problem was to find a parent craft to replace surface transport; the submarine was the obvious answer. UDT swimmers had operated from a *surfaced* submarine at night during the Yap mission. However, it was now realized that in future war radar would immediately reveal surfaced submarines; the operations must be conducted while completely submerged. It was known that underwater escape could be made, but the problem of re-entry had not been pursued in our Navy. Information of foreign techniques had not as yet been made available to UDT. This factor was imposing.

Fane first contacted a former UDT staff officer, Commander Margetts (an ex-submariner), who believed the scheme possible, though he had no knowledge of an accomplishment.

By chance Fane met his old friend Commander Kauffman in the corridors of the Pentagon. With facility he grasped the import of Fane's idea and said, "For the safety of your men, if for no other reason, you will have to go under water. Operations from submarines are the only possible way of conducting secret UDT missions."

It was one thing to envision an entirely new method of conducting naval warfare, but to have a new system adopted by the U.S. Navy is another story altogether. In the Navy there is a term "the operational requirement" which governs all development. To the layman this means the reason for doing things; the reason for using cruisers rather than destroyers for a certain tactical mission; or for the use of 16" shellfire rather than bombs to destroy an enemy emplacement. Of equal importance is the phrase "operational readiness." This means the readiness of the Fleet for combat, and of every unit within it to do its job. A new concept of warfare, therefore, must satisfy a valid operational requirement, and increase the operational readiness of the Fleet.

Tactical changes are scrutinized with great care in the Navy Department, as are new proposals for the design of equipment. The lives of men are dependent on the correct evaluation of new techniques and equipment. Fane entered the Amphibious Type Conference with considerable apprehension in January 1947. The agenda items were placed before various committees, and received a thorough going-over. The theory that UDT swimmers would become "men-fish," diving to deep depths and pursuing their course in small underwater craft, met skepticism except as a remote future development.

The proposals were recorded, however, including Fane's ideas for the employment of assault swimmers, who would attack enemy harbor shipping and installations under water and tow powerful explosive weapons by submersible craft. Though the UDT submersible plans were not then accepted as doctrine, the way was left open for the unit to conduct trials.

During planning for the following winter's Amphibious Force maneuvers in the Caribbean, Fane asked Captain Wales, Commander of Submarine Squadron Two, if his UDT swimmers might try to enter and leave a submerged submarine. To the surprise of those present, the submarine commander agreed. "What goes on inside the submarine is our responsibility. What you do once you are out of the escape hatch is your responsibility, and," the veteran submariner added with a slight pause, "God be with you."

In planning the UDT submersible operation, there were no past records available. It was a step into an unknown element, the underwater world. Divers in conventional dress, heavy suits and helmets, have plumbed the ocean depths to 500 feet, dangling on the end of a line, with a hose furnishing air, and with telephone connections to the surface, tenders, recompression chambers, doctors and boats standing by.

Free-diving is another matter entirely. The free-diver carries his own limited air supply in tanks on his back, has no lines to the surface, may be unattended, has no "squawk box" for communications; he is independent of the surface in all respects. His maneuverability is greatly increased, limited only by his own strength, skill, and "the depth-time factor" which all divers face. From a military standpoint, the free-diver has a tremendous advantage in combat areas. All this, however, had still to be learned.

The world of the underwater expert is so small that the leading figures eventually become known to each other. Fane, who needed expert advice, heard that Dr. Christian J. Lambertson was in Fort Knox, Kentucky, training Army personnel to use his lung. Lambertson had been in OSS during the war as an underwater swimming instructor, and later as a pilot of the British "Sleeping Beauty" in combat. He was now specializing in the study of respiratory diseases and the effects of oxygen toxicity at the University of Pennsylvania.

Fane brought Lambertson to the Naval Amphibious Base at Norfolk in January 1948, for a medical demonstration of diver's diseases. The UDT men watched their swim buddies suffer under carbon-dioxide poisoning, and collapse from anoxia (lack of oxygen). In swimming-pool tests, they learned to recognize the preliminary symptoms in themselves. Training was stepped up until they could make mile swims under water on oxygen.

Next Fane arranged with the Submarine Medical Research Laboratory in New London, Connecticut, to study free-escape techniques in the Submarine Escape Training Tank—a nuge cylindrical water tank 100 feet high, with air locks for entrance and escape at various depths. Men of the teams qualified in free-escape training to a depth of 100 feet. Then they took oxygen susceptibility tests in dry pressure chambers, breathing pure oxygen for thirty minutes at a depth of 60 feet.

The oxygen tests were continuing while Fane was conferring with Admiral Fife (Commander Submarine Force, Atlantic Fleet, and an outstanding wartime submarine flotilla commander), Dr. Lamberston, and an expert on submarine and diving medicine, Captain T. L. Willmon (MC).

The conference on the proposed UDT submarine experiments was interrupted by a phone call for Dr. Willmon. One of the UDT men had convulsed in the pressure tank. The doctor gave quick instructions for his care, and the conference resumed. Shortly the phone rang again—another man had convulsed. Repeating his instructions over the phone, Dr. Willmon gave Fane a knowing look; after all, this was what they were here to find out—how long men could take pressure. A few minutes later the phone rang again. Dr. Willmon nodded his head, and the Admiral hurriedly adjourned the conference; word had been received that the sight of thrashing bodies being carried out of the pressure chamber was affecting the morale of personnel reporting for sub duty. Dr. Willmon directed thereafter that the UDT cases be treated in a back room of the tank until recovery.

It is horrible to see a man suffering *grand mal* convulsions from oxygen toxicity. His limbs thrash, his face muscles twitch spasmodically, his mouth foams. His pulse races, he breathes in rapid pants, then the body stiffens and slowly relaxes into unconsciousness. The treatment is simple: Bring the man to the surface and allow him to breathe air. Consciousness is regained within twenty to thirty minutes.

Ten men volunteered to act as human guinea pigs during the tests. For hours on end they swam in pairs around the circumference of the pressure chamber until stricken with either carbon-dioxide poisoning or oxygen toxicity. Doctors of the medical research laboratory closely watched them, noted pulse and respiration at intervals, and waited for the inevitable spasmodic twitching of facial muscles which signaled the approaching convulsion. Some men experienced a feeling of euphoria, a sense of high elation, just prior to being poleaxed by oxygen poisoning. The interval between this happy state of intoxication and the condition of a racing, pounding heart (often at a pulse rate of 140-150) and lungs frantically panting in the vain attempt of the human system to beat off the effects of poisoning, was generally but one minute!

Fane had far exceeded the swimming times of other men at a depth of 60 feet, when he convulsed. "I can assure you it is entirely painless to the victim," he says. "In fact, just before the attack there is a general feeling of well-being. I am told my last words were, 'I don't need help, there is nothing wrong with me!' Then all went black. Again while in the stretcher being carried out of the chamber I said, 'This is all so absurd,' and then again collapsed. I felt no pain, but it is a fearful thing to see happen to another.

"It was the only way to learn how deep we could dive on pure oxygen, and how long and how hard we could swim under water. As a result of the knowledge gained in these and other tests, there has not been a single fatality under water during the thousands of man-hours of diving operations which I have conducted; however, we had our close ones."

Training in the 100-foot-deep escape tank was pursued. All hands learned to enter and leave escape hatches. They learned the effects of too-rapid descent which caused squeeze, and the dangers of rapid ascent (air embolism). They learned to "pop their ears," equalizing pressure in the inner drum—men who cannot perform this simple exercise or who have defective ears are disqualified from diving.

They learned to squeeze into the small round tube of a submarine escape trunk which could hold two men in lungs and the operator. When the steel hatches slammed shut and water flooded in, the hatch could be a perfect claustrophobia machine. In fact, during the war, submariners had preferred to stay in the boat and die rather than to attempt an escape through the trunk.

All of the various "divers' diseases," the dangers of oxygen toxicity, CO_2 poisoning, anoxia, and air embolism (a most vicious killer, since it strikes without any warning symptoms as does anoxia) were thoroughly indoctrinated into all hands. Bends and nitrogen narcosis were at first not a matter of concern, as diving would be confined to the relatively shallow depths of 50 feet.

Captain Willmon declared the men to be fully qualified to undertake submerged operations. Fane gave the unit the designation of "Submersible Operations Platoon," the first fully qualified detachment of underwater swim-divers in the U.S. Navy. Captain Wales took the men on board the submarine *Grouper,* commanded by Commander Miles Refo, Jr., whom they would meet in the clear, warm waters of Saint Thomas in the Virgin Islands, in February 1948.

This Caribbean area, near the scene of the Amphibious Force, Marine Corps, and Atlantic Fleet winter maneuvers, has probably the best year-round weather conditions in the world. The water is clear, with little current or tide, and there is good bottoming ground for submarines—it was a Navy submarine base in World War II.

The UDT tests included directional swimming under water to an objective by wrist compass, submersible approach to a beach, deep-channel clearance and salvage problems, and the demolition of underwater obstacles. Then came submarine exercises in Pillsbury Sound, between the islands of St. Thomas and St. John.

There Commander Refo submerged the *Grouper* on the bottom in 52 feet of water. Wearing oxygen lungs, Fane and Lambertson safely escaped from the hatch, swimming around in the clear waters filled with fish; they then re-entered the hatch, and it closed to let them back into the submarine.

As they repeated the test, they met their first barracuda. He appeared out of nowhere with an escort of small fish waiting to pick up crumbs from his meals. Almost as long as a swimmer, steel-gray with silver patches on his sides, he followed the swimmers with his cold eyes steadily fixed on them. His undershot jaw had teeth like a tiger's. When struck at, he darted off—to reappear instantly behind them, a dozen feet away. When the swimmers realized he was not coming any closer, they went about their tests. Finally the wolf of the sea cruised majestically away about his business.

Once when Fane entered the submerged submarine, an enlisted man in the sub's crew asked him if he couldn't keep the Sleeping Beauty farther away from a small beach nearby. Fane assured the man that there were no reefs or shallows to endanger the boat.

"That isn't it," the embarrassed submariner admitted. "You see, sir, the men off duty have been taking turns at the periscope. There's a beautiful blonde living on that beach and she likes to sun-bathe nude. When your boat circled too close, she ran into the house and got dressed."

The UDT men had been so intent on their underwater duties that for once they had missed a trick in reconnaissance.

The preliminary submarine tests were smoothly successful. On February 22, 1948, the swimmers commenced the next test. No records were available that this had ever been done before.

The *Grouper* submerged to periscope depth, and proceeded on a straight course at minimum speed. Fane and Lambertson in lungs entered the escape hatch with Lieutenant Nicholson of the *Grouper* as the operator. The trunk flooded up over the lip of the escape hatch, pressure was equalized, and Nicholson opened the outer door.

The bright sunlight illuminated the submarine's super-structure. It was dead quiet. Out into the sunlight went the two swimmers, holding onto the coaming of the torpedo loading hatch. The water was crystal-clear. Almost the entire length of the submarine could be seen, bathed in sunlight, black and somber. She was making a little over two knots, drifting along at dead slow, a silent shape in the blue water. The men shouted with joy in their face masks. They rose to the surface and signaled to the protruding periscope. Down they swam to re-enter the hatch, close it, and drop into the submarine. It had seemed ridiculously easy—but this was the first escape and re-entrance that had ever been made while a USN submarine was running submerged.

The Underwater Demolition Teams were justifying their name. The Navy, however, demands conclusive evidence before accepting a new tactical concept. Proof is requested, visual proof!

A solution appeared in the form of a reserve officer who had pioneered in studies of underwater light and photography, Lieutenant Commander E. R. Fenimore Johnson. This man wandered into Fane's office one day "just looking around" while on Reserve training. "Fen" Johnson, as he came to be known in UDT, greatly influenced and assisted in the submersible development. He was a man of many outstanding talents, in fields as diverse as vice-president of the Victor Talking Machine Company (which had been founded by his father) to scientific research on underwater visibility. In World War II, he had donated the services of his laboratory, his scientific staff, and his research vessel to the Navy, at no cost. Johnson, on being apprised of the SUBOP project, became enthused and again volunteered his services and precious underwater camera equipment to the Navy at no cost; he nearly gave his life as well.

In October, Fane, Fen Johnson, Doc Lambertson plus a half ton of underwater photo equipment, the UDT detachment, and a Sleeping Beauty flew to St. Thomas. The old, patched-up World War II "submersible canoe" was a cranky and hazardous craft, in which some British operators had lost their lives. One blew up due to hydrogen gas accumulation while being driven by Rollins, a UDT SUBOP diver. However, it was the only small submersible available. The versatile Doc Lambertson was the Sleeping Beauty instructor.

Fen Johnson knew well the problems to be faced in underwater photography. In many years of expeditions in Florida, the Bahamas, and Puerto Rico, he had found that a man standing on the bottom in shallow water could get pictures only on one to fifteen days a month, depending on storms. Sand and fine coral particles make the water murky or "milky," sometimes for days following a blow. Even a man walking on the bottom kicks up sand. No such delays could be permitted in the Navy's tight schedule for the UDT-sub tests.

Lieutenant Commander Johnson's solution was to build a light tower on the sea floor where it was fifty feet deep, and the water transparency remained good to fair except in actual stormy weather. The UDT lungmen fastened Johnson's aluminum extension ladder and platform to the sea floor by heavy weights.

"By that time I had made three dives with the lung," Lieutenant Commander Johnson says, "and in view of my long experience in diving with full-dress and shallow-water rig, I was confident that I should have no trouble in setting up my camera, and waiting for the Sleeping Beauty to pass. Nevertheless, Fane assigned F. Keppesser, BM3/c, to be my watchdog. This turned out to be a most sound precaution. I made the platform at the top of the ladder without difficulty, and Kep duly handed me my camera.

"A line of buoys had been set up twenty feet off the ladder, and I had given instructions for the Sleeping Beauty to pass close on the ladder side of the buoys. Anyone who has operated her or watched Sleeping Beauty in operation knows that she is indeed a sleeper. The diving planes can be set hard up or down, and at least ten seconds elapse before she snaps out of her doze and gets going in the required direction. The rudder is almost as sluggish. I was not surprised when the first pass was from the wrong side of the line of buoys, so I settled down to wait for the next.

"After a few minutes in a position of complete rest, I was much surprised to note that my respiration had markedly increased. There was no feeling of confusion and indecision such as comes with asphyxia, so I decided to stick, and attempt to control my rate of breathing. Nevertheless, the rate and depth of respiration increased until I was in acute distress. Several minutes had passed, and I was expecting Sleeping Beauty to come by at any moment—not knowing that she had sunk!

"Presently some instinct warned me that loss of consciousness was not far off. Handing my camera to Keppesser, I managed to make the launch. When I was hauled out, I was pasty-white and turning blue. I've felt worse in my life, but not much, and thought that my diving days were over, at the young age of forty-nine. Fortunately, a big, husky chief picked up my lung and went overboard with it. In less than two minutes he came up with his lungs going like a pair of bellows. This aroused my suspicion that my trouble was not entirely due to advancing years.

"Dr. Lambertson was aboard the J-boat, and I asked him to inspect my lung. He found nothing wrong but took it with him to help Fane, who with the assistance of my technician, A. C. Dyer, had taken over the camera work.

"I timed Lambertson's dive. He was down less than three minutes. When he came up, he hailed me across the water, telling me that the trouble was not with me. The lung was examined and the fault found to be due to a used charge of baralyme which had failed to fully absorb carbon dioxide; I had built up carbon-dioxide poison. Although still somewhat shaky, I was able to resume diving the next day."

The submarine *Quillback* arrived on Sunday. Johnson stripped the legs off his ladder and erected the platform above the submarine's starboard torpedo gates. The submarine bottomed, and Johnson took his post on the platform, checking his underwater light meter and the external manual adjustments (shutter opening, film speed, distance, filter, and trigger) on the thirty-pound camera—which only weighs a pound under water.

The plan was to photograph lungmen slipping in and out of the water-filled torpedo tube entrance. The swimmers would end the test by attempting to enter the submarine through the tubes.

"The torpedo gates were opened," Johnson reported. "Fane entered the tube feet first. The plan was to close and reopen the gates by hand, as a preliminary experiment in handling the lungs while inside a torpedo tube, and incidentally to get pictures of men entering and leaving the tubes.

"No sooner had Fane entered the tube than he came out like a shot and drove desperately for the surface.

"With plenty of hands topside, Keppesser and I stuck to our posts. Presently Fane returned and re-entered the tube, feet first and face down. Later I learned that his oxygen supply valve had been knocked shut in the process of working into the cramped quarters. Unable to breathe and not knowing what had happened, he was forced to surface. After such an experience his feelings could not have been too good about being shut up in the black darkness of a torpedo tube; nevertheless, he gave the hammer tap signals to close the gates.

"The operation of entering, closing the gates, reopening and exiting from the tubes could not have been much over two minutes since the camera holds only 1 1/10 minute film supply, and I was shooting most of the time. The fraction of a minute he spent in the tube was by far the longest in my entire life. Imagine for yourself what it was in his, cramped as he was into 21 inches of space, unable to see or move.

"Having gotten the outside pictures and having made several dry runs with manual handling of the air valves, Fane dove down and alone entered the lower starboard forward torpedo tube. The gate was shut, the water was drained off, and, much to the relief of all hands, Fane slipped himself into the forward torpedo room unharmed but, I suspect, a little shaken.

"The drainage of the tube had been pretty fast, and had lifted the mask away from his face. Yet it was not so rapid but that he would have drowned had he not succeeded in getting a little oxygen after the mask snapped back in position. It was his opinion that had he elected to lie on his back instead of his face, the mask would have been torn off completely. This probably was the first successful entrance of a submarine via the torpedo tubes."

The next pioneer experiment was to have the Sleeping Beauty land and take off while the submerged submarine was under way. Several officers and men had qualified, and been duly recorded by underwater camera, going in and out of the submarine's escape trunk.

Dr. Lambertson, by far the most experienced operator present, would pilot the yellow-painted Sleeping Beauty. With the sub under way, Fane and Johnson would leave the escape trunk and take stations on the forward gun platform as photographers. On either side of the main deck would be the boat handlers, Gunner's Mate Baily, and Ensign George Atcheson III (who was later to be the first UDT man in action in Korea). Gunner's Mate Piotrowski had to grab a line, release a buoy and ride it to the surface to act as hook-on man, riding the Sleeping Beauty down to the submarine's deck. Two underwater cameras and light meters and a camera tripod were fastened near the gun, with the aluminum ladder lashed crosswise as a back rest for the two photographers. The submarine dove to 50 feet and started running down on the Sleeping Beauty's station at sea. A mile away it slowed to two knots, leaving half an hour for the men to operate under water.

Johnson reported what happened on that submerged deck: "Fane and I were then locked out. It had been proven that a speed of two knots would not tear off our face masks if we kept facing the current, but no one knew whether they would tear off or flood if we turned. We backed aft to the gun platform. The full force of the current on our bodies drove us back into the ladder. The flow of the water plastered our swim fins flat onto the slatted deck. By fitting our backs between the rungs of the ladder, it was possible to let go with both hands and work at the cameras. Metering the adjustments of the camera took two or three minutes, and there was then time to glance about.

"Baily and Atcheson were just reaching their stations. Piotrowski succeeded in releasing the buoy and rose to the surface, some twenty-five feet above the main deck. I could see that he was taking a severe beating and wondered how he could hang on. This wonder turned to sheer admiration as minute after minute rolled by. The sea was what is known as channel chop—short, steep-sided, and for the most part crested. The waves were not very high, probably six feet from trough to crest. Nevertheless, their action reached down to our position and alternately lifted and slapped our oxygen bottles against our chests.

"There was a sensation of tremendous speed. I gingerly experimented with turning my head a little to one side. The downstream edge of the mask began to vibrate, but no water leaked in so I was able to see Fane. His red hair was streamed back, his ears were flapping in the submarine breeze, his trunks and lung were bellied out behind and whipping about. I could think of no better simile than Ben Hur driving his chariot in his race around the Roman Colosseum. I was tempted to turn the camera on him, but decided I could not afford to use the film on anything but the operation.

"The underwater visibility was good. It extended almost to the bow of the ship. Particles of Gulf weed and bubbles streamed toward and by us. Nantucket sleigh riders certainly had no greater thrill than a man on his first ride on the deck of a submerged submarine under way. I first thought the submarine's speed had been increased to three or four knots.

Fane remarked about it. We both looked up at the weeds at the under side of the surface, and decided that speed was being held, as ordered, to about two knots. However, the moment we looked ahead, the sensation of really high speed returned, like looking at the water rushing by a fast launch with a low freeboard."

They had a long, tensely watchful wait before the submarine closed with the approaching Sleeping Beauty.

"To conserve oxygen," Johnson continued, "Lambertson elected to stay on air for some minutes. The slight but steep-sided seas swept clear over his head as soon as he had trimmed Sleeping Beauty to an awash condition, consequently he could only inhale in the trough of the waves. While he was undergoing this ordeal, and struggling to keep his sluggish craft in line with the submarine periscopes, Piotrowski was being dragged along the surface.

"Suddenly I saw a blur of yellow. It was the Sleeping Beauty. I was unable to bring my tripod-mounted camera to bear, so I tapped Fane on the shoulder, signaling him to use his hand-held camera.

"Somehow Lambertson made contact with the buoy, and Piotrowski hooked it on. Lambertson at once dove Sleeping Beauty. The descent was a little off angle and the craft hung, bow down, from the main deck rail.

"Baily, a brawny giant, wrapped both arms around its stern and hauled it inboard. All three men on deck wrestled her into the dolly and made it fast. Lambertson got out and stood by for a moment. Under the necessity of fast action, he and the others faced aft at times and sometimes failed to hold onto their masks. Thus, inadvertently, they proved the ability to face aft without flooding or losing a mask.

"Lambertson re-entered the Sleeping Beauty. It was cast loose. He ascended and was unhooked by Piotrowski. He had way enough to steer clear before the advancing periscope overtook him.

"We of the underwater detail all stood at our stations, and the submarine surfaced. Never have I seen the sun shine brighter. There was no shock and no turbulence at my post as we burst through. The relief was vast, but the fatigue was nil.

"Some underwater pictures had previously been taken by means of remotely controlled cameras fixed to the outside of a submarine, but we were the first to accomplish such photography personally with hand-controlled cameras.

"Obviously the day when diver fights diver undersea, and raiding parties march out of the sea to attack beaches, and divers in submersible craft will reconnoiter coasts and harbors, is not far off."

Weather conditions worsened, but the undersea photographers took pictures of UDT men working around the propellers of a bottomed submarine, and incidental shots of big barracuda. Familiarity was breeding contempt with this fish of terrible reputation.

At night the UDT men did well in large groups, but they showed some hesitation about diving singly or in pairs after dark in waters where they had seen shark and barracuda. There was a slaughterhouse in the harbor which attracted large shark. To set an example, since UDT operations cannot be limited to "safe" waters, Fane and Johnson made a night dive with Lambertson lungs in Charlotte Amalie Harbor to take special flash-bulb photographs of the propellers of a docked submarine. There was no record of a shark attacking a helmet diver, but many cases of shark attacks on swimmers; whether a shark would regard a lung-diver as a diver or swimmer was unknown. As an experienced French fisherman in the Virgin Islands said to Fane, "Who can say what is in the mind of a shark?"

As Lieutenant Commander Johnson noted, "Fane has on more than one occasion swum directly over a bottomed shark without receiving unwanted attention. Nevertheless the possible presence of a large shark is a mental hazard, especially at night.

"Curiously enough, visibility under water at night is not completely absent. On the night we chose for the special photographic experiment there was a little moonlight. Familiar objects could be distinguished at a distance of about six feet when we submerged.

"I was to stand on the after edge of the diving plane and operate the camera while Fane seated himself on the leading edge with the flash-lamp holder. The two were connected by eight feet of rubber-covered electric conductor. We then dove.

"When I reached my position, I was horrified to see the ghostly bulk of a large fish which was quite obviously interested in our activities. Beyond seeing that it was bulky, had a broad head, and was big enough for its body to extend out of sight into the darkness, I could distinguish nothing about it. Something about the angle it hung in the water looked vaguely familiar, as did also the indistinct outlines of its head.

"I continued to contemplate this unwelcome sight," Johnson admits, "until Fane, by a tug on the electric conductor, informed me that he had reached position. It required all of my will power to turn my back and go about the business of photography.

"When the lamps had flashed, and I was again able to look around, the specter was gone. Probably this most unwelcome kibitzer was a jewfish and not a shark, as the submarine crew later told me they often saw a jewfish hanging around that particular dock."

The next day was the last of the submarine tests, and the underwater work was particularly prolonged. A couple of men were forced to the surface by toxicity toward the end of the run, and Lieutenant Commander Johnson noted that one had mild but noticeable symptoms of oxygen poisoning. Keppesser lost control and ripped off his face mask while under water! Fane grabbed him and swam him to the surface float buoy, then returned below, hauling himself down the line. At one time the submarine nearly "broached" to the surface, and the commanding officer was forced to increase speed to nearly six knots to hold her down. The force on the divers was tremendous; one by one they were torn off the deck by the surging submarine. Finally only Fane and Piotrowski were left, both severely battered, and partly overcome by carbon dioxide. Fane came to his senses enough to give the emergency signal to surface.

"When I climbed aboard," Johnson reported, "I was astonished to see Fane sitting down in one of the gunners' seats of the aft 40mm gun. This, I knew, was not natural to him. He is seldom off his feet, especially during an operation. Upon closer approach, I observed that his face was flushed and that he not only was shivering violently but that his muscles were dancing in knotty bunches to an extent far beyond that which can be accounted for by the chill of even a long submersion.

"He was talking in jerks and obviously didn't know exactly what he was saying. I called the corpsman and got him a drink of brandy. His symptoms were also those of oxygen poisoning, but far from mild."

This brought to an end the second series of tests.

After the conclusion of the maneuvers, Lieutenant Commander Fane remained in St. Thomas for further training of one team. It was at this time that the other author of this book, Don Moore, became familiar with the less classified phases of UDT operations, since he shared with Fane and a local Army man, Captain (now Major) John Jouett, an off-duty interest in barracudas, sharks, and langustas.

UDT swimmers dove for hours and swam for miles under water in their indoctrination to the underwater element, so fascinated by the natural beauty of their newly acquired environment that they forgot all fears of oxygen toxicity, CO_2 poisoning, squeeze, embolism, and the other unseen but ever-present dangers. There was no problem in requiring men to dive; when given a day off, they invariably spent the time spearfishing.

Captain Jouett led the explorers to his favorite shark hole, where the swimmers found the mako shark, as advertised. Stingrays, mantas, the dread moray eels changed from terrors to trophies. More and more, the men were indoctrinated into the knowledge that the sea was their own brave new world, in which the denizens of the deep usually accepted them as equals, if not masters.

Popularizing undersea sport was of course an inadvertent by-product of the UDT work. The underwater photographic record by Lieutenant Commanders Johnson and Fane proved thoroughly convincing to the interested Navy officials, and further development of the program was approved.

As pioneers in underwater photography and diving operations, Johnson and Fane were startled to read James Dugan's story in a scientific magazine, about the independent, parallel work by Commandant Jacques-Yves Cousteau and his French "men-fish," using his compressed-air lung, and French underwater cameras. It was their first inkling of undersea operations by other enthusiasts.

With the French Navy sunk or interned, Cousteau had turned to undersea diving, which the American writer Guy Gilpatric had popularized on the Riviera. Cousteau developed the lung for military use against the Germans in Toulon. Using compressed air eliminates the immediate 30-60 foot depth limitation of pure oxygen. A diaphragm controlled by the surrounding water pressure enables the diver to breathe air at the same pressure; the "hard" air in his lungs equalizes the weight of water pressing on him in sensitive balance.

Fane thought Cousteau's apparatus sounded good, and arranged to meet the French diver, who was arriving in New York. They proved to be charter members of the natural fraternity of brother divers. Fane acquired a Cousteau lung (the American model became known as the "aqualung") and took it to the New London escape tank to test it. He dove 100 feet to the bottom on his first try, and came up convinced of the lung's usefulness, despite natural official Navy skepticism about new, untested devices.

In December of that year (1949) came a practical occasion for UDT employment of the aqualung. A menacing wreck 60 feet deep in Chesapeake Bay had caused difficulty for conventional full-dress (helmet, suit, and hose) divers, because of the swift tidal currents. They could only work during half an hour of slack tide. Wearing the compressed-air lung, Fane dove to the wreck. In successive dives, he and his men loaded the hull with tons of explosives and demolished it, in an impressive demonstration of UDT submersible techniques.

Recognition of the merit of this conquest of the hydrosphere by UDT swimmers came from Admiral W. H. P. Blandy, USN, who addressed letters of commendation to Fane, Fenimore Johnson, Chiefs Devine and Foster, and petty officers Baily, Piotrowski, Petway, and Keppesser.

Although there was still much to be done, the aqualung had opened the door to safe deep-diving operations. Procurement of this equipment from the French resulted in huge strides ahead in submersible swimmer developments. In that next winter's Atlantic Fleet Exercises, UDT swimmers operated the Sleeping Beauty in far-ranging maneuvers. Lieutenant Bruce B. Dunning performed a remarkable feat of underwater navigation, piloting an SB two miles through coral reefs to the beach, and safely returned. Divers in aqualungs reached greater depths as their skill and confidence in the underwater world developed. Theoretically, any depth reached by a deep-sea diver in conventional hard-hat dress can be reached by a free-diver in his naked hide.

A significant development occurred in the summer of 1950. A British X-Craft, the midget submarine responsible for sinking the German battleship *Tirpitz*, visited the Amphibious Base at Little Creek, Virginia. The UDT SUBOPS Detachment quickly made themselves at home on this craft. Joint exercises were conducted, including the penetration of a harbor defense net in the Norfolk ship channel. Fane and the British diver worked hand-in-hand under water, with a strong current forcing the XE7 hard against the net. Finally the last grommet was severed and the submersible sliced through. Such exercises were routine for the British, who had accomplished similar deeds in combat; they were a new experience for UDT.

The joint X-Craft-UDT exercises proved successful, all

hands of the SUBOPS Detachment making underwater exits through the "wet and dry," the British term for their escape trunk. It consisted of a tube leading vertically out of the craft. It had a double purpose, serving as a "john" as well. It would accommodate one diver, who crawled in, shut the hatch on the interior of the craft, sat down, and flooded the entire chamber by means of a pump. Then a valve was operated to equalize pressure. Quite simple, but a bit eerie sitting in the dark submerging oneself. However, as the British said, "If all goes well you pop out of the hatch, one mistake and you go down the drain."

No UDT personnel were flushed out of the "wet and dry" the wrong way. The X-Craft proved to be an excellent mother ship for UDT submersible operations. As a result, plans were made for the construction of the first American midget submarine, the X-1, which has an exit for UDT swim-divers. This craft has been recently launched in Long Island Sound by the Fairchild Engineering Corporation.

In his garage in the town of Glendora, California, a transplanted Yankee engineer and inventor, Calvin Gongwer, and his colleague G. McRoberts labored over a device which his fellow engineers had named "The Thing." Designed as a propulsive device for swimmers, it was truly an underwater airplane. Its control surfaces resembled wings; for propulsion it was driven by contrarotating aircraft-type propellers. Steering was by a "joy stick," and the sensation of handling the craft under water was similar to that of flying a light airplane. The Swimmers Propulsive Unit was named SPU for short. The first SPU showed the limitations of family garage construction. But although he nearly drowned in a reservoir during the first tests, Fane fell in love with it at first sight.

Gongwer and McRoberts went "back to the drawing board." On their own, they built SPU Mark II on the garage floor, and put it into the test tank of the submarine engineering section of Aerojet General Manufacturing Co. By the application of aerodynamic principles to the field of hydrodynamic propulsion, a submersible was built which could "fly" under water. The SPU is one of the most remarkable of all recent developments in the rapidly expanding underwater conquest.

The design proved so good in tests that Fane arranged for sea trials in the Hawaiian Islands. There, with plenty of sea room to maneuver in, the Aerojet pilot Harold Osborn put the craft through its paces. Osborn, a hot-rodder of some renown, gave the SPU a thorough "flight test." A CO_2 motor had been added which gave spurts of high speed. Osborn performed every maneuver under water with the craft that could be done in the air. He looped the loop, did snap rolls, Immelmann turns, vertical dives, inverted passes, all while dodging coral heads at top speed. To the underwater photographers, Fen Johnson and Fane, the SPU had all the appearance of a jet aircraft as Osborn buzzed by.

The SPU II was finally demonstrated before Admiral Momsen, Commander Submarine Force, U.S. Pacific Fleet, noted inventor of the Momsen Lung, who gave the SPU high praise.

No longer "The Thing," a new, smoothly streamlined two-place model is called the "MiniSub." It had required 150 years of technical progress to develop a small submersible craft which exceeded the capabilities of Fulton's Nautilus.

In September 1952, a B-36 crashed in 253 feet of water off Mission Beach, California. Divers in standard deep-sea diving suits had difficulty in locating the wreckage because the stirred-up muddy sediment blinded them as they stumbled around in their heavy lead boots. An ex-UDT officer, Mack Boynton, then in charge of the deep-sea diving school at San Diego, telephoned Fane, "This appears to be a good chance for your aqualungers to make a real deep dive."

No free-diver had ever worked at that depth before. The French had reached 300 feet, but only as an experiment, immediately returning to the surface.

Fane studied the problem with the submarine medical officer on his staff. It was decided that a mixture of helium, oxygen, and nitrogen would be used in the aqualung, in

suitable proportions for the great depth and hard work conditions. A careful timetable for decompression was worked
out, with a slow ascent, the first "stop" scheduled at 20 feet.
Leonard E. McLarty, Boatswain's Mate First Class, known
as "Big Mac" due to his tremendous girth, volunteered to
make the dive with Fane.

An underwater television camera was being used from
the submarine rescue vessel *Florikan* with floodlights attached,
to try to locate the wreckage. Fane planned a five-minute
swim at 250 feet using the TV camera lights to illuminate the
bottom for his own photography. He carried the latest
Fenjohn camera, the "Bantam," a small compact motion-
picture camera with splendid controls. As well as a search
for wreckage, the dive would be a depth test for camera and
men, and the Cousteau constant-volume diving suit worn
by Fane.

"Hard-hat" divers of the old school watched Fane and
McLarty don their gear, McLarty squeezing into a skin-tight
Pirelli rubber suit. Not a word was spoken, but a whisper
was heard from a master diver, "You would never get me
to go down in one of those phony rigs."

At 1515 Fane and McLarty stepped over the gunwale
of the *Florikan*. They were connected by a "buddy line."
Fane signaled for the plunge, and two minutes and two
seconds later they hit bottom! It was black dark, but far off
in the gloom the lights of the TV camera glowed eerily. Fane
took the end of the "buddy line" and swam over, photo-
graphing the sea floor under the lights of the TV camera
until a signal from McLarty indicated time was up. Back
to the descending line he swam, lingering to plow his fingers
through the mud, hoping to contact wreckage. No luck. Then
the long, slow ascent at 25 feet per minute, to allow their
bodies to throw off accumulated nitrogen. There was none
of the "rapture of the depth" on this dive; just another cold,
uneasy penetration of the deep gloom of the sea, which both
divers had often experienced.

The first decompression stop was reached. To Fane it

appeared too dark for 20 feet. Looking at his depth gauge, he saw that it registered 80 feet. This meant that for minutes his body tissue had been absorbing additional nitrogen. An error had been made. One of the hard-hat divers who was acting as tender had stopped the stage at 80 feet instead of 20, a mistake which could have resulted in a severe case of the bends. Fane signaled to be brought up to complete decompression on oxygen in the recompression chamber. "Hard hat, hard head," he said in disgust to the attendants, as the lungs and suits were stripped off and he and McLarty started a one-hour decompression soak.

Despite the mishap on time, there were no ill aftereffects, and another record was in the books. This dive broke the ice of resistance to the aqualung; deep free-diving had to be accepted as a reasonable risk. Hard-hat divers, jealous of the monopoly they had held on the art of deep diving, were reluctantly forced to make room in the manual for a new technique.

Recently free-divers of Underwater Demolition Unit One were responsible for the location and recovery of the wreck of a new F-100A Super Sabre jet airplane being tested for North American Aviation. It lay in 150 feet of water off Laguna Beach, California. When electronic detecting devices failed to locate the wreck after days of search, UDT divers in aqualungs went down and did the job. In thirty days of diving they located over 4,000 small fragments of the jet, constituting 90 per cent of the vitally important aircraft.

In recognition of this important task, the UDT divers each received a letter from the Secretary of the Navy, the Honorable C. S. Thomas, in which he said: "It is just such fine public service as this that goes to make the U.S. Navy the fine organization that it is and I wish to express to . . . those directly involved in this salvage operation my own personal and official appreciation."

As a clincher to the event, the location of the wreckage was made through a photograph taken by a UDT man on liberty, Dean Boggess. Trained in observation of all hydrographic details, he photographed the slick of the jet where it hit the sea. This man was later one of the divers on the job.

The Bureau of Naval Personnel has placed what amounts to the final seal of approval on free-diving, through the establishment of an Underwater Swimmer School in Key West, Florida, under the command of Lieutenant Commander John C. Roe, USN, formerly commanding officer of UDT 12. The development of underwater techniques also is being pushed hard by Commander Dave Saunders, the former commanding officer of UDT 27 in World War II. Saunders carried UDT to new heights, recently qualifying swimmers as parachutists.

Dr. Lambertson has for years been active in interesting scientists in the problems of divers, particularly in eliminating the dread divers' diseases caused by the tremendous pressures of the depths. He has proposed the use of apparatus reducing the problem of oxygen poisoning, a dread hazard, by decreasing the alternate exposure of the diver to low and high tensions of inert gases, thereby decreasing the possibility of bends. Along more practical lines, Doctor Edward Lanphier of the Naval Experimental Diving Unit in Washington, D.C., has done a tremendous amount of work in basic research on diving physiology. Science and medicine will, through the endeavors of these and other zealots, solve the problems and enable men-fish to plumb the abyss.

UDT swim-divers have played a major part in rolling back the last great unexplored frontier of this narrowing world. Now the individual Homo Sapiens can return briefly to his ancestral home in the sea. Men can be truly amphibious, swimming on somewhat equal terms with the fish who seem to accept their presence without fear—one more air-breathing mammal joining the whale, the porpoise, and the seal.

Index

NOTE: Most World II personnel listed below rank of Captain were USNR unless otherwise noted. Officers are listed with highest rank noted in book.

Acheson, Chief "Bill," 31, 32, 39
Adams, Ensign J. C. ("Jack"), 98, 102, 103, 104
Almond, Maj. General Edward M., USA, 248
Anderson, A. E., 179
Anderson, Capt. Carl E., USNR, 106, 107, 108, 186, 188
Anderson, Lt. (jg) Lloyd, 24, 211
Andrews, Ensign E. F., 184
Aquadro, Lt. Charles F., 274
Archer, Cdr. S. M., USN, 257
Atcheson, Lt. (jg) George, III, USN, 236, 237, 238, 239, 240, 241, 243, 290, 291
Atlantic Fleet Amphibious Force, 9, 10, 13
Audibert, Gunner's Mate B. B., 153
Austin, L. A., SF1, 240

Baily, Samuel, GM1, USN, 290, 291, 292, 297
Ball, Chief, 134, 135
Barbey, Vice Admiral Daniel E., USN, 132, 149, 150, 156, 162, 165, 211, 226, 228
Barbour, Chief Aviation Ordnanceman Loran E., 60, 61, 66

Barnes, Lt. Cdr. J. S., USN, 270
Barnhill, Leonard L., 135, 137
Barr, Maj. Gen. David G., USA, 257
Bass, Gunner's Mate Robert W., 55, 56, 66
Bender, George, 219, 224
Bentley, J. L., CM1, 153
Berkey, Rear Admiral R. S., USN, 213, 218
Bess, Lt. (jg), 245
Black, Robert, 135, 137
Blackwell, Lt. (jg) Lane, 41
Blanchard, Lt. Cdr., 115
Blandy, Vice Admiral William H. P., USN, 17, 144, 146, 172, 180, 190, 270, 297
Blettel, D., MM1, 168
Blowers, Chief Warrant Officer R. A., 114
Blumberg, Ensign, 79
Boggess, Dean, 301
Bohne, Lt. L. H., 69, 70
Bostock, Air Marshall, RAAF, 226
Boswell, QM 3/c, 245
Boyd, Lt. (jg) R. M. S., 183
Boynton, Lt. Cdr. Mack M., USN, 245, 247, 256, 257, 259, 272, 299

Brewster, Commander Edward D., 25, 26, 40

Brooks, Lt. Cdr. Houston F., 158, 172, 181, 185

Bryan, Wallace, 155, 156

Burke, Admiral Arleigh A., U. S. Navy, Chief of Naval Operations, 1, 236, 277

Burke, Lt. Cdr. Richard F., 88, 90, 92, 99, 100, 101, 105, 107, 125, 129, 139, 142, 194

Bryam, Carpenter Morris H., 80

Carberry, Lt. Cdr. William Gordon, 27, 34, 36, 83, 86, 107, 115, 116, 117, 118, 119, 122, 152, 196

Carpenter, Emmett L., 135

Carusi, Commander Eugene, 45

Cashion, 2d Lt. Dana, USMC, 243

Castillo, G., S1/c, 168

Chace, Lt. Cdr. J. F., 262, 263, 265, 266

Chandler, Lt. Cdr. Daniel F., 245, 254, 264

Choate, Lt. Arthur O., Jr., 132, 133, 143, 146, 154

Christensen, Robert, 98

Christensen, Warren, 135, 137

Clark, Lt. Eugene, USN, 244

Clayton, Lt. Cdr. Edward P., USN, 77, 79, 196, 208, 228

Cleland, Capt. J. B., USNR, 230, 232

Commander, Underwater Demolition Teams, Amphibious Forces, Pacific (ComUDTsPhibsPac, "Mudpac"), 159, 161, 171, 181, 183, 187, 190, 206. *See also* Hanlon, Capt. B. Hall.

Commander, Underwater Demolition Teams and Underwater Demolition Flotilla, Amphibious Forces, U. S. Pacific Fleet, 227. *See also* Rodgers, Capt. R. H.

Conolly, Rear Admiral Richard L., USN, 27, 34, 35, 37, 109, 112, 114, 115, 118, 119, 120, 121, 122, 158

Conrad, Chief Samuel, 203, 225

Construction Battalions, 8, 13, 18, 24, 25, 26, 31, 43, 65, 83, 130

Cook, Lt. Cdr. Marshall, 274

Coombs, Lt. Cdr. Charles E., 218, 221, 225, 228

Cooper, Lt. Cdr. Walter, 42, 44, 64, 230, 234, 269, 270

Couble, Capt. A. J., USN, 170

Cousteau, Commandant Jacques-Yves, 252, 268, 296, 300

COXE (Combined Operations Experimental Establishment), 42

Crist, Lt. Thomas C., 25, 26, 34, 36, 82, 83, 86, 107, 109, 118, 119, 121, 122, 152

Cruzen, Capt. Richard A., USN, 271

Cullen, Ensign William T., 193

Culver, Lt. Harold W., 144

Culver, Lt. William H., 211

Curry, Capt. C. N. E., Royal Navy, 16

Darroch, Lt. James W., 10

Davenport, E. J. ("Red"), 96, 98

Davis, Chief E. M., 95

De Bold, Lt. John K., 91, 97, 126, 153, 163

De Forest, Lt. Cdr. Don C., USN, 255

Deiner, Ensign Frederick G., 202, 219, 220, 224, 225, 267

Demolition Research Unit (DRU), 20, 21

Devine, Chief J. A., 297

DOLO Committee (Demolition of Obstacles to Landing Operations), 20

Donovan, Maj. Gen. William J., USA (OSS), 133

Downes, Lt. Arthur M., Jr., 195

Doyle, Rear Admiral James H., USN, 238, 239

Dunning, Lt. Bruce B., 297

Dupras, Maj. Edward F., USMC, 240, 241, 242

Duquette, Lt. Cdr. Herbert E., 63

Dyer, A. C., 288

Dynamiting and Demolition School, Camp Perry, Va., 13, 18

Eaton, Lt. Cdr. James B., 155, 158, 159, 164

Edwards, Lt., 267

Eisenhower, General Dwight D., 46

Eleventh Amphibious Force, 45

Emery, Lt. (jg) C. F., 158

Fairbairn, Major Richard, Royal Engineers, 21, 41, 46

Fane, Cdr. Francis Douglas, 28, 230, 235, 252, 263, 264, 265, 266, 269, 271, 274, 277, 278, 279, 280, 281, 282, 283, 284, 285, 286, 287, 288, 289, 290, 291, 292, 293, 294, 295, 296, 297, 299, 300, 301

Fielding, Lt. (jg) T. R., 243, 245

Fife, Admiral James, Jr., USN, Commander Submarine Force, Atlantic Fleet, 282

Fifth Amphibious Force, 3, 27, 28, 38

Flynn, Lt. William F., 170

Foley, Boatswain's Mate Warren, 239, 240

Forrestal, James, Secretary of the Navy, 188

Fort, Rear Admiral George H., USN, 138

Foster, Chief A. W., 78, 297

Francis, Ensign John, 17

Freeman, Ensign William R., 11, 53, 54, 55, 56, 57, 58, 66, 74, 75

Frey, Lt. (jg) Edward, USN, 261

Gagnon, Emile, 252, 268

Gamache, Chief W. D., 168

Gammill, Lt. Floyd P., 279

Garren, Lt. Herman, 271

Garrett, Ensign Arthur O., 145

Giannotti, William, 252

Gibbons, Lt. Cdr. Joseph H., 47, 64, 74, 75

Gongwer, Calvin, 298

Gordon, Chief Carpenter W. L., 25

Gregory, Lt., USA, 59, 60

Griffin, Rear Admiral R. M., USN, 32

Guinnee, Ensign John W., 153

Gulbransen, Capt. Clarence, USN, 17

Hagenson, Lt. (jg) Carl P., 43, 44, 67

Hall, Harold, 97

Halsey, Admiral William F., USN, 149, 162, 228

Hanlon, Capt. B. Hall, USN, 158, 159, 160, 163, 164, 170, 171, 172, 173, 174, 178, 180, 181, 183, 189, 192, 193, 201, 202, 206, 208, 269

Hannigan, Thomas, 152

Harris, Chief Carpenter Earl, 25

Hawkins, 1st Lt. William Deane, USMCR, 5

Hawks, Lt. William Lambert, 17, 25, 36, 112, 171, 187

Hayler, Rear Admiral Robert W., USN, 146

Heideman, Lt. (jg) Lawrence L., 41, 42, 53, 64

Heil, R. E., GM1, 98, 99

Higgins, Edward, 200, 225

Hill, Capt. Tom B., USN, 7, 8, 25, 26, 82, 158

Hill, Vice Admiral Harry L., USN, 28, 38, 40, 102, 106, 127, 128, 184, 205, 228

Hochuli, Cdr. Edward S., 171, 191, 192, 194, 198, 207

Hoffman, Ensign Walter B., 116

Hopkins, R. L., CM3, 168

Horner, Cdr. J. S., USN, 105

Hutson, Cdr. Albert L., 148

Hyatt, Lt. Cdr. Bruce, USN, 250

Isley, Maj., USA, 64

Jacobson, Chief, 58, 59

Jacobson, Ensign Martin, 112

Jameson, Ensign Frank, 198, 222

JANET, see Joint Army-Navy Experimental and Testing Board

Janowicz, 70

Jenkins, Lt. (jg) William M., 58, 66

Jewett, Maj., USA, 64

Jirka, Ensign Frank, 176

Johnson, Coxswain, 36

Johnson, Lt. Cdr. E. R. Fenimore, 286, 287, 288, 289, 290, 292, 293, 294, 295, 296, 297, 299

Johnson, Lt. T. R., 262, 263, 266, 269

Joint Army-Navy Experimental and Testing Board (JANET), 20, 21, 42, 82, 186

Jones, Lt. (jg) Albert H., 274

Jones, maj. James L., USMCR, 124, 125, 128, 193, 208

Jouett, Maj. John, USA, 295

Joy, Vice Admiral C. Turner, USN, Commander of Naval Forces, Far East, 239

Kaine, Lt. (jg) Frank, 24, 211

Karnowski, Ensign Lawrence S., 59, 60, 66

Kasman, B. W., 152

Kauffman, Commander Draper L. (later Captain, USN), 14, 15, 16, 17, 18, 19, 20, 22, 23, 87, 88, 89, 90, 91, 94, 95, 96, 97, 98, 99, 100, 101, 102, 103, 104, 107, 123, 124, 127, 128, 129, 131, 153, 159, 174, 175, 176, 183, 186, 187, 190, 196, 206, 208, 230, 233, 279

Kauffman, Vice Admiral James L., USN, 15, 87, 88, 90, 97

Kenney, Lt. Gen. George, USAAF, 149

Keppesser, BM 3/c, 287, 288, 289, 294, 297

Kiland, Rear Admiral I. N., USN, 191

Killough, Ensign Robert F., 193, 194

King, Ensign Myles, 25

King, Fleet Admiral Ernest J., USN, Commander in Chief, U. S. Fleet, and Chief of Naval Operations, 13, 14, 20

Kingman, Rear Admiral Howard F., USN, 143

Kinkaid, Admiral Thomas C., USN, 149, 150, 156, 157, 161, 165

Kirk, Rear Admiral Alan G., USN, 87

Kirtpatric, Lt. Cdr. C. E., 133

Knowles, Capt. H. B., USN, 32

Koehler, Commander John T., 27, 34, 36, 37, 40, 81, 82, 83, 89, 90, 91, 133, 134, 137, 170, 174, 229

Kramer, Maj. R. V., USMC, 263, 264, 265, 266

Kreuger, Lt. Gen. Walter, USA, 149

Lahr, 1st Lt. Frank F., USMCR, 111, 118, 121, 233

Lambertson, Dr. Christian J., 281, 282, 285, 286, 287, 288, 290, 292, 302

Lanphier, Dr. Edward, 302

Lauderdale, K. B., 155

LeBoutiller, Lt. P., Jr., 182

Leslie, 1st Lt. Alan Gordon, USMCR, 5, 90, 103, 104

Lewis, Rear Admiral Spencer S., USN, 79

Lewis, W. R., SM3, 168

Lindbergh, Anne, 273, 274

Lindbergh, Charles, 273

Lindbergh, Ensign Jon, 273, 274

Line, Gunner's Mate John H., 61, 66

Loban, Chief Carpenter Walter K., 119, 120, 205, 207

Logsdon, Lt. DeEarle M., 90, 107, 120, 138, 140, 142, 155

Lowry, Rear Admiral Frank J., USN, 76

Luehrs, Lt. (jg) Lewis F., 18, 25, 31, 32, 39, 218

Lynch, Francis, 200

Lyon, Lt. (jg) J. O., 258

Lyon, Lt. Richard, 267

MacArthur, General of the Army Douglas, 24, 149, 150, 156, 157, 194, 226, 228, 229, 232, 237, 239, 242, 243, 260

McCallum, Ensign R. H., 184

McCormick, QM 3/c, 236, 240

McKinney, Lt. Cdr. William R., USN, 245, 246, 248, 249, 251, 254, 259

McKnight, Chief T. R., 168

McLarty, Boatswain's Mate 1/c Leonard E., 300, 301

MacMahon, John, 134, 135, 137

McRoberts, G., 298

Magill, Ensign Clark, 79

Malanaphy, Cdr. M. S., USN, 174, 176, 180

Malfeo, Ensign M. A., 168

Margetts, Cdr. Richard, USN, 279

Marine Amphibious Reconnaissance Battalion, 193, 208

Marine Fifth Amphibious Corps, 86, 179

Marion, Lt. George T., 191, 193

Markham, Chief Jerry N., 61

Marshall, General George C., USA, 20

Marshall, Lt. R. P., 96, 153

Martin, Lt. William, 93, 95

Masden, Coxswain Charles, 216

Massey, Lt. (jg) M. R., 133, 134, 135

Metzel, Capt., USN, 15

Meyers, Lester J., 60

Mitchell, Lt. Edward A., 195, 201

Mitscher, Rear Admiral Marc A., USN, 28

Modesett, Gunner's Mate Jackson, 69, 71

Momsen, Rear Admiral C. B., USN, Commander Submarine Force, U. S. Pacific Fleet, 299

Montgomery, Field Marshall B. L., 46

Moon, Rear Admiral Don P., USN, 69

Moore, Don, 295

Moore, William E., 135, 137

Moranz, Lt. Cdr. Vincent J., 171, 173, 191, 193, 194

Morgan, Cdr. C. C., 151

Morrison, Fred, 243

Morshead, Gen., 1st Australian Corps, 226

"Mudpac," see Commander, Underwater Demolition Teams, Amphibious Forces, Pacific

Nash, Lt. Cdr. W. V., 175, 180

Naval Amphibious Training Base, Fort Pierce, Fla., 13, 14, 17, 18, 20, 21, 23, 24, 25, 26, 31, 35, 40, 41, 42, 45, 47, 75, 83, 86, 87, 90, 91, 132, 170, 186, 211, 227, 229, 230, 231

Naval Amphibious Training Base, Solomons Island, Md., 13, 17

Naval Combat Demolition Training and Experimental Base, Maui, T. H., 81, 83, 86, 88, 90, 132, 133, 137, 138, 148, 151, 158, 170, 195, 212, 227, 229
Naval Combat Demolition Unit (NCDU), 13, 14, 22, 24, 25, 41, 43, 44, 45, 46, 48, 66, 67, 74, 196
Navy Bomb Disposal School, 14, 17
Nicholson, Lt. Charles, USN, 285
Nimitz, Fleet Admiral Chester W., Commander in Chief of the Pacific Fleet and the Pacific Ocean Area (CINCPAC), 7, 8, 25, 38, 88, 133, 158, 159, 228
Nixon, Ensign Thomas D., 117, 121
Noble, Rear Admiral A. G., USN, 212, 224, 226
Nourse, Lt. (jg) Donald G., 153
Nowack, Lt. Cdr. Harry F., 245, 249, 251, 256

O'Connor, Lt. Cdr. D. K., 184
Oddstad, Chief Andres F., Jr., 117
Oldendorf, Vice Admiral Jesse B., 102, 138, 150, 154, 157, 158, 159, 160, 161, 162
Onderdonk, Lt. Bruce, 100, 125, 142, 158, 172, 194, 198
O'Neill, Lt. Col. John T., USA, 42, 64
Orr, Chief, 128
Osborn, Harold, 299
OSS Maritime Unit, 132, 133

Parmelee, Ensign Robert, 145
Peterson, Lt. Cdr. Herbert A., 47, 67, 68, 74, 75
Petway, Jimmy J., USN, 297
Phelps, Ensign Robert M., 142
Phillips, Cdr. George, 176
Piotrowski, Gunner's Mate Henry L., USN, 290, 291, 292, 295, 297

Pope, Lt. (jg) R. G., 261
Powell, Rear Admiral Paulus P., USN, 133, 134
Prewitt, Chief Leland A., 71, 72
Pyle, Ernie, 71, 207

Raymor, Chief Carpenter William H., 59
Refo, Cdr. Miles, Jr., USN, 284, 285
Riggs, Rear Admiral R. S., USN, 212
Robbins, Lt. (jg) Sidney, 100, 101
Rodgers, Capt. R. H., USN, 8, 208, 227, 228, 230, 232, 234
Rodgers, Rear Admiral Bertram J., USN, 77
Rodriquez, J. O., MoMM2, 168
Roe, Lt. Cdr. John C., USN, 302
Roeder, Chief Howard L., 26, 82, 133, 134, 135, 137
Roosevelt, Lt. Gen. T. R., Jr., USA, 47
Root, A. H., GM2, 98
Rosenthal, Joe, 188
Rossart, J. W., MM2, 168
Rupertus, Maj. Gen. W. H., USMC, 138
Ryan, 1st Lt. Edward, USMCR, 93
Rybski, Ensign E. B., 184

Satterfield, Paul, 261
Saunders, Lt. Cdr. David, 230, 302
Schmitt, Lt. Robert J., 266
Scoggins, F. P., SK1, 168
Scouts-and-Raiders, 18, 21
"SeaBees," see Construction Battalions
Sears, Lt. Alfred R., 61, 75
Seventh Amphibious Force, 24, 132, 149
Shinners, Carpenter George, 211
Shouldice, Lt. Cdr. D'Arcy, USN, 248, 251
Sieminski, Walter, 155

Smith, Lt. (jg) Edwin P., USN, 240, 241, 243, 245, 261

Smith, Lt. Gen. Holland M., USMC, 102, 124, 127, 128

Smith, Lt. Robert C., 41, 45, 68

Solomon, Capt., 213

Soto, Gilbert, 203

Spruance, Admiral Raymond A., USN, 28, 30, 228

Starkweather, Lt. Mark W., 10, 11

States, Lt. Cdr. Louis A., 197, 201, 202, 212, 213, 214, 215, 216, 217, 218, 219, 221, 224, 225, 267, 268

Stocking, Ensign H. B., 61, 62, 63

Struble, Rear Admiral A. D., USN, 169

Sugden, W. L., GM3, 168

Suhrland, Lt. (jg) George, 126

Sullivan, Lt. Cdr. A. W., Jr., 268

Sumpter, Frank W., 179

Swygert, "S" "O," MM2, 153

Taylor, Capt. Jack McN., USN, 8, 82

Thackrey, Rear Admiral Lyman A., USN, 257

Thede, Lt. W. L., 239, 258, 259

Third Amphibious Force, 7, 132, 149

Thomas, C. E., Secretary of the Navy, 301

Thompson, Chief J. D., 152

Tilton, Edward, 153

Towner, Rear Admiral George C., USN, 273

Turner, Admiral Richmond Kelly, USN, v, 3, 4, 7, 8, 24, 25, 27, 28, 29, 30, 31, 32, 34, 37, 38, 40, 81, 83, 86, 87, 88, 89, 102, 109, 115, 118, 122, 123, 124, 128, 131, 158, 159, 163, 181, 189, 195, 203, 205, 208, 228, 230

Underwater Demolition Team (UDT)

— "Able," 132, 137, 172

— One, 25, 28, 29, 30, 33, 39, 40

— One (Korea), 240, 244, 245, 257, 258, 262, 263

— One (postwar), 301

— Two, 25, 26, 27, 35, 81

— Three, 83, 86, 108, 109, 111, 117, 118, 121, 132, 151, 152, 191, 233

— Three (postwar, Korea), 236, 244, 245, 248, 262, 266, 268, 270

— Four, 83, 86, 108, 113, 117, 119, 121, 132, 195, 196, 200, 205, 206

— Four (postwar), 271

— Five, 83, 86, 87, 88, 89, 91, 94, 105, 107, 125, 131, 132, 136, 153, 162

— Five (Korea), 267, 268

— Six, 86, 89, 90, 107, 108, 120, 122, 132, 137, 138, 140, 147, 148, 155

— Seven, 86, 88, 89, 90, 91, 94, 99, 100, 103, 125, 131, 132, 137, 138, 139, 141, 142, 147, 148, 194, 199, 200, 201, 206

— Eight, 132, 138, 143, 153, 162

— Nine, 132, 155, 156, 157, 162, 165, 167, 168, 231

— Ten, 132, 133, 137, 138, 143, 145, 146, 154, 162, 164, 166, 167, 168, 169

— Eleven, 197, 198, 200, 201, 202, 203, 209, 210, 211, 212, 213, 218, 219, 220, 224, 225, 226, 267

— Eleven (postwar), 272

— Twelve, 171, 174, 190, 198, 199, 207, 226, 231, 302

— Thirteen, 171, 173, 174, 190, 194, 230

— Fourteen, 158, 162, 172, 174, 190, 198, 199

— Fifteen, 158, 162, 172, 174, 179, 181, 182

— Sixteen, 195, 200, 201, 207
— Seventeen, 195, 200
— Eighteen, 209, 212, 218, 219, 221, 224, 228, 229, 230, 261
— Nineteen, 190, 192, 193
— Twenty-one, 196, 200, 205, 206, 207, 208, 228
— Twenty-seven, 302
Underwater Swimming School, Key West, Fla., 301
U. S. Naval Amphibious Base, Little Creek, Va., 10

Wales, Capt. George H., USN, Commander Submarine Squadron Two, 280, 284
Walker, Maj. Gen. Walton H., USA, 248, 257
Warnock, Lt. (jg) James, 17
Watson, Maj. Gen. Thomas E., USMC, 38, 90, 102, 103
Weidner, Coxswain Albert, 101
Welch, Lt. Cdr. D. F., USN, 240, 241, 245, 257, 258

Wellings, Capt. T. F., USN, 47
Wells, Lt. (jg) Robert F., 197, 212, 213, 216, 224, 225
Wetenkamp, Chief William R., 246, 251
Wetzel, Lt. (jg) James, 17
Wilkinson, Vice Admiral Theodore S., 24, 132, 133, 149, 150, 156, 157, 165, 228
Williams, Capt. R. D., USN, 191, 206, 229
Williams, Lt. (jg) J. H., 203
Willmon, Capt. T. L., MC, USN, 282, 284
Wilson, Lt. (jg) P. A., USN, 240, 241
Wirwohn, Chief H. E., 71
Wise, Lt. Fred A., 13, 14
Wood, Lt. Jack R., 205
Wood, Maj. T. W., 186

Yates, Lt. (jg) Lee C., 176
Young, Lt. Cdr. Donald E., 143, 144, 153, 154, 164

(1)

About the Authors

Cdr. Francis Douglas Fane, USNR (Ret.), commanded UDT 1 and was instrumental in initiating underwater swimmer operations in the U.S. Navy. Born in Scotland and a merchant mariner at the age of sixteen, he brought scuba-diving technology to the United States from Italy. In 1952 he reached a depth of 250 feet while free diving—a record at the time. He celebrated his eighty-sixth birthday in 1995.

Don Moore was the eastern story writer for RKO Radio Pictures when *The Naked Warriors* was first published. He served in the U.S. Army during World War II.

the searchlight illuminated the submarine's super-